# AllEtiquette.com

## A Power Guide

by **Fredrica Cere Kussin**

Published and printed in Victoria, Canada

Co-published by Crofton Capital Corporation

**Canadian Cataloguing in Publication Data**

Kussin, Fredrica Cere,
Allettiquette.com

Includes bibliographical references and index.
ISBN 1-55212-380-4

1. Etiquette. 2. Manners and customs. I. Title.
II. Title: Allettiquette.com
BJ1838.K87 2000 395 C00-910517-4

TRAFFORD

**This book was published *on-demand* in cooperation with Trafford Publishing.**
On-demand publishing is a unique process and service of making a book available for retail sale to the public taking advantage of on-demand manufacturing and Internet marketing.
**On-demand publishing** includes promotions, retail sales, manufacturing, order fulfilment, accounting and collecting royalties on behalf of the author.

Suite 6E, 2333 Government St., Victoria, B.C. V8T 4P4, CANADA
Phone 250-383-6864 Toll-free 1-888-232-4444 (Canada & US)
Fax 250-383-6804 E-mail sales@trafford.com
Web site www.trafford.com TRAFFORD PUBLISHING IS A DIVISION OF TRAFFORD HOLDINGS LTD.
Trafford Catalogue #00-0044 www.trafford.com/robots/00-0044.html

10 9 8 7

"Timing. Just as important as knowing how to present your card is knowing when, says Fredrica Cere Kussin, author of AllEtiquette.com - A Power Guide. Offer your card when you are first introduced to someone at the beginning of a meeting or meal, never during, she advises. And don't act offended if you don't receive a card in return. Finally, a hint: If you would like to give your card to someone but can't find an appropriate moment, ask for the other person's card."

Jennifer Saranow, The Asian Wall Street Journal

"People should never kiss at business-related functions, says Fredrica Cere Kussin, author of AllEtiquette.com. In fact, Kussin is aggressively opposed to this public cheekiness. She recommends women fend off kissers. Put your hand out to be shaken, but keep your arm straight to literally keep any potential kisser at arm's length."

Daphne Bramham, Southam Newspapers

## Acknowledgements

In the years that it has taken me to write this book, I always had enormous support, love, and encouragement from the people close to me, and from those who became friends while working on the text.

I dedicate this book to my loving husband, Irving, who totally supports me in everything that I do.

Many thanks to all the wonderful people who spent hours doing research, typing, correcting, editing, designing, and giving advice.

Bernie Abromaitis

Sandee Greatrex

Trude LaBossiere Huebner

Joanne Kellock

Caroline Lahoski

Virginia Leeming

Terri Raymond

Samm Chan

Sabrina Silverstone

Jacqueline Wood


In the end, all we really have are manners.
*Carmel Berkson*

Acknowledgements

# Table of Contents

Table of Contents

**ALL ETIQUETTE.COM**
By **FREDRICA CERE KUSSIN**

## TABLE OF CONTENTS

# Chapter 1

# BasicManners

BasicManners

Good manners will open many doors for you. They are a passport to a world that is otherwise closed. Good manners signal that you have respect for others, and that you will rise to every occasion with grace. They suggest to everyone you come into contact with, including business associates, that you have taken the trouble to learn the social graces and can do them effortlessly. People with good manners do not have to stop and think about their actions. They come naturally. Your manners will help you achieve your goals, for without them, you are placing stumbling blocks in your path.

Basic manners are best learned when growing up. Needless to say, not everyone has them. The simple use of "please" and "thank you" can change the way people respond to you. "Please" changes an order into a request and "thank you" expresses gratitude. Showing appreciation and respect will help you get along with others.

Have you ever been in a situation of uneasiness because you or someone else did not practice correct table manners? Most likely you have. Knowing proper etiquette inspires trust, and that can give you the edge you need to move ahead in life.

Everyone should have enough assurance to introduce himself or herself properly, take clients out for lunch, attend the opera, ballet, and sports events without thinking twice about conduct.

Good manners = Consideration for yourself and others.

Good manners = Good business.

## THE ART OF INTRODUCING PEOPLE

An introduction is the first impression you make on someone, so it is significant that you do it adequately. If your name gets mispronounced when you are introduced to others, repeat your name when you acknowledge them.

### Basic Rules

A man is always introduced to a woman:

> Mrs. Ann Dawson, may I present Mr. Tom Ford, our neighbour.

A young person is always introduced to an older person:

Dr. Kelly, I would like you to meet my nephew, Blair Scott.

A less important person by title is always introduced to a more important person by title:

Judge Maurice Brown, may I introduce to you the president of our company, Mr. Alex Barnett.

### Introducing Executives

- The most important executive is always introduced first, regardless of gender.
- Introduce a non-official to an official person.
- Introduce a junior executive to a senior executive.
- Introduce a fellow executive to a customer or client.
- Explain who the people are when introducing them.

## ADDRESSING CORRESPONDENCE

### Married Couples

To a husband and wife:

Mr. and Mrs. Blair Scott
Home address

Mr. Blair Scott and Mrs. Jane Scott
Home address

Mr. Blair Scott
Mrs. Jane Scott
Home address

When the wife has kept her maiden name:

Mr. Blair Scott and Mrs. Jane Smith
Home address

BasicManners

When the wife has a title and the husband does not:

> Mr. Blair Scott and Dr. Jane Smith
> Home address

When both have titles:

> Dr. Blair Scott and Dr. Jane Smith
> Home address

When the husband is a "Jr.":

> Mr. Blair Scott, Jr., and Mrs. Jane Scott
> Home address

**Business Letters**

To non-official people:

Without a job title:

> Mr. Blair Scott
> Name of Company
> Address

With a job title:

> Mr. Blair Scott
> President, Name of Company
> Address

When a professional title follows the name (do not use Dr., Mr., Mrs., Miss, or Ms.):

> Jane Smith, M.D. (not Ms. Jane Smith, M.D.)
> Office Address

> Blair Smith, Ph.D. (not Dr. Blair Smith, Ph.D.)
> Address

> David Jones, Esq. (not Mr. Blair Smith, Esq.)
> Address

When a title goes before the name:

President David Jones
ABC Co.
Address

## THE USE OF MS.

### *And addressing a woman who is widowed or divorced*:

Ms. is now commonly used in the workplace for married, divorced, widowed, and single women. Some women prefer to use Mrs. once they are married, but may choose to use Ms. after being widowed or divorced. In general, if a woman wants to use Ms., her wishes should be respected.

## THE HANDSHAKE

The most important thing to remember about a handshake is to use it when you are introduced to someone. Get into the habit of shaking hands; not only when you meet someone but when you leave them.

A proper Western handshake is a full-hand grip that is both firm and warm with an understated downward snap. In the Western Hemisphere, a person with a poor handshake will be immediately judged by his peers. Do not send the message that you are a wimp — or the opposite, a macho person with a bone-crunching grip.

Shaking Hands with Women:

> No difference in the grip, but convention has it that you should wait for her to extend her hand first.

Emily Post once said, "Never forget that a handshake can create a feeling of friendliness or irritation between two strangers." Shaking hands is a relatively universal gesture of greeting, but the way to do it varies around the globe. See chapters on general etiquette worldwide for more on appropriate handshakes for different cultures.

## TABLE MANNERS

Good table manners will show that you are sophisticated and in control. There is nothing more pleasant then enjoying a meal with people who observe table etiquette.

Two important rules to remember when eating with Westerners and Europeans:

1. Do not let people see what you have in your mouth.
2. Do not make noises when chewing or with your utensils.

**Menu Terms:**

| | |
|---|---|
| Appetizer | Food served before the main meal. |
| Entré | In North America it is the main dish and in Europe it is the appetizer. |
| A La Carte | Each item is priced separately. |
| Fixed Price | A set price for a complete meal. |
| Market Price | Ask the waiter for the current price. |

## Do:

Be thoughtful and help your guest or date to be seated.

Place the napkin on your lap as soon as you are seated. At a formal dinner, wait for the host to take his or her napkin first.

Place the napkin on the left or right side of your plate when leaving the table during the meal. On your return place it back on your lap.

## Don't:

Take your jacket off in a formal setting.

Tuck your napkin into your collar, belt, or shirt.

Wipe your mouth as if the napkin were a washcloth, or use it to clean the tableware.

## Do:

Start with the implement that is farthest from the plate, and with each course work your way in.

Know the appropriate table setting. The bread plate is always on the left.

Leave a used utensil on the plate, not half on or half off the plate.

Leave your fork resting on the left of your plate and your knife on the right to indicate you have not finished eating.

Eat slowly, quietly, and gracefully.

Say please and thank you when you need something.

Excuse yourself if you leave the table during the meal. Sit straight; your hands should lie on your lap when not eating.

Reach only for items that are in front of you. Ask for things that are farther away to be passed to you once others have helped themselves.

## Don't:

Put utensils that you have used back on the table. If ever a waiter does that, he or she does not know how to serve and you should ask for clean utensils.

Make noises with your utensils against a plate or bowl while eating.

Leave a spoon in your cup while you are drinking from it.

Slouch or lean too far forward.

Put your elbows on the table while eating.

Talk with your mouth full of food. Slurp or make a noise while eating.

Drink something when your mouth has food in it. Eat, then drink.

| Do: | Don't: |
|---|---|
| Break your bread with your hands, one piece at a time; and butter it one piece at a time as well. | Encircle your plate with your left arm at any time. |
| Complain quietly if you have not been served properly, or the food is cold or badly prepared. | Crook your little finger when drinking. |
| Cut meat one bite at a time. | Cut up a large piece of meat all at once. |
| Fill the spoon by moving it away from you when eating soup. Leave the spoon on the serving plate when finished. | Mash your vegetables, or salt the food before tasting it. |
| Turn your head away from the table to remove something from your mouth that was un-chewable or not good. You may use your fork or fingers and hide the process with your napkin. You may put the food on the side of your plate if it is not gross or leave it in the napkin and ask for a fresh one. | Leave your napkin on your chair, ever. Order food at a restaurant that is difficult to eat politely, such as corn or spareribs. |
| Use one of the two accepted ways of eating spaghetti: the Italian method is to roll it onto the fork against the plate; in America, diners roll it onto the fork against a spoon. | Blow your nose into a napkin. If you need to blow your nose, excuse yourself and do it in the washroom. |

## Do:

Use your fingers to eat only asparagus, baby lamb chops, french fries, sushi, and any canapé smaller than your mouth.

Lift the shell of an oyster to your mouth with your hand — or use a fork — and eat it whole. Eat mussels whole as well.

Cut your vegetables and salads with a knife and fork a piece at a time.

Place your knife and fork parallel to each other on the right side of your plate with the fork prongs up or down when you have finished your meal.

Put your hand in front of your mouth while using a toothpick to clean your teeth. It is, however, preferable not to use a toothpick at the table.

Show your appreciation if the food is outstanding and the service is good.

Pay your bill privately. If you are going to pick up the tab, inform your guests and the waiter at the beginning of the meal.

## Don't:

Put butter on bread that you are eating with cheese.

Cut an oyster.

Transfer vegetables or salads to your plate if they are served on a separate plate.

Have food on a utensil while you are listening or talking, or hold it in mid-air.

Lick your knife or fork when you are finished a meal.

Push back your plate or say that you are full or stuffed when you are finished.

Use a comb at the table, or touch your hair while in a public place.

## Do:

Check the bill before paying. Base your tip on the total cost of the meal, not the total after tax. The usual tip is 15 percent.

## Don't:

Put your briefcase on the dinner table.

Make phone calls or receive them when you are with a client.

**Eating the Western Way:**

Although the American tradition of switching the fork from the left hand to the right after cutting the food is quite acceptable, it seems a complicated process. The simpler, easy-to-do European custom of retaining the fork in the left hand after cutting the food is more pleasing.

### CHOPSTICKS

The utensils of the Orient are very practical and one should make a point of learning to eat with them.

Practice using chopsticks at home. Hold them by the wide ends and eat with the narrow ends. Pick up one chopstick and place it between your thumb and your index finger. Use the second chopstick as a lever while the first one remains firm.

When helping yourself to food, use the large ends of your chopsticks to remove pieces from the centre dish to your plate. When finished eating, place your chopsticks parallel across your plate or bowl.

## Don't:

- Rub wooden chopsticks together — it is not useful and can raise splinters.
- Point with your chopsticks or wave them in the air.
- Suck on your chopsticks.
- Stick them upright in your rice.

## SUSHI

Eat sushi in one or two bites. Sushi can be a finger food but sashimi is always eaten with chopsticks. Do not set down a half-eaten piece of sushi on your plate.

## WINE

There are two schools of thought as to how to hold a glass of wine. Both schools agree that white wine and champagne should be picked up by the stem of the glass, as this helps to keep the wine cool. As for red wine, some say the glass should be held by the bowl, while others say that to appreciate the colour, the glass should be held by the stem. The latter, however, is much more elegant.

### Wine tips:

Wines age best in cool, dark places with good air circulation.

When storing wine, lay the bottles on their sides to keep the corks wet. If the bottle is left standing upright, the cork will get dry and allow air to get inside, which will turn the wine into vinegar.

It is important to serve wine at the right temperature:

Red wines should be served cool at the storage temperature of 55°F (12.8°C).

The best way to chill white wine is in a bucket filled half with ice and half with cold water. The bottle should be submerged up to its neck. To get the ideal 50°F (10°C) for white wine, the bottle should be in the bucket for 25 minutes.

The adage that white wine goes with fish and red wine with meat is false. The body of the wine, not the colour, is the main factor in matching wines with food.

Never rinse your glass with water and then use it for another type of wine. For each wine use a clean glass.

White wines do not require aging. Do not bother aging cheap red wines, they will not usually improve to any degree.

A wine glass should not be more than half filled when it is served with a meal.

Learn how to choose and comment on fine wines.

In December of '87, former U.S. president Ronald Reagan and former Soviet president Mikhail Gorbachev were at a black-tie affair in the White House.





BasicManners

Members of the media and experts on protocol criticized Gorbachev for not wearing a tuxedo. Perhaps he should have, but he did one thing right, he held his glass of white wine properly. Reagan, on the other hand, did not. Both leaders could have learned something from the other.

## CHAMPAGNE

Store your champagne the same way as wine. Champagne must be cooled slowly in a bucket of cold water and ice, no more than 30 minutes. To open, undo the wire hood, firmly grasped the top with a white cotton napkin and rotate the bottle around the cork. The cork will be forced out by the pressure of the gas. Serve the champagne in a flute or tulip-shaped glass. Tilt the bottle and pour slowly — to appreciate its bouquet, fill the glasses only half or two-thirds full.

### Don't:

- Place the bottle on ice or put it in the freezer.
- Serve too cold; it will lose its flavour.
- Serve too warm; it will lose its effervescence and aroma.
- Open the bottle with a loud popping sound.
- Chill the glasses.
- Leave detergent on the glasses; it will kill the bubbles.

## THE BUSINESS DINNER

Entertaining is part of doing business. It is important to remember, however, that your guests are clients, or prospective clients, and they will be observing the way you handle the situation. The more favourable your behaviour is, the better chance you will have of obtaining the results you want.

### Do:

Request a quiet table and find out who will be at the restaurant to greet you. When you arrive, say hello to that person by name — it gets you known right from the start.

### Don't:

Arrive late — whether you are the guest or the host, it would be embarrassing for everyone.

## Do:

Dress the part. People will treat you with respect if you are well groomed. When your appearance indicates that you are well off, servers see a chance to get a big tip — and the better the tip the server expects, the better the service you will receive.

Choose a seat where you can see everyone and everything that is going on — a must do for a host.

Get hosts, maitre d's captains, and waiters to notice you. Smile, make eye contact, and engage in friendly banter.

Be a proper host, place the highest ranking guest on your right, the second highest on your left, and the others at random (but put men next to women, not to other men).

Give servers your complete attention. When he or she comes to your table, put conversation on hold — it will reinforce the connection you made earlier and allow the server to tell you the specials.

Let your guests order first.

## Don't:

Bring your cellphone or answer it while having a business dinner.

Sit just any place at the table; if you are a guest, wait to be seated.

Talk only about business if spouses are present.

Interrupt when someone is speaking. Wait for your turn.

Talk all the time. Let other guests express themselves equally.

Order more courses or more expensive items than the others.

## Do:

Order the drinks if you are the host. When ordering wine, order a bottle of red and white.

As host, put your napkin on your lap to indicate dinner is starting. Put the napkin on the table to signal that dinner is over.

Pick up the check if you are the host.

Tell the waiter to give your compliments to the chef.

## Don't:

Drink too much or fill a glass of wine to the top.

Call the waiter to the table if there is a problem and you are a guest.

Argue about the cheque if you are a guest.

(See general etiquette around the world for more table manners).

### THE POWER LUNCH

The term "power lunch" is now part of the modern vernacular. What is it that differentiates it from an ordinary meal? The distinguishing feature is the motivation. You are there to sell something or get what you want on the table. In other words, it is an opportunity to embark on a discussion with your guest in a pleasant social setting.

You can pick up many clues over lunch that will assist you in achieving your objectives.

1. Body language:
   Is the person easy or uneasy? Is there limited or no eye contact? Does your lunch guest exude or lack self-confidence?
2. Ordering:
   A person who cannot decide what to eat will probably have a hard time making a decision in a business deal.
3. Table manners:
   What does it say about a person who salts and peppers his food before tasting it?

| Do: | Don't: |
| --- | --- |
| Call and invite someone out, citing the purpose of your lunch. | Invite someone to a club that discriminates on the basis of sex, religion, or race. |
| Make a reservation. Choose a restaurant you know. | Keep your guest waiting. |
| Make sure you arrive at the restaurant before your guest. | Choose a table near the door, the kitchen, washroom, in front of a mirror, or in a place where everyone can hear you. |
| Choose a table in advance. Ask for a quiet table. | |
| Order your meal if your guest has not shown up after 20 minutes. | Order or eat before your guest arrives, unless they are late. |
| Order smart — choose food that is light and that will give you energy. | Order food that is difficult to eat or finger food. |
| Offer your guest a cocktail, wine, or mineral water. | Order alcohol for yourself. |
| Start business negotiations as soon as the waiter has taken your order. | Tell your guest your life story or indulge in small talk. |
| Get to the point before dessert. | Smoke in front of a client. |
| Take only an hour for lunch. | Leave the table to talk to people you know. |
| Pay your bill privately. | Place or receive phone calls at the table. |

BasicManners

In some countries people usually consume alcohol during lunch, but it is no longer a common practice in Canada, the United States, and Northern Europe.

A lot of work is done over meals. Do not underestimate the business breakfast, an old trademark of the financial community in North America. A business breakfast is usually held early in the day and lasts no longer than one hour.

Doing business at tea time is also gaining in popularity. According to the New York Times, "Hotel dining rooms at tea times are full of open briefcases, stacks of paper, and men and women in business suits." In fact, the "power tea" just might replace the "power breakfast" and the "power lunch" as the ideal meal over which to make deals.

Whatever occasion you choose, make sure you close the deal before leaving the table. Good luck!

## THE THEATRE

Keep yourself informed about the world of theatre, especially in London and New York. Find out what the hits are by reading the reviews, then go see them with a client. Support your local theatre as well.

### Do:

Invite your guest for dinner or cocktails before the theatre.

Have the tickets in your hands ready to show the usher.

Arrange for tickets in advance. Tell your guests the seating arrangements beforehand.

Seat a woman next to a guest other than her husband.

Let the women exit the theatre first.

### Don't:

Walk in front of your guests when entering the theatre.

Arrive late.

Make comments to your guest during the play.

Bring your cellphone in the theatre.

Precede your guests out the door once the performance is over.

Do:

Follow the dress code for opening nights, which are black-tie events.

In Northern and Eastern Europe, always face the people who are sitting in your row when you pass them to get to your seat.

Always say "please," "thank you," and "I'm sorry" if you must leave and return to your seat.

Applaud at the end of each act and at the end of the performance. The first appearance of a star can be greeted with applause, as can the first viewing of a set.

Don't:

Let your date wear a hat.

Make noises or talk during the performance.

Use a flashlight or a camera.

### THE OPERA

Operas are the most extravagant of the performing arts. Rise to the occasion and dress well.

Do:

Subscribe to seasons tickets if you go often.

Applaud at the end of every act and after each curtain. A great aria deserves applause; you may say "brava" for a female singer and "bravo" for a male.

Don't:

Arrive late for the start of the performance or after intermission.

Talk during the performance.

Eat candies, make noise, or wear a watch that beeps.

**Do:**

Wear business or cocktail attire in balconies.

Dress black or white tie if you are going to an opening night or gala performance. The same attire is appropriate for the orchestra box.

Throw flowers onto the stage to your favourite performer when he or she takes his or her final bow (only if you wish, of course).

When sending flowers, make sure the name of the performer, opera house, and stage number are written on the card.

**Don't:**

Applaud at the entrance or exit of a performer.

Dash out of the theatre the minute the performance is over.

Bring a bouquet backstage without an invitation or knowing in advance that the prima donna is receiving after the performance.

Leave the theatre until everyone has left the stage.

## THE BALLET

You should make a point of attending at least one ballet a year. As with all of the other performing arts, you should keep yourself informed enough to be able to talk about it intelligently. The more cultivated you are, the more interesting you will be.

**Do:**

Arrive on time; late arrivals are not acceptable.

Wear cocktail or business attire for regular evenings. On opening nights, black-tie and dressy outfits are de rigueur.

**Don't:**

Talk during the performance.

Wear running shoes, sandals and casual wear to a ballet.

Do:

Applaud individual performers when they bow at the end of the ballet. Hold your applause until the end of an act or the performance.

Don't:

Applaud before a dance is complete or a scene is over.

**CONCERTS**

Whether you are going to a matinee or evening concert, the etiquette is the same.

Do:

Be especially quiet, as concerts are an auditory rather than visual performance.

Applaud the conductor or guest soloists when they walk onto the stage.

Stop applauding when the conductor steps onto the podium and raises the baton.

Applaud when the conductor turns towards the audience and bows.

Don't:

Arrive late.

Talk or make any kind of noise.

Applaud the music before the end of each selection.

Bring your cellphone with you.

**MOVIES**

Going to the movies is different from watching television at home; it is public entertainment and therefore consideration for others is very important.

BasicManners

BasicManners

## Do:

Arrive before the film begins.

Excuse yourself if you must leave during the film.

Get your popcorn before the film starts.

Keep conversation to a minimum before the beginning of the film.

## Don't:

Talk during the show.

Make noise with beverages and food, as it is really annoying to other people.

Applaud at the end if there is nobody there to take the credit.

Bring little children to an adult-oriented film merely because you do not have a sitter.

Bring your cellphone to the movies.

### SPORTS & GAMES

The degree of sportsmanlike behaviour that one displays, either as a spectator or as a player, is a true mark of a gracious, civilized person.

## Do:

Be on time.

Be neat and wear proper clothing.

Play because you enjoy it, not for the sake of winning.

Be considerate toward other players.

Be a gracious winner.

## Don't:

Cancel at the last minute.

Grunt, whistle, or make sounds while playing.

Lose your temper.

Stop in the middle of a game to complain.

Make inappropriate comments to anyone.

## TENNIS

**Do:**

Dress in proper tennis attire. Inquire about the club's dress code before arriving.

Change sides of the court every other game.

Wait until other players have finished their play, before retrieving a ball that went into their court.

Ask your opponent if he or she is ready for your serve.

Congratulate your opponent at the end.

**Don't:**

Take your shirt off.

Question the referee.

Use a court longer than the appropriate time.

Brag about how good you are at the sport. Use excessive force with a smaller opponent.

## GOLF

With so many public courses nowadays, golf is no longer just a rich man's game. It has also become a very popular sport all over the world.

**Do:**

Let any player tee off at the first hole. After that, the person with the lowest score tees off first. He has "honours."

Look before you swing. If your shot approaches a player ahead of you, call out "Four."

**Don't:**

Make noise or talk loudly, as it will distract the players.

Step anywhere in the area between another player's ball and the cup.

Do:

Don't:

On the green or the fairway, allow the person whose ball is farthest from the hole or cup play first. He is "away."

Repair as much of the course as you can, including divots, pits made by high shots, and the bunkers.

Ask your caddy to repair the course.

Hold up the game if you are a slow player. Let faster foursomes play through if yours is very slow.

Have fits or show uncontrolled rage.

Hit your shot until the group ahead of you is out of range.

**SKIING**

Good manners on the slopes means ensuring others' safety.

Do:

Don't:

Be in control at all times.

Wear proper ski attire.

Offer to pair off with another skier if you are alone in the lift line.

Call out "On your left," or "On your right," or "Track left," or "Track right" when skiing around someone.

Apologize and help, if by your mistake someone fell. Make sure there are no injuries.

Ski alone.

Ski on a closed trail, or outside the boundaries.

Laugh at a beginner.

Ski on a slope that you cannot tackle.

Move an injured skier. Wait instead for the ski patrol to arrive.

## BASEBALL

| | |
|---|---|
| When faced with a bad call: | forget it as soon as possible and get refocused. |
| When questioning a call: | never turn and face the umpire. State your objection looking at the pitcher. |
| When discussing a call: | direct your comments towards the call, not the umpire. |

## JOGGING

Give the right of way to pedestrians — unless you are on a track designed for jogging, then pedestrians have to give you the right of way. Always stay on the right side of a city track when jogging or speed walking.

## MOUNTAIN BIKING

The growth in popularity of mountain biking means adopting good trail etiquette.

| Do: | Don't: |
|---|---|
| Slow down or stop and pull over when you encounter hikers on the trail. | Skid around corners; it is not safe and ruins the trails. Turn slowly or dismount and walk. |
| Call out or ring your bicycle bell when approaching hikers from the rear, then slowly pass them. | Use trails that are not open to mountain bikers. |
| When approaching people on horseback from the front, pull over and let them pass. If you are coming up the trail from behind, ask which side is best to pass them on. | Behave like a boor; be polite to others on the trail; say "Hi." |

BasicManners

| Do: | Don't: |
| --- | --- |
| Take a bicycle pump, tools, a spare tube, a small first aid kit, and some food and water. Plan your route. | Overdo it; know your abilities. |
| Leave the trail clean. | Scare the animals. |

# Office Politics



Office Politics

With the new world order and the freelance economy, one must work much harder to stay or, better yet, get ahead of the game. There will be many individuals looking for the same job that you want. Everything is more specialized and a lot of work is now done on a contractual basis. Therefore, the first product to sell is yourself. Keep up with the changes and adapt to them. Your job will be more secure if you have the ability to add value to your employer's company.

Mastering and practising business etiquette gives you an edge when you are being considered for employment or advancement.

You will earn the respect and cooperation of co-workers, bosses, or partners by using the skills that encourage a positive response from others.

You will enhance your success rate by putting that "something extra" into your way of doing business. People want a role model to look up to and admire. When you become that person, you are on your way to being a very successful individual.

Etiquette is based on common sense and mutual respect. Good manners and good business go hand in hand; they are partners.

A well-mannered executive will have more opportunity to progress in his or her career and social life.

## THE RÉSUMÉ

Your résumé is the interviewer's first opportunity to get to know you. It must be well organized, simple, easy to read, clean with no typos. List your skills (computer programs that you know), knowledge (all of your academic degrees), interests (all personal development courses, hobbies, sports), job titles, names of previous employers, and references.

### The Cover Letter

**Do:**

Use the first paragraph to state the position that you are applying for and any referral. This paragraph can include a statement about why you are interested in the position.

## Do:

Use the second paragraph to briefly explain why you are qualified for the position.

Use the final paragraph for a polite request for an interview. It is acceptable to include a closing sentence saying that you will call the prospective employer to make an appointment. If you indicate that you will call the employer on a specific date, make sure you do so.

Send originals only, not photocopies.

## Don't:

Include your height, weight, or description of your physical appearance or health.

Use professional buzzwords unless you are sure the person who will read your résumé is going to understand them.

### The Hardcopy Résumé

Be aware that some companies are now using résumé-scanning software because they get too many applications.

## Do:

Make sure your résumé is only one to two pages long.

Use white paper with a common font and a typeface of 12 to 16 points.

Use only one typeface and either boldface or all capital letters for headings.

Ensure that your left and right margins are at least 1" wide, as companies may scan your résumé into a database.

Tailor your résumé to specific industries or jobs.

List your most recent work experience first, except in the case where earlier experience bears directly on the company's needs.

Use meaningful words.

## Don't:

Underline or italicize words or handwrite or fax your résumé.

Disregard the importance of your past experience, job-related or otherwise.

Include exact dates. Months and years are enough.

Add "References available on request." It is assumed and clutters the page.

**The Online Résumé**

## Do:

Apply online whenever possible. If you don't the job may go to an e-mail competitor.

Use appropriate nouns in your résumé. Employers tend to plug nouns, not verbs, into the computer when doing a search.

Survey the words you see in the job ads, then use these in your résumé. Potential employers will likely use the same words in their electronic search.

## Don't:

Send your résumé without a subject line.

Use acronyms or other words that only the geek culture understands.

Use columns, graphics, or shading.

Bold, capitalize or underline too many words or entire sentences.

OfficePolitics

## THE INTERVIEW (appearance)

A good job interview depends on your appearance, personality, skills, and how well you can handle a conversation. An interview is unlike any other tête-a-tête encounter because you are going to be judged throughout it.

The interview begins the moment you open the door. If you show up with unwashed hair, unkempt fingernails, rumpled clothing, dirty shoes, or excessive jewellery, you are putting your future in jeopardy.

What you wear will affect the interviewer's decision-making process. Do not dress as if you were going to a wedding, or wear something that you have never worn before. Dress in a way that does not bring attention to yourself. When you are dressed properly, the interviewer will not be distracted by your clothes and focus instead on what you have to offer. Your clothing image should reflect the position to which you aspire. You must convey a feeling of accessibility and friendliness.

Both genders should avoid garments that are too tight, too loose, too big, or too small.

A man may wear a blazer or sports jacket with soft wool pants. To look more conservative and serious, then a suit is in order, preferably a European cut. Unless you want an investment banking or a top-level position, avoid suspenders, a three-piece suit, a strong pinstripe, or a double-breasted jacket.

Wear a good shirt in pure cotton, white or blue, nothing trendy, no monograms, no button-down collars (too preppy). Your silk tie should express your personality without being too flamboyant. Leave your pocket square at home. Socks must be long enough to hide your skin when crossing your legs; the best colour is black.

Avoid penny loafers, wing tips, and boots. Go for a lace-up shoe instead. Shoes, belts, and briefcases should only be black, brown, or burgundy, and in good condition.

Women may wear a business suit or jacket and skirt made of light wool. Keep to solid neutral colours (navy, black, taupe, grey, tan, and khaki.) Stay away from maxi or mini skirts. The blouse or sweater should reflect a high quality fabric such as silk or cotton. Hosiery should be tan or black. A low-heel black pump is best. Avoid stilettoes, high-legged boots or big platforms.

Jewellery should be minimal: small earrings, a nice watch, a pin on your lapel is a nice touch. Never wear more than one ring on each hand. Make-up and hair should look natural.

When a person dresses in a manner unlike his or her normal custom, it invariably shows. The interviewer will look for someone who is at ease with himself or herself.

## THE INTERVIEW (personality)

The personal interview will be the first one you have and it is mostly geared to getting to know your personality.

The questions usually asked by the interviewer fall into these categories:

1. Work background
2. Level of education
3. Family
4. Interests and hobbies

## THE INTERVIEW

**Do:**

Find out background information about the company before the interview, know how to pronounce the interviewer's name.

Practice in advance your responses to expected questions.

Dress for the job you want; on the conservative side.

Be on time, and no more than 10 minutes early.

**Don't:**

Put your feet on the table while waiting to be interviewed.

Dress poorly, it may signal that you do not want or cannot do the job.

Slouch, smoke, or chew gum.

| Do: | Don't: |
|---|---|
| Be polite to everyone when entering the reception area. | Sit until asked when entering the room. |
| Give a firm handshake when arriving and leaving; stand up to greet the interviewer. | Ask for tea, coffee, or water if it is not offered. |
| Maintain eye contact throughout the interview. Lean forward and project your voice. | Talk too much, or discuss your personal life in details. |
| Keep your poise. Hold your head up. | Put anything on the interviewer's desk without first asking "May I?" |
| Show enthusiasm and a willingness to learn. | |
| Be sure to exhibit strength if the position requires a strong personality. | Put down a former boss. |
| Listen carefully. Turn negative questions into positive. | Play Mr. Nice Guy or be a bore. |
| Be truthful but positive when answering a question about why you are looking for a new job. | |
| Ignore all interruptions, do not listen if the interviewer takes a call. | Give too long an answer. |
| Bring copies of your résumé. | Use slang or jargon. |
| Have your career goals in mind. Know why you are interested in the job. Emphasize your accomplishments and the contributions you can make. | Overdo it. |



OfficePolitics

| Do: | Don't: |
|---|---|
| Give examples of how you can use your skills in the job you are applying for. | Shift in your chair. It will make you appear nervous. |
| Sell your potential. Know your strengths and weaknesses. | Provide generic answers such as "I'm a hard worker". |
| Be honest if you are asked to describe a weakness and describe strengths that are relevant to the position. | Cite perfectionism as your weakness – it is not a fault. |
| Ask questions that show your interest in the job. Prepare at least two questions about the company. These should be open-ended but direct. | Lose the interviewer's attention. |
| Evaluate the interviewer and the company to assess the quality of the opportunity before you commit yourself to it. | Press for an answer right away. |
| Give a realistic answer to a question about your salary expectations. | Lie about what you are now getting paid. |
| Follow up job interviews with an e-mail or personal note to explain anything negative that may have occurred during the interview, or to reaffirm your suitability to the position. | |
| Write a thank-you note and send it the same day. | |

OfficePolitics

You may be asked back for a second, third, or more interviews, especially if you have applied for a top position. In the near future, you may even have to go through an interview via the computer before you get one in person.

Companies today will make you jump through hoops, but if you refuse, the job will go to the next person. An executive was once recruited by a high-tech firm in Boston and had to endure 17 interviews — but he finally got the job.

## JOB TESTS

In an article in the National Post (May 10, 1999), Lorne Sulsky, associate professor of industrial and organizational psychology at the University of Calgary says companies are looking for the "big five" personality traits in employees: social adaptability; agreeableness; conscientiousness; emotional stability, and imagination. "These personality traits are supposedly predictive of success in a variety of jobs."

Sulsky, who is also the president of the Canadian Society for Industrial Organizational Psychology, adds that a well chosen test or tests can improve employers chances of hiring the best people.

The most common job tests are as follows:

### The Psychological Test

The second interview would most likely be a psychological test to see whether you would fit in with the corporation. Are you a problem solver? Do you have leadership and communication skills? How will you act on the job? — not how you think you might. How effective are you when dealing with a demanding client?

### The Work Test

Numerous enterprises require applicants to perform a work test. In the U.S., the American Telephone & Telegraph Co. requires some job aspirants to deliver presentations or lead meetings. Managerial applicants at Massachusetts Mutual Life Insurance Co. have to pretend to be the boss for a day.

### The HDS Test

If you want to be promoted to a leadership position, the company may ask you to pass an HDS (Hogan Development Survey) test developed by psychologists Robert and Joyce Hogan of Tulsa, Oklahoma. It detects bad bosses.

The HDS assesses 11 patterns of behaviour that have been noted among managers when they are overworked and experiencing stress. The test also identifies the characteristics that make good leaders and can determine how well a manager is suited to teamwork.

## THE LUNCH INTERVIEW

If you get asked for a lunch interview, be prepared — not only will you have to perform but you are going to have to eat properly too. Table manners may be the factor that determines whether you get hired for the job. In the U.S., 30 percent of all job interview failures stem from poor manners (*Wall Street Journal*).

The most common mistakes made during a lunch interview are:

- Holding a fork incorrectly.
- Talking with your mouth full.
- Not putting your napkin on your lap.
- Using your napkin as a flag.
- Buttering a whole piece of bread instead of breaking it into small pieces.
- Pushing food onto the fork with your thumb.

(See Chapter 1: **Basic Manners** for more advice on table manners and power lunches.)

## NEGOTIATING FOR MORE MONEY WHEN A JOB IS OFFERED

| Do: | Don't: |
| --- | --- |
| Ask, it is acceptable. The first offer is the starting point to counteroffers. | Assume the initial offer is a take it or leave it deal. |
| Be reasonable; you may ask for a 5 to 10 percent increase. | Alienate the employer by asking for too much. |

Always negotiate for other benefits if you cannot get the salary you want:

- a bonus at the end of the year
- an early opportunity for a raise
- more paid vacation
- tuition reimbursement
- career development (training courses)
- flexible work hours
- a company-paid membership to a private club
- some company-paid gadgets (cellular phone, notebook, laptop)
- some stock options
- a paid relocation
- a prominent job title

(For more information, see "Asking For A Raise," p. 60)

## MAIL & LETTER ETIQUETTE

| Do: | Don't: |
|---|---|
| Use quality paper; white or ecru, unless a more artistic image is desired. Black ink is best. | Use quality paper for everyday use. |
| Write a letter that is brief, thoughtful, honest, and to the point. Clearly reveal your purpose from the beginning. | Use jargon, foul language, or exaggeration in order to persuade. |
| Be prompt and proofread memos and letters carefully. | Misspell anyone's name. |
| Answer important mail within four days, and less important mail within two weeks. | Send out a sloppy-looking business letter. |
| Answer thank-you notes for gifts no later than 3 months. | Write many words, sentences, or paragraphs where one will do. |



Office Politics

Do:

Respond to written invitations as soon as you can especially for lunches, dinners, or weddings.

Use company letterhead for business only.

Don't:

Send a thank-you note on printed letterhead.

A thank-you note should be proper, personal, meaningful, sincere, and timely.

**BUSINESS CARDS**

Do:

Display the relevant information about your business. Use print large enough to read easily. Always include the area code with your telephone number.

Give it to someone to let him or her know who you are and where you can be reached.

Hand out your card at the beginning or at the end of a meeting or meal.

Don't:

Exchange business cards during a meal.

Force your card on senior executives.

Give your card too readily to someone you hardly know or to a group of strangers.

(See chapters 5 to 12 for business card etiquette in different countries.)





OfficePolitics

## FACSIMILES (FAXES)

**Do:**

Use a cover sheet when sending a fax, specifying the number of pages being sent.

Send less than five pages unless the recipient is expecting more.

Use light-coloured paper.

Reply immediately to a fax even if only to acknowledge receipt and advise when to expect a reply.

Send only typewritten business letters by fax (12- to 16-point type size is the best).

**Don't:**

Use someone's fax without permission or use the office fax for personal communication.

Ask everyone to fax you this and that.

Send a messy looking fax that has dark patches because you forgot to cut the photographs out.

Send thank-you notes by fax. A card is preferable.

Transmit letters of complaint by fax.

## COMPUTERS

Always investigate before buying — read a lot of material on different companies and what they have to offer. Invest in a large colour screen and get the most drive and memory. Check the warranty. Upgrade when needed.

**Do:**

Read the user's guide.

Protect your material against electrical surges. Get a backup system to safeguard the data. Make copies of all data on diskettes.

**Don't:**

Buy a computer based on price alone.

Leave your computer in a very cold place or in the sunlight.

OfficePolitics

## Do:

Devise complicated passwords using different cases, numbers, and other symbols, and make them as long as possible.

Create a password in another language that you speak.

## Don't:

Use the same password more than once. If someone cracks your password for one thing, they have access to everything else that uses the same password.

Use proper words or names.

Choose passwords that are easy to find out, such as your pet's name, car registration number, or your child's birth date.

Assume that your private information is not worth finding out—it is.

(See p. 115 for more information on laptops and PC cards.)

### THE INTERNET & E-MAIL

When you are part of an online service, you are not alone. One must be civil and respect other people's privacy. If you have your own Web site, manage it as if it was a business. Link your site to many places.

## Do:

Avoid problems by analyzing what others are doing when starting to use the Internet.

Send messages that are clear, short, and to the point — no longer than one screen.

## Don't:

Use the system to transmit your personal views or send unfriendly messages.

Capitalize your whole memorandum.

## Do:

Speak face to face or make a telephone call rather than labour over an e-mail.

Explain the purpose of your e-mail in the first sentence.

Make e-mails easy to read. Use short paragraphs and bullet points.

Say what you have to say in a positive manner. Insults accomplish little and make it difficult for the recipient to read the rest of your message with an open mind.

Use a spell check, re-read before pressing on the send button.

Use the "blind carbon copy" (Bcc) field when sending group e-mails. This way you won't divulge the names of the other people you are writing to.

Add your own note to messages that you are forwarding, don't just pass them along. Take the time to delete the extra e-mail addresses at the top and the extra symbols before each line.

Check your e-mail often.

Make subject fields relevant.

## Don't:

Forward a message unless it truly warrants passing on.

Forward jokes and chain letters.

E-mail acronyms to people who do not know what the symbols mean.

Use a lot of cute acronyms, such as LOL (laughing out loud), or any that are not likely going to be understood.

Send a potentially contentious e-mail without sleeping on it first.

Respond to someone's e-mail by copying it to other parties who you think should be casually informed or just to show that you are working.

Answer e-mail queries directly after each question in the original text—they will be hard to find. If you prefer to answer this way, leave a line space between the text and your responses.

Expect responses too soon.

## Do:

Find out what your office e-mail policy is and, by all means, use common sense.

Use your work e-mail for business topics only.

Ask the receiver if is okay to send attachment files before including them in your e-mail.

Ask first-time recipients of your e-mails whether they can receive messages that are HTML formatted. HTML messages look more like web pages and show bolding and different fonts. Otherwise, send them in plain text.

Only give your e-mail address to people you trust — unless you like junk mail.

Send short birthday greetings electronically.

If you require an urgent response, make sure you say it in the subject heading.

## Don't:

Use inter-office e-mails for personal matters. There are exceptions, such as alerting someone that their car lights are on, or letting your colleagues know that you are looking for your lost car keys.

Try to sell items via e-mail while at work.

Assume that everybody is using the Internet.

Give out your credit card number unless you know the site is secure.

Send formal invitations on the Net.

Get hooked on the Net.

## HOW TO FIGHT SPAM (JUNK E-MAILS)

If your are receiving unwanted junk e-mail and you would like to stop it, here are several things to consider:

### Do:

Ask acquaintances who include your e-mail address in mass mailings to hide your name by using the "blind carbon copy" (Bcc) feature. Tell the sender of a chain letter to remove your name from the list.

Find out if spam filters are in place at work, or try any free filter services that are available. Report spammers to anti-spam organizations.

Consider using an online e-mail service that advertises spam-free mail.

### Don't:

Respond to junk e-mail by asking to be removed from the sender's list unless you know the organization. Your reply may confirm that your address represents a "live" e-mail account, which then becomes more valuable to the spammer.

Sign up for newsletters or Web site notifications before finding out whether it means you will also receive e-mails.

Post your e-mail address on Internet discussion groups or web sites.

## NET ACRONYMS

AFK — Away from keyboard

BAK — Back at keyboard

BBL — Be back later

BD — Big deal

BFN — Bye for now

BRB — Be right back

BTW — By the way

CUL8R or L8R — See you later

CYA — See ya

FAQ — Frequently asked question

FWIW — For what it's worth

FYI — For your information

GAL — Get a life

GDM8 — G'day mate

GRD or GR&D — Grinning, running, and ducking

GR8 — Great

GTRM — Going to read mail

HTH — Hope this helps

IAE — In any event

IANAL — I am not a lawyer

IMNSHO — In my NOT so humble opinion

IMHO — In my humble opinion

IYSWIM — If you see what I mean

IOW — In other words

LOL — Lots of luck or laughing out loud

MHOTY — My hat's off to you

NRN — No reply necessary

NW — No way

OIC — Oh, I see

OOTB — Out of the box

OTOH — On the other hand

OTTH — On the third hand

PBT — Pay back time

PMFJI — Pardon me for jumping in

RSN — real soon now (which may be a long time coming)

RTM — Read the manual

SITD — Still in the dark

SOL — Sooner or later

TIA — Thanks in advance

TANSTAAFL — There ain't no such thing as a free lunch

TIC — Tongue in cheek

TLA — Three-letter acronym

TTFN — Ta ta for now

TTYL — Talk to you later

TYVM — Thank you very much

WYSIWYG — What you see is what you get

## E-BUSINESS

When designing your e-business strategy, take the following things into consideration:

- E-business is still about business—you have to consider it within the larger context.
- Define the concept. What is the idea fuelling the business?
- If you don't have a strategy, you may not be able to maintain significant returns on investment.
- Create a business plan. Potential investors will need to know the company's vision and the milestones for achieving success.
- Make sure it is feasible. Is the idea worth pursuing?

- It usually takes more time and money than is estimated to successfully launch an e-business.
- Appoint the right leader. Startups need strong leadership to advance an idea. Investors are usually betting on the management team.
- Arrange the financing. Raise the necessary capital by looking for investors who share the company's vision.
- Customers in foreign countries may order your products and services online, but you will still have to deliver them the old-fashioned way. And you will still have to provide good customer service.
- A well-designed Web site increases visibility; it doesn't guarantee new customers.
- Implement the plan. Proper implementation requires an aggressive strategic plan that can be clearly tracked by investors.
- Establish business practices. The right business infrastructure is critical to building and maintaining a successful business.

## WEB PROFESSIONALS DEFINED

**Web Technician:** Sets up and maintains a web server, links a local area network to the Internet, acquires domain names, implements security measures, publishes content to the Web, registers sites with search engines, analyzes network traffic and monitors network connectivity.

**Web Designer:** Researches, plans and designs web pages, integrates all components into web sites, writes HTML (Hypertext Markup Language), has knowledge of Internet tools and protocols, uses graphic packages for photo enhancement, image generation optimization, and format conversion. The web designer creates the web site's look and flow, incorporating usability and client needs.

**Web Manager:** Co-ordinates the planning, creation, organization, implementation, maintenance, and control of a web site. Monitors project progress, administers company policy, documents goals and direction, and arranges for resources as needed. The web manager also develops a project plan and supervises the development of content.

## TELEPHONE MANNERS

How your telephone is answered says a lot about you and your company. Some surveys show that the caller will form an opinion within the first four to six seconds.

Just as you are easily judged by your appearance, you do not get a second chance to make a good first impression on the telephone.

| Do: | Don't: |
| --- | --- |
| Identify yourself immediately when calling: "Hello, this is Thomas Scott, may I speak with Mr. Brown. He's expecting my call." | Say: "Hello this is Mr. Thomas Scott," when Thomas Scott will do just fine. |
| Ask the person right away if it is a convenient time to talk. Give the person your complete attention. | Engage in other activities while you talk on the phone. |
| Answer a business colleague's telephone by saying: "May I tell Bob\Joan who is calling?" | Call people at home for business matters unless it is critical or you have their prior permission. |
| Apologize to the person you have disturbed when you dial a wrong number. | Interrupt someone's meeting with a phone call unless it is an emergency. |
| Return your calls the same day if possible, but no later than 48 hours, or have someone else do it for you. | Be rude to anyone when you dial the wrong number. Never ask "What number is this?" Instead, ask "Is this 222-5555?" |
| Pick up the receiver immediately, first ring is best, three or more is sloppy. | Call early in the morning or late at night, unless it has been pre-arranged. |



OfficePolitics

| Do: | Don't: |
|---|---|
| If you get disconnected, the person who originally placed the call should call again. | Leave someone on hold for more than fifteen seconds. |
| Give your undivided attention to the caller. | Have your calls forwarded when you are with a client or in a business meeting. |
| Keep your personal calls to a minimum while at the office. | Make personal calls on an 800 number. |
| Write the time of the call and the caller's name, company, and telephone number when taking a message. | Get upset if a person does not want to leave a message. |
| Get to the point quickly and end your call in a positive, upbeat note. | Eat or chew into the mouthpiece. |
| Always ask first before you put someone on a speaker phone. | Switch to a speaker phone in the middle of a conversation. |

If you have an **answering service**, make sure that you know the names of the people taking care of your line and treat them cordially. Show your appreciation at Christmas with flowers or chocolate. This courtesy will help you get the best service.

## CELLPHONES

Using a cellphone while driving is increasingly under fire. A 1997 study in the *New England Journal of Medicine* found the chance of a car accident was four times greater when the driver held a cellphone. Similarly, *Knight Ridder* news service reported in 1999 that cellphone chatting drivers were five times more likely to have an accident than non-chatting ones.

In at least 23 countries, including Australia, Brazil, Germany, Great Britain, Italy, Israel, and Japan it is now illegal to use a hand-held cellphone while driving. The debate over banning cellphones while driving has also made its way to North America.

Brooklyn, Ohio, was the first American city to make it a misdemeanour. As of June 2001, New York passed a "state-wide law banning the use of hand-held cellphones while driving but allows hands-free phones."

Many studies have shown that talking on a hand-held or hands-free cellphone are both dangerous because the person is distracted and more liable to have an accident.

## Do:

Park your car before you call someone, use the speakerphone, or get a passenger in the car to place the call for you.

Make sure your phone is easy to reach. Consider the traffic before you answer or make a call.

Use the speed dial for frequently called numbers.

Place your car phone securely in its cradle so that it does not become a projectile in a crash.

Tell emergency operators whether you are reporting a medical or police emergency, and in the case of an accident, whether there appear to be injuries.

## Don't:

Call from your car and say, "I'm on the car phone." Use something else to impress, like your personality.

Make unnecessary calls while driving, chat at home.

Have long conversations on your car phone; only short ones are suitable.

Take notes while driving, or punch in numbers when there is poor visibility.

Interfere, or show a lack of respect for other drivers: e.g., you indicate that you will turn right, but then you do not because you are too busy talking on the phone.

## Do:

Turn off your cellphone at social and sporting events, the theatre, and the cinema.

## Don't:

Bring your telephone into a restaurant unless you are expecting an emergency call.

Ask to use someone's cellphone. Wait for the person to offer.

Scream or speak loudly when there are people around you.

Interrupt a face to face conversation to pick up your cellphone.

### VOICE MAIL & ANSWERING MACHINES

Do not use the voice chip that comes with some answering systems. Make a personalized message, or if you have a home-based business, consider getting a professional to do your outgoing message. Never have loud music or jokes on your machine. When you go out of town, leave the details on your business line. Be attentive to your voice mail system. A client will play telephone tag for only so long.

If you want to get around using a person's voice mail, try the following:

- Call someone else who works in the same company and ask them if they can help you reach your contact directly.
- Send e-mails or faxes.

## Do:

When you leave a message on someone's voice mail or answering machine, the following information should be included:

- Your name.
- Your telephone number including area code and extension.
- The time and date of your call.
- The name of the person for whom the message is intended.

Do:

- A brief message, enunciated clearly.
- Say "good-bye" at the end of your message to let the person know that you are finished.

Don't:

- Leave a complicated message.
- Try to be cute or funny.
- Leave bad news on an answering machine.
- Assume that people who do not answer the phone are screening their calls.

## CALL WAITING

The first caller has priority. The second caller should be handled as rapidly and efficiently as possible, but with as much consideration as the first caller. You may want to consider turning off call waiting during important calls.

## HOW MEN SHOULD DEAL WITH WOMEN AT THE OFFICE

Women play an important and expanding role in business. Unlike the previous generation, women today are generally more independent, assertive, and competitive. They are well educated, career-oriented, and quite capable of doing what used to be considered a man's job.

Because of this evolution, some men are a bit confused about how to interact with women on a professional level. Remember, the only thing women want is to be treated with respect and equality. Forget sexual distinctions — treat women as people.

Do:

Help a woman colleague with her coat or open a door, and accept gracefully if she does it for you.

Don't:

Flirt in the office. Whether you are a co-worker or the boss, it will only bring trouble.



OfficePolitics

| Do: | Don't: |
|---|---|
| Respect the ideas of the women with whom you work. | Tell a woman in your office who is married or regularly dating someone that you would love to go out alone with her. |
| Address women at the office using Ms., Miss, or Mrs., until asked to do otherwise. | Call women in the office by pet names such as "dear," "honey," "sweetie," etc. |
| Go out for dinner or drinks after work as part of a group. | Go to a bar alone with a female co-worker. |
| Keep your dialogue and body language on a professional level when dealing with female bosses. | Discuss your sexual life at the office. |
| Speak to a woman privately if you are concerned about her working habits. Do so only if you are the person in charge. | Mistreat or put down your wife, girlfriend, or a female worker in front of others. |
| It is always better to say that your secretary works "with you," rather than works "for you." Treat her with respect. | Tell off-colour jokes or make sarcastic comments. |
| Regard women in the office as team members. | Become a harmful gossip. |
| Assist women without patronizing them. | Assign note-taking in meetings to women only. |
| Praise, congratulate, and spotlight achievements. | Play the psychologist, e.g., your problem is... |

| Do: | Don't: |
|---|---|
| Expect your secretary to serve coffee when you have visitors or when you are very busy. Clarify this when you hire her. | Expect your secretary to serve your coffee daily. |
| Be honest and develop trust in order to remove any road blocks to communication. | Order or threaten by using such phrases as " you must," "you have to," "you had better," or "if you don't..." |
| | Touch another person in a business setting. When it is not reciprocal, touching can be seen as a power play or harassment. |

## PERSONAL QUESTIONS

Questions that are too personal to ask a person at the office:

- What someone's salary is.
- The age of a person who is over thirty.
- The details of a divorce, especially on the custody of children or alimony.
- Whether a person has had a facelift or laser surgery.
- What religion someone practices.
- What someone's political choices are.
- About someone's sexual orientation or lifestyle.

## ROMANCE AT THE OFFICE

Research done in the last couple of years shows that many couples met at the office. Even with sexual harassment cases on the rise, office romance is going strong — mainly because people do not have the time to look elsewhere. Combined with a fear of disease, people are looking for partners at work more than ever before.

A survey in Fortune magazine showed that three-quarters of the CEOs interviewed on the subject of romance between workers said it was none of the company's business. In some workplaces, however, office romance is frowned upon. You should know your company's rules, both the formal and the unwritten ones.

| Do: | Don't: |
|---|---|
| Keep an office romance discreet. | Hold hands, kiss, or fax each other love notes while at the office. |
| Act professionally, and sustain a high level of productivity. | Make telephone calls to each other at the office. |
| Keep your affair under wraps until you have committed to a long-term relationship. | Arrive or leave with your lover, or sit next to him or her at meetings. |
| Ask for a transfer if love is interfering with your work. | Discuss with co-workers what happened on your date. |
| Be aware that some co-workers won't approve of an office romance and you could lose some credibility. | Have an intimate relationship with a subordinate — it could end in a lawsuit or someone getting ousted. |
| Make sure that your office romance does not create an unbusinesslike atmosphere. | Get involve with someone who is married or known as the office flirt. |
| Realize that an affair at work could prevent you from getting promoted. | Ask for another date if you know the relationship will never be serious. |

OfficePolitics

## GETTING FIRED

Even if you knew you might get fired, or hoped you would, the moment will have a huge emotional impact. Here are some guidelines to help you get through the ordeal:

| Do: | Don't: |
| --- | --- |
| Save questions and comments for later. Just listen. | Try to read your severance letter in the meeting with your boss. If you are a longtime employee, you might want to take a quick look at the dollar amount. Otherwise, wait until you get home and read it in privacy. |
| Be clear about what is expected of you on your last day of work. If you do not know, ask. | Use this time to confront your boss. |
| Compose yourself before you leave the office and walk out with dignity. | Say your good-byes before you leave for home. Call your co-workers later. |

## DEALING WITH BULLYING AT THE OFFICE

Bullying is any of the following behaviours: yelling, rudeness, severe criticism, threats, harassment (usually sexual or racial) or even physical assault. The actions are frequent enough to affect an employee's ability to do his or her job.

Here are some suggestions for dealing with bullies:

- **Communicate with the bully:** Politely tell the bully that their behaviour is inappropriate and ask them to stop immediately. This should be enough to change the way the bully acts toward you. If not, try communicating in writing, and consider sending a copy to his or her supervisor. This approach is a lot more aggressive, so be sure you know where you stand.

- **Document the behaviour:** Bullying usually comes down to credibility — yours versus the bully's. Keep detailed notes of the objectionable behaviour, when and where it occurred, and the names of any witnesses. This will help you prove your case later on.
- **File an internal complaint:** Find out whether your company has any administration related to bullying — such as a sexual harassment or workplace harassment policy. Such procedures commonly deal with discrimination and are particularly focused on race, gender, disability, and sexual orientation.
- **File an external complaint:** If you haven't stopped the bullying by other means, consider filing an external complaint. If your complaint is based on conduct that is discriminatory — for example, sexual or racial harassment — you can file a complaint with a human rights commission. There is usually a limitation period for filing, so check with the commission to avoid missing the cut-off date.
- **Launch a civil action:** Lawsuits are expensive and, in most cases, you will have to leave your job. Depending on the nature of the bullying and its consequences, you may be able to claim "constructive dismissal," which entitles you to sue for "reasonable notice" damages.
- **Consider resigning:** If the bullying is causing significant emotional and psychological harm, and your company has failed to take action, it is probably best to simply resign. Even though you won't be entitled to compensation if you resign, it may be necessary to your well being.

## BUILDING RAPPORT WITH YOUR BOSS

When hired for a new job, establish who you will be working for. Find out right away what is expected of you by getting to know the corporate culture.

What you should try to know about your boss without personally asking him:

1. His or her personal style; how people view him or her.
2. His or her values on family, religion, social issues, and politics.
3. His or her interests and hobbies.

## Do:

Always address your boss and co-workers with Mr., Mrs., Ms., or Miss, unless they tell you otherwise.

Learn the boss's style. Try to understand him or her. Find out his or her true objectives.

Be honest and dependable. Show enthusiasm, tact, and sensitivity.

Be willing to learn and change. Listen when your boss makes a suggestion.

Spread the word about your boss's success. Voice public support for his or her goals.

Be accountable and responsible for you actions. Observe deadlines.

Accept full responsibility for the things you do. Take criticism positively.

Admire a boss who delegates — it shows strength.

Be supportive and a good listener. When your boss has a problem, try to help solve it.

Treat your boss's feelings with care and try to understand them. Praise his or her good points.

## Don't:

Walk into his or her office without an appointment.

Say, "We always did it that way." Never bring old problems to your new job.

Overreact when a crisis occurs.

Become too friendly, take over, or try to fight your boss's battles.

Be the bearer of bad news unless you have to.

Go around your boss's decisions or complain to her or his superiors.

Spring something on your boss if at all possible and don't upstage him or her.

Underestimate your employer.

Criticize your boss in front of other staff, clients, and suppliers.

Use your boss as a confidant, do not burden him or her with personal problems. Your boss is not your best friend.

OfficePolitics

## Do:

Deal with a dislikable boss by ignoring his or her rages. Catch your boss doing something positive and thank him or her. Develop a support network with co-workers. Hold your ground and stay rational when bullied.

Take legal action if you are abused by your boss.

Adjust to the situation if your boss is younger than you — show adaptability and work harder.

Share your accomplishments with him or her.

Learn to manage your boss; adapt to that individual's personality and needs.

Be understanding of your boss's quirks; show compassion.

Send a card or a note if your boss is sick or hospitalized.

## Don't:

Wait until you are really angry to ask for a personal meeting.

Drop into your boss's home without a proper invitation.

Patronize a young boss or have a know-it-all attitude.

Talk negatively to your boss about people you work with.

Lecture your employer or try to go over his or her head to get something approved.

Invite your boss out socially before he or she asks you.

Visit your boss in a hospital unless invited.

### THE BOSS'S SPOUSE

## Do:

Note that the boss may sometimes bring his or her spouse to the office to get a feel for the employees.

## Don't:

Underestimate the power of the boss's wife or husband.

## Do:

Keep a professional distance from the boss's spouse should he or she work in the same office.

Mind your own business when the boss's spouse is in a powerful position at your office.

Treat spouses who attend office parties as real people. Make an effort to meet and chat. Try to find out their interests.

## Don't:

Forget that when a man and woman run a business together there will always be one who plays the role of the "bad cop," and it is usually the woman.

Imagine that just because everyone else thinks the boss's wife/ husband is a pain it means the boss would agree. Not so!

Tell the spouse of your boss that her husband/his wife is having an affair with an employee.

Give the boss's spouse the details of what's happening in the office over the telephone. Tell the spouse that you are busy and connect him or her with the husband or wife.

Take sides if there is an argument between the boss and his or her spouse.

### EXECUTIVE ETIQUETTE

Job protection in the corporate world and other business sectors has changed enormously from previous decades. There are no more job guaranties: long-term employment is not a sure thing and the "no lay offs" policy is dead and buried.

In this millennium you must take responsibility for what you want in life. Self-management is what it is all about — you cannot wait for directions, or expect to be trained by a company or sent all-expenses paid to special programs.

At the executive level, you are in charge of people, projects, and decisions. You have to be in control, bring yourself up to speed, master your skills, and see yourself as a business entity.

Remember the old adage: In a company no one should complain, everyone should perform.

| Do: | Don't: |
|---|---|
| Have an image that is credible and consistent. | Expect people to follow rules if you do not follow them yourself. |
| Realize that you are the living advertisement of your company. You are only influential if you are perceived to be. | Step on another's territory or read papers on other people's desks. |
| Keep your promises. Respect the ideas of others. | Accept anything until you are sure it is the best. |
| Be a good teacher. | Pretend to be an expert if you are not one. |
| Learn to work with people you don't like. Show people they matter. | Make negative assumptions. |
| Return borrowed property. | |
| Show compassion when there is bad news in a colleague's personal life. | Be arrogant or threatening. |
| Go out of your way to help people in the organization. Treat them fairly, equally, and with respect. | Become the office doormat or give a reason for everything that you do. |
| Be a team player. Exhibit leadership qualities. | Drop in on a business associate without an appointment. |
| Involve everyone in continuous improvement. Listen to people's suggestions. | Keep people waiting for an appointment outside your office, or show up late. |
| Handle decisions quickly. | Procrastinate. |

## Do:

Let people know you appreciate them. Keep them happy.

Look for ways to make new ideas work.

Accept responsibility, follow through.

Speak positively about your company.

Remain ethical, honest, and have integrity.

Be willing to work hard; your success depends on it.

Commit to your work one hundred percent.

Communicate clearly with co-workers if a disagreement arises.

Have allies and make sure that people know it.

Work hard at being polite. The nicer you are the more opportunities you will get.

## Don't:

Have any employee as an intimate personal friend.

Be proud of stupid things.

Patronize or play the psychologist, saying things such as "Your problem is..."

Borrow money from someone in the office.

Give criticism or confront an employee in front of others.

Mistreat a business associate's secretary.

Use sarcastic remarks to make a point, such as "I'm glad that you finally made it on time."

Get other people involved when resolving a problem with a colleague.

Avoid issues; we have all heard, "Let me check it out and get back to you."

## ASKING FOR A RAISE

Always negotiate with a winning hand. You must be able to convince your boss that you deserve that pay increase. Prove to him that you are an important player in the company.

(See p. 34 for information on this subject.)

| Do: | Don't: |
| --- | --- |
| Find out what you are worth by doing some market research. | Ask for an appointment by fax or e-mail. |
| Make your request in person. If the secretary asks what you want to see your boss about, tell her it is about your performance or career. If she wants more details, say "It's personal." | Ask for a raise if you just bungled an important deal.<br>Count on a raise to be automatic or guaranteed. |
| Ask for a raise after a major coup or at your yearly review. Use your business acumen to sell yourself. | Whine, as in "My wife will leave me if I don't get a raise," "I have been with the company twenty years and I deserve a raise," or "Everyone else got one." |
| Show your accomplishments; have a list of how your work has benefited the company. | Get on the defensive or be aggressive if your boss shows some opposition to your demand. |
| Ask at a later date if you are refused the first time. Never give up. | Get too annoyed if the boss offers you a car, a big office, or a new title instead. |

## NAME TAGS

There are certain situations such as conventions, corporate gatherings and business parties when one needs to wear a name tag.

| Do: | Don't: |
| --- | --- |
| Place the name tag on your right shoulder. When you shake hands your name will be more visible on the right than on the left. | Include Mr., Mrs., or any other gender designations on the tag. |
| Put your professional title, such as "President" or "Doctor," or the company name on the tag — if you wish. | Use a soiled or torn name tag. |

## MAKING MEETINGS WORK FOR YOU

Many people think that meetings are a waste of time. The fact is, they will not go away. They are conducted to exchange information, to make announcements, or to vote on a direction. There will always be a meeting when a decision has to be made.

Today meetings are smarter, more focused, shorter, and less costly. The idea is still the same, however — goals must be attained.

| Do: | Don't: |
| --- | --- |
| Hold meetings in the morning when everyone is fresh with ideas. | Hold meetings on Friday afternoons. |
| Make the meeting convenient for others — show consideration for the schedules of the individuals attending. | Call a meeting at the last minute; allow people a chance to prepare. |
| Let the chairperson show you to your seat. | Arrive late. |
| Understand quickly what's going on and where everybody fits in the larger scheme of things. | Request refreshments if not offered. |

| Do: | Don't: |
|---|---|
| Have the confidence to present your ideas with wit and wisdom. Be as specific as possible. | Take too long to make your move. |
| Tell a person that is interrupting that they are making a valuable point, but it will have to be discussed at another time. | Interrupt or quarrel with someone who is angry, and do not sit across from a colleague who you have just had an argument with. |
| Accept responsibility. Supply background information and reasons for changes. | Confuse toughness with bullying by making someone feel bad in front of others. |
| Keep your talk to a minimum and speak only to the matter at hand. | Daydream, look disinterested, or slump in your seat. |
| Thank the chairperson on your way out. | Make offensive noises with your pen or drum your fingers. |
| | Be a Mr. Goody Two Shoes or a know-it-all. You will drive everyone mad. |

**When in charge of a meeting:**

- devise a meeting plan
- open the meeting forcefully
- give clear directions
- establish your goals
- listen to others
- keep to the agenda and time allotted
- stay in control
- keep meetings productive and focussed
- read the signals
- bring to a close
- thank everyone for their input
- evaluate every meeting
- follow up

## TRADITIONAL POWER POSITIONING IN MEETINGS

The head of the table is the most important spot, this is where the chairperson sits. At a table for eight, the other important power spots are the foot of the table and the centre seat on either side — these seats provide a direct line of sight with the chairperson. A seat at the foot of the table is the best for a person making a presentation.

Chairs on the right and left of the chairperson are reserved for guests; of these, the chair on the right is the most important. At a round table, the power spots are the seats nearest to the left or right of the chairperson.

| Do: | Don't: |
|---|---|
| Wait to be seated if you are a junior executive. | Sit at the head of the table or in any of the power spots unless you belong there or are invited to do so. |
| Move to the seat you are given and say, "thank you." | Sit until senior persons have taken their seats. |
| | Hunch in your seat at meetings. It shows disrespect to others. |

## OFFICES OF THE NEW MILLENNIUM

Power positioning in offices is not so important today as it was in the 1980's and '90s. Managers who once could not live without corner offices are now working from their cars. Status is out.

Today people are rewarded for the work they do and the initiative they take. Values have shifted. Companies are downsizing, reorganizing, and trying to get rid of old-school attitudes. Management is pushing teamwork and cooperation.

Welcome to the age of the cubicle. Office planners in Canada and the U.S. are now designating about 100 to 150 square feet per worker — some 100 square feet less than a decade ago. Many companies are trying to get the most value out of their real estate dollars.

Dividers are coming down and some executive offices are being eliminated. The tendency is to have smaller meeting rooms and to get rid of big conference spaces.

This transition is very difficult for workers who are used to working alone or who perform better privately. Some companies have to train employees about the importance of respecting others' personal space before moving them to smaller workspaces. Communicate with the staff. Inform them about the reason behind the change. Begin with a pilot program. Find out whether the new design is actually going to work. Be realistic — a new office look won't solve all your management problems. Provide your employees with proper environment layouts, ergonomic furniture, clean air, distilled water, windows, natural light, user friendly washrooms, good food facilities, adequate parking or access to transit. Show you care. Find out who needs quiet space, who needs to interact with others. Give the employees workplaces that are easy to use.

A major trend at more sophisticated companies is toward "hotelling." A concierge allocates available space in a hotel for consultants that are in and out of the office a lot. When the consultant makes a reservation, the concierge gets the person's files, sets up a computer, and an instant office is ready when he or she arrives.

The concierge may provide other services such as calling the dry-cleaning service, or making a dinner or theatre reservation when a consultant has to entertain a client.

Another trend, especially in the U.S., is the satellite office. The head office is electronically linked to smaller offices in different cities. This is especially good for consultants that are on the road.

## EUROPEAN OFFICES

Rules concerning office space differ all over Europe. Compared to North Americans, Europeans are more status driven. It will be a while before open-plan offices take a hold in Europe, but there is a move towards a common standard. For impact and recognition, big companies want all of their international offices to have the same design.

In Germany and the Netherlands, workers must be seated at least seven metres from the window. In Germany, office space of more than 100 square metres must have a three-metre high ceiling.

In France, there is no written policy but a person who does not see daylight gets to take extra days of vacation. A non-smoking building must set up one smoking room per floor.

In Spain, every employee must have at least 10 square metres of space.

There are no rules on natural light in Britain. Office building there may be constructed deeper and the floor plans divided into smaller areas.

And in Belgium, the ceilings of office buildings must be 2.5 metres high.

## HOME OFFICES

### Do:

Set up a home office only if you have the discipline.

Project a competent image. When meeting with customers, dress as if you were in a downtown office.

Get business cards done by a professional printer. Add a picture to a brochure.

Get your own telephone line. Use voice-mail — it sounds more professional.

### Don't:

Set up an office near the kitchen or a bedroom.

Invite clients to your home unless your office looks very professional.

Get involved in family matters, house repairs, or cleaning while working.

Let family members answer you business line.

Do:

Market yourself. Approach your local newspapers, radio, and television.

Reach your clients the way they like to communicate. Have an e-mail address and establish a web site.

Don't:

Let your children open the door for clients or interrupt you during a meeting.

**NETWORKING**

Networking is a skill that can produce tremendous results for you or your company. To network means to exchange information, contacts, and experiences for business or social purposes. Whether in your personal life or at work, meet regularly with people to talk, as well as to support and advise each other. You will learn to do things better and solve problems. Network with a group in your company — it is less expensive than hiring a private consultant.

Stay alert and follow your instincts. Take the time to talk to people you encounter often; opportunities are everywhere. Build up your relationships; one day you might need them. Networking is more than just accumulating business cards.

Do:

Network everywhere. Talk to as many people as you can. Tell people what you do.

Join a breakfast club or volunteer for a charity. Become involved in local activities — be part of what's going on.

Act like a host, not a guest. Introduce yourself.

Don't:

Do business while networking. Make a later appointment.

Say too much about your personal life or your problems.

Impose yourself on people or be too pushy.

## Do:

Jot down facts about the people you network with. Follow up, keep in touch.

Advertise yourself. Promote others. Develop and edit your contacts.

Remember to thank people who help you.

## Don't:

Network on a date.

Overburden your contacts.

## NETWORKING ABROAD

Networking with people in other countries can help you do your job better. It will keep you informed, give you new ideas, and enhance your influence with others. It will also give you an idea of your market value, which gives you negotiating power.

International networking can also lead to other job offers. You may decide you want to change careers, or simply want a safety net in case you lose a job or miss out on an opportunity.

## Do:

Spend a great deal of time networking.

Get an internationally accepted credential. Attend an executive degree program at a well known business school or, barring that, even a three-day course is useful.

## Don't:

Leak information or provide a bad referral. These kinds of things will give you a bad reputation.

Call up just to say hello — in Europe, it is simply not done.

Neglect your in-house networks.

**Office**Politics

## THE ETIQUETTE OF AMBITION

Competition is inevitable and every one of us will engage in it at some time. Some qualities are required to get ahead: self-esteem, organizational skills, positive work ethics, being a good team player, an ability to take risks, and having a talent for seizing opportunities.

| Do: | Don't: |
|---|---|
| Use common sense; being aware and thinking ahead are elements of a person's success, development, and leadership. | Be pushy, rude, and insensitive. |
| Face hostility with poise. | Get angry. |
| Make friends with your competitors. | Stomp on your contenders. |
| Remember to work as part of a team. | |
| Listen, be courteous, and get along with others. | Spend too much time making your move. |
| Stay on the path of self-improvement. | Stop learning — ever. |
| Make the right connections. Attract a mentor. | |
| Let people know your goals. | |
| Ask for feed back on your job performance. | |
| Excel in what you do. Seek high visibility. | Compromise on quality. |
| Publicize your achievements. Become known for something. Develop expertise. | |





OfficePolitics

You do not have to be ruthless to make it to the top. As Eliza G.C.Collins, a senior editor of the Harvard Business Review pointed out: "Etiquette may take you farther than aggressiveness, and integrity can take you all the way."

## WINNING

To be successful one must know who one is and who one is not.

One must recognize one's true persona and develop a personal style and charisma.

Think big and win big. "I like to think big, I always have," said Donald Trump. "To me it's very simple: If you are going to be thinking anyway, you might as well think big."

Make your dream become reality, there is magic in the power of belief. Have a purpose and a vision for the future, develop a plan with specific goals, and do everything in your power to reach them. Stay focused, do not get caught up in what you should have done yesterday, concentrate on what you can do today. Take risks! If you fail, get back up again — achievement knows no age limit.

Connect with winners, use your contacts, and develop alliances with the most powerful people you know. High achievers and powerful people have a driving force that is usually larger than themselves — they use it to focus and direct all of their energy. They create their own luck.

When you cannot make a decision, trust your feelings, the answer is within you. Intuition is a great asset. A person who knows how to use it will always come out ahead. Success is easier for those who trust their intuition for they make fewer mistakes.

Look, speak, and act like a winner.

> "Never surrender the belief that good guys can — and increasingly will — finish first." (Owen Edwards, Upward Nobility.)

# Your Public Image

YourPublicImage

# Chapter 3

## NON-VERBAL COMMUNICATION

To develop a winning image you must communicate effectively. Good body language, which sends the appropriate message at the correct time, goes a long way toward making the proper impression. Do not hinder yourself by the way your body talks, walks, and gestures. If your posture is bad, it will affect the way you speak, and send out the message that you are insecure, scared — not in control.

Non-verbal communication has been described as the music that accompanies the words. It's not what you say that is significant at first, it's how you say it! Words express roles; non-verbal communication expresses feelings and attitudes.

In face-to-face interactions, body language communicates 60 percent of our message, our tone of voice accounts for 30 percent, and our words, only 10 percent. It is vital, therefore, that our body language reflect our spoken message.

## FACE

In dealing with other people, it is important to be able to read their mood. It is equally important to know what signals your gestures and facial expressions may be sending.

### Do:

Show warmth and intelligence through facial expressions.

Look directly at the person with whom you are speaking. Eye contact is extremely important. For one-on-one meetings, eye contact is recommended as much as 95 percent of the time.

### Don't:

Cover your mouth when speaking. It suggests that you are not sure of what you are saying.

Overpower another person by the way you look at them — don't stare.

Do: Learn to read others' every movement: the slight raise of an eyebrow, the tilt of the head.

Don't: Blink excessively, it may be interpreted as a sign of guilt, fear, anger, or lying. Research suggests that a good lie detector is whether someone blinks too much.

Do: Look natural. Your facial expressions should reinforce what you are saying.

Don't: Blush, giggle, or contract your facial muscles, as these show tension.

Do: Smile, it is the best way to create a rapport and will make you look comfortable.

Don't: Frown or look scornful, it will make you appear too serious.

Don't: Constantly touch your face, or bite your lips or nails, as these are associated with insecurity.

Don't: Hold your head down or look down to the left, it signals submission.

Don't: Cough frequently, it implies nervousness or covering up a lie.

### HANDS & ARMS

Do: Make a point by using an open palm. The gesture that shows rather than points, transmits a much more acceptable message.

Don't: Point at another person. Pointing is associated with making an accusation and gives out a negative signal.

Do: Signal sincerity with open hands. It shows you want to listen.

Don't: Drum on a paper to make a point, or point at a document for emphasis.

## Do:

Be aware that if someone is scratching his chin, or has his hand next to his chin and one finger touching his temple or cheek, he is probably evaluating what's been said.

Lean forward when sitting at a conference table, it indicates that you are interested.

Keep your fingers together when gesturing.

Use your hand gestures to capture attention and convince your audience when speaking in public.

Keep your hands at your sides or on the lectern when speaking to an audience.

Find out which gesture works best for you and use it to make an impact.

## Don't:

Put your hands behind your back. It signifies defiance of authority.

Put your hands behind your head. It gives the impression that you think you are superior.

Back away from the table at a meeting, it means that you don't feel part of the group and are not interested.

Cross your arms when listening to someone, it suggests you are not willing to communicate.

Cross your arms with tight fists, it is a defensive position.

Flail your arms, it shows awkwardness.

Hold your arms and elbows too close to the body, it signals tension.

Fidget with your ring, pick at your cuticles, play with your hair, pull at one ear. These gestures suggest you are bored.

YourPublicImage

Do:

Carry yourself with confidence — maintain good posture and movement.

Don't:

Touch or rub your nose with your index finger. It shows doubt and uncertainty.

Put your hands on your hips when speaking with someone. You will be perceived as a know-it-all.

Wring your hands. This gesture shows a lack of confidence and people will have trouble relating to you.

**LEGS & FEET**

Do:

Keep your feet flat on the floor and the legs closed together — the proper position for a woman.

Cross your legs only if it is acceptable in the country you are visiting.

Keep your knees apart when both legs are on the floor — the proper position for a man.

Sit up straight when you want to make a point.

Practice walking in front of a mirror. Keep your head up and look ahead; stomach in, chest out.

Don't:

Lock your ankles. It means you are holding back.

Cross your legs in some countries — some people are offended if you point your feet or the soles of your shoes at them.

Cross and uncross your legs.

Put your leg over the arm of a chair or sofa. It shows indifference.

YourPublicImage

# Do:

Walk tall and you will have the respect of your peers. Deliberate movement reflects confidence.

## PERSONAL SPACE

Every person is "encased" in a bubble of personal space. The size of the bubble depends on the degree of intimacy between people and varies with culture. In general, however, people do not want their personal space to be invaded. Respect everyone's personal space — three to five feet is the perfect distance.

Edward T. Hall, an American anthropologist, views personal space as an extension of the human body. He defined the following four distinct zones:

The Intimate Zone (within 18 inches of your body) — for whispering and embracing.

The Personal Zone (18 inches to four feet) — for conversing with close friends.

The Social Zone (four to 10 feet) — for conversing with acquaintances.

The Public Zone (10 to 25 feet) — for interacting with strangers.

These zones are mostly appropriate for people in North America and Europe. The distances are closer in Latin and Asian cultures. In general, however, it is always important to respect other people's personal space.

# Don't:

Invade a person's personal space by standing too close to them.

Pick up or touch objects on someone else's desk. It is private property.

Touch people with whom you work. Any gestures of affection that are not wanted become very uncomfortable for other people.

Interfere when someone is talking.

(See chapters 5 to 12 for more on "personal space" in different countries.)

YourPublicImage

### The Rules of Standing in Line

From *The Waiting Game* by Amy Finnerty.

Some essential truths about the mind of the involuntary idler:

1. Unoccupied time feels longer than occupied time.
2. "First contact" with a service provider (for instance, checking in with a host in a crowded restaurant) makes people who are waiting feel better, even if it gets them no closer to their goal.
3. Human beings have a natural fear of being forgotten.
4. Anxiety makes a wait seem longer.
5. Any unexplained event or circumstance increases anxiety.
6. Perceived unfairness makes waiting seem longer.
7. Waiting alone is worse than waiting with one or more companions.
8. The greater the ratio of the patron's personal wealth to the value of the service, the more impatient she will be. (In other words, the rich won't wait around for just anything.)
9. An unexpected wait feels longer.

## CONFRONTATION

| Do: | Don't: |
|---|---|
| Ask the person confronting you if you can talk later in private. Deal with emotions first. | Argue or confront someone in public. |
| Be open and receptive when dealing with conflict, it will make the other person less hostile and defensive. | Say things in the heat of the moment that you would regret later. |
| Avoid further interaction with someone you have had a recent confrontation with. Avoid eye contact with that person by sitting on the same side of the table at a meeting. | Sit across from a person with whom you have just had a confrontation. |

## Do:

Seek a compromise in a conflict. Acknowledge the other person's needs.

## Don't:

Confront anyone on the telephone or by e-mail.

## PUBLIC SPEAKING

Speeches and presentations are an increasingly common feature of corporate life and can make a big difference to a career. Speaking skills are essential to advance in your profession. Public speaking is a learned art. World famous motivational author Dale Carnegie said, "Speaking in public makes us come to grip with our fears."

Surveys reveal that 10 percent of the audience pays attention to the content of the speech, 40 percent to the speaker's appearance, and 50 percent to how the person speaks.

The only way to become an effective public speaker is to read your speech over and over before you present it. Tape and video yourself — learn from your mistakes.

### Preparation & Voice

Always know beforehand what the occasion is, the location, who the other speakers are, their topics, and who the audience is. Approach your presentation from the audience's point of view. Know what interests them and what they expect to get out of your speech. Tailor your message for that specific audience. Be credible. Talk from experience. Fill your talk with examples. Use vivid language and dramatic effects. Be consistent with your material.

Be aware that you may get an audience that:

a) loves you
b) has already decided they do not believe in your subject
c) does not care about your presentation at all.

| Do: | Don't: |
|---|---|
| Practice impromptu talks. Personalize your speech. Know your subject. Rehearse until you are comfortable. Time your presentation. | Practice too much in front of a mirror — try and create an imaginary audience for yourself. |
| Develop a tone of voice that conveys trust, confidence, and warmth. | Look too relaxed — you may sound dull. |
| Practice focusing by controlling the emotional and physical aspects of yourself. This can be achieved through physical and vocal exercises. | Create tension in your body or strain your vocal cords by shouting. |
| Modulate your voice more than you normally would. Speak loudly, clearly, and evenly. | Speak too fast; you will appear nervous and the audience will not understand what you are saying. |
| Use good grammar and pronunciation. Say "we" not "you." | Slump or slouch, as it will affect the quality of your voice. It will tell the audience you are scared or insecure. |
| Use 4" x 6" or 3" x 5" cards. Write the word "pause" into your speech notes as a reminder. | |

**Developing Confidence**

Tips for developing confidence as a public speaker:

- Prepare yourself and your speech beforehand.
- Memorize your introduction or opening.
- Get rid of fear — get centred.
- Be alert, relaxed, and focused.



YourPublicImage

- Act confidently — as if you were talking to friends.
- Visualize your presentation; imagine a smooth delivery.
- Use your own language and sense of humour.
- Get excited about your subject — it is contagious.
- Speak from the heart.

### The Parts of a Speech

The introduction of your speech should take up five percent of your speaking time. Establish a rapport with your audience right from the start. Seize the audience's attention and stimulate their interest. Tell the audience what you are going to talk about by using one of the three methods below.

Start with:

1. A humorous story or anecdote about yourself.
2. A startling fact to get attention.
3. A question for the audience (if you dare).

The middle, or body, of your speech tells the story or the main plot. Develop three points, three goals, or three steps to support your theory or theme.

If you use visual aids (pictures, charts, or slides) to make your point, keep them simple and brief. Make certain everyone can see them. Always stand to the side. The climax of the speech secures your main plot and can be told in one sentence. It is done for effect, so the audience understands and remembers your point, as in Martin Luther King's speech "I have a Dream." The climax can come at the end of the middle of your speech or at its conclusion.

The conclusion summarizes or answers your introduction. It should comprise 10 percent of your speaking time and should neatly wrap up your presentation. Remind the audience of what you have already told them. Bring your speech to a dramatic conclusion. It, and you, will be unforgettable.

### Delivering Your Speech

## Do:

Arrive one hour in advance to familiarize yourself with the room (size, seating arrangements, microphone). Make sure all the equipment you need is there (spare bulb for projector, glass of water). Visualize yourself with the room full of people.

# Do:

Think of how you will stand so that you appear relaxed: with your legs slightly apart, your weight on the balls of your feet, and body tilted forward. Your stance should remain constant and still.

Connect with your audience by immediately making eye contact. Throughout your delivery, get the audience involved, communicate with them. Be animated and interesting.

Hand out printed material even if it is only one page, but only at the end of your presentation.

Make yourself available after your talk.

# Don't:

Talk to anyone on your way to the podium.

Start with "Tonight, I'm going to talk to you about."

Stare at the same people or look only at those sitting in the centre of the front row.

Read your text or have it memorized word for word.

Take yourself too seriously by lecturing or talking down to your audience.

Sound hesitant or apologize if you make a mistake.

Read your speech past the allotted time.

Rush through your speech and finish half an hour early, then expect your audience to ask questions.

Put your hands in your pockets or clasp them at groin level.

Overuse hand movements, or use pointers and pens as props.

Show your visual material in total darkness, face your material while you talk, or show too many things. Another no-no is to pass out reading material during your presentation.

## Don't:

Talk with a glass of water in your hands or drink while looking toward your audience.

Lean back, sink back on your heels, or turn your back to the audience.

Stand immobile behind a podium.

Say, "I'm done" or "I'm finished" at the end.

**Using a Microphone**

## Do:

Make sure the microphone is working perfectly before people come into the room.

Tap gently on the microphone to test it. Take time to adjust the position of the mike so that it is at the proper height.

Arrange for a portable microphone if the lectern is too tall, and stand to the side of the lectern while delivering your speech.

Speak directly into the microphone from a distance of about four to six inches.

Adjust a lapel mike so that it is a few inches below your chin.

## Don't:

Hold or fondle the microphone stand.

Blow on the microphone to see if it works.

Handle the mike unless you are sure it is designed to be hand held.

Rustle your notes close to the mike or speak under, over, or to either side of the microphone.

Get too close to the mike, because you will hear a popping sound when using the letter "p" and a hissing sound when you use an "s."

## PRESS RELEASES

A press release is a news story. State the facts: Who you are and what your business is about to do. When and where it will happen. Why it is happening and how it will be accomplished.

### Do:

Network for contacts in the medium you plan to use: TV, radio, or newspapers. Personal contact is the essence of good public relations.

Make sure you have an angle that will make your story unique. Sending a release does not guarantee news coverage.

Write "FOR IMMEDIATE RELEASE" at the top of each 8.5" x 11" page. Type "-30-" or "###" and centre horizontally at the end of the release. Double space the lines.

Be sure that your facts are absolutely accurate.

Make sure that you have correctly spelled the name of the person to whom you are sending the press release.

Send a photograph (newspapers) or video clip (TV) of you and the product you are selling.

Fax or courier your release to the assignment editor at least one week before the event.

The assignment editor will pass the release on to a reporter who may or may not cover the event.

### Don't:

Make spelling mistakes or use jargon in your text.

Write more than two pages.

State that you are the best, the least expensive, or the only one — avoid statements of belief.

Use the company executive for quotes — they may have the expertise, but they will appear biased.



YourPublicImage

## INTERVIEWS: RADIO & TELEVISION

To achieve a winning impression on radio and television you must have confidence (and for TV you must have presence as well). Your vision must be clear, and the ability to react quickly is a wonderful asset.

### Preparation

Here is a list of questions to ask the producer or interviewer a week or two before the program:

Will the interview be live or taped? If it is live, is there an audience and will the audience pose questions?

Who is the audience of the program?

What time of day will the program air? If it is taped, when will it be shown?

How long will I be on the air?

Will I be part of a panel, and if so, who are the other panelists?

What will be the background of the set?

Will I be standing or sitting?

Will I be behind a desk or console?

What kind of chair will I be seated on?

If it is a swivel-type chair, remember not to swivel back and forth.

## Do:

Ask to see previous interviews conducted by the person who will interview you. Study his or her previous work; find out the tone of the program.

Prepare a detailed list of the questions that you may be asked.

Know your subject.

Rehearse aloud in the same way you would for public speaking.

Video or tape yourself — it is a very good practice.

Train yourself to appear sincere.

### The Interview

| Do: | Don't: |
|---|---|
| Arrive early: 10 minutes before a radio show and 15 to 30 minutes before a TV show. | Look too stiff or formal, or appear tense by folding your arms across your chest — you will project a poor image or attitude. |
| Immediately establish a rapport with the reporter or interviewer. Smile and thank him or her for having you on the show. | Have an alcoholic drink or eat a big meal before a show. |
| Be aware of your tone of voice. Be direct, it will also convey that you are sincere and trust-worthy. | Use jargon or slang, repeatedly say "well" or "you know", or use negative phrases such as "I don't know" and "I don't think so." |
| Sit with your derriere well back into the chair and lean forward. It will give you an air of credibility and authority. | Slouch in your chair, it shows that you do not care. Avoid rocking or wriggling your head. |
| Stand with shoulders back and head held high. | Move your hands about unnecessarily or display awkward mannerisms; you will appear nervous. |
| Be brief and ready for difficult questions. Try to have the last word. | Try to convey too much information. |
| Take charge — make three positive points with examples from a story or anecdote. | Pretend you know everything, or answer a question with another question. |
| Be relaxed and in control. | Be passive or defensive. |

## Do:

Show enthusiasm, emotion, energy, and positiveness. If the viewers like you they will listen to you.

Look at the interviewer. Choose to answer just one question if many are solicited. Ask the interviewer which question he or she would like you to answer.

Bring notes if necessary; write your main ideas on 3" x 5" or 5" x 8" cards.

Try to understand clearly the interviewer's questions. Learn to respond in short, crisp sentences of about 20 to 40 seconds.

Remember your objective, the purpose of the interview, and exactly what you came to say.

Be informal, talk as you would with a friend. End on a positive note.

## Don't:

Sound out of touch.

Be caught off-guard by an interviewer who bombards you with too many questions.

Read all of your points, it would look as if you didn't know your subject.

Lose your cool, get angry, or overreact because of a difficult question.

Let an interviewer put words in your mouth or distort what you just said.

### THE TV CAMERA

The camera can be a friend or a foe! What you say is one thing, what the camera picks up is another. A bold pattern in your attire or an emotional reaction will jump right out from the TV screen — everything is dramatically magnified through a camera lens. TV will make you appear heavier and some glasses will make you look older. (Men should avoid a five o'clock shadow.)

Make-up will be necessary; powder takes the shine off your face.

## Do:

Keep eye contact with the person you are speaking to, whether it is the interviewer or the other panelists.

Be aware that radio and television operates on the basis of experience, spontaneity, and impressions.

Show confidence — a lack of it will be intensified by the camera.

Sit with both feet on the ground. Women may cross their legs.

Fold your hands one over the other, place them on your lap, or palm down on each leg.

Rise and shake the hand of the interviewer at the end of the program, as you will still be on TV while the credits are rolling.

## Don't:

Look down, it shows you are fearful. If you look up and away, you will appear shifty. Never look directly into the camera.

Interrupt, raise your voice, or look bored. These reactions will be caught by the camera and amplified.

Shift on your seat, it will imply that you are not comfortable with the question.

Cross your legs at the ankle or the thigh (men.) In some countries, crossing one's leg over the thigh is not acceptable for anyone.

Cross your arms or put the palm of your hand on one side of your face.

Play with your hair, chew on a pen, or twiddle your fingers; such mannerisms will make you appear insecure.

### WHAT TO WEAR

On television or a video clip, your appearance is as important as what you have to say. Sometimes the way a person looks can get in the way of the message. The audience will have no respect for you or your ideas if you look like a slob. Make sure your hair is perfectly trimmed and coiffed and that you are comfortable in your clothes. You will appear confident, authoritative, and credible.



YourPublicImage

## Do:

Stick to classic items, that way you won't look outdated if the clip is used much later.

Wear a suit — it looks good in close-ups. Suits are preferable to sports jackets or dresses.

Wear medium tones. Suitable colours are navy, teal, brown, taupe, camel, grey, khaki, plum, and burgundy.

Wear textured fabrics or weaves; they look richer on television. A light pattern or a small pinstripe is also acceptable.

Sit on the tail of your jacket, that way you will not look hunched.

Keep your jacket buttoned (men when standing up, women at all times); it conveys to the viewers that you are in control.

Wear long-sleeve shirts in solids pastels. For adequate breathing space you should be able to insert two fingers between the collar and your throat.

## Don't:

Appear in wrinkled clothes or poorly groomed.

Wear a very dark suit, it will make you look older.

Wear very light or very bright colours, or strong contrasts such as black and white.

Wear hound's-tooth, checks, or plaids; they vibrate on the screen.

Wear a double-breasted jacket if you are overweight; it will make you look bigger.

Wear dark shirts, or blouses with bold patterns or stripes or fabrics that shine or glitter under lights.

Allow your tie or scarf to take over the screen. Avoid big patterns, flowers and stripes, plaids and checks.

YourPublicImage

## Do:

Wear conservative ties with small patterns. Make sure the tie is a fashionable width.

Wear a slip-on shoe (men). Women should wear a low heel. Black is the best colour.

Wear knee-length, black executive socks (men). Women should wear nylons (black, grey or skin tone).

## Don't:

Wear too much jewellery. Men should stay away from chains, pins, bracelets, or earrings. Neither sex should wear more than two rings. Women should avoid wearing jewels that dangle.

Wear wing-tips (men). Women should not wear clunky shoes — they will appear too heavy on TV, or white shoes — they draw attention to the feet.

Wear mini-skirts, see-through or low cut garments (women.)

### INTRODUCING SPEAKERS

## Do:

Have all the facts: the name of the person and the proper pronunciation, the subject of his or her talk, and the background of the speaker. Find out how the speaker likes to be introduced.

The ideal M.C. will make the audience eager to hear the speaker.

## Don't:

Read the introduction. (You should have it memorized.)

Make long introductions that will take time away from the speech or other speakers. An introduction should not take more than three minutes.



YourPublicImage

Do:

Be enthusiastic and sincere.

Turn and look at the speaker after the introduction, indicating that he now has the floor.

Conclude your introduction by saying "Let's welcome our speaker (name of the person) and start the applause.

Don't:

Use humour that patronizes the speaker or the audience.

Tell the audience to "pay attention" that they "will learn something", or anything else that would make them feel ignorant.

**PRESENTING AN AWARD**

Do:

Reassure the recipient that he or she is really deserving of the award.

Tell the recipient:

- Why he or she is getting the award.
- Why the award is important and how the group feels about him or her.
- Why he or she deserves it.
- Congratulate and wish him or her well.

Don't:

Exaggerate or praise the award itself.

Talk about yourself or other matters that are not related.

**ACCEPTING AN AWARD**

Do:

Thank the host and guests.

Be sincere.

Make your acceptance speech three to five minutes in length.

Don't:

Overdo it.

## COMPANY EVENTS & CELEBRATIONS

Whether it is a birthday, promotion, Christmas party, picnic, or office party, you should always seize the opportunity to get to know your co-workers better and advance your career. Remember that even the most casual party is still a business function.

There are rules and regulations to observe. And if you plan the event, provide transportation for the employees who drink.

| Do: | Don't: |
| --- | --- |
| Go! No-shows are considered disloyal. You will be seen as a person who is not a team player. | Bring someone that has not been invited. |
| Arrive a little late if you choose. | Talk shop excessively. |
| Leave early rather than stay too long. | Flirt or become too intimate with the other guests. |
| Wear appropriate attire. | Indulge in office gossip. |
| Introduce yourself to the CEO or the people in charge (if you have not already met them.) | Try to pitch proposals or score points with your boss. |
| Talk about travel, hobbies, sports, and current events. | Call your boss by his or her first name, unless you always have. |
| Chat with many people and smile frequently. | Drink too much, or reveal personal secrets. You may regret it later. |
| Develop a bond with co-workers. Compliment them. | Make a toast unless you have been asked to do so. |
| Apologize if you have offended someone because of your behaviour during the party. | Become the "life of the party" or tell obscene jokes. |

## Do:

Send a thank you note to your host.

## Don't:

Offer constant advice on the rules of any games that are played.

Repeatedly ask the same person to dance.

**PRIVATE CLUBS**

Private clubs are ideal places to hold business and social functions. Most clubs have very expensive membership fees and many companies pay for their executives. These clubs are the perfect place to bring an out-of-town associate, or take employees in appreciation of a job well done. Most people are honoured when invited to a private club for lunch.

Cash is never used in private clubs. Only members can sign the bill. Never belong or invite someone to a club that discriminates against a person's race, sex, or religion.

## Hosts:

You must be sponsored by a friend or your company to be eligible to join.

Invite a business colleague to lunch at a club and arrive early to greet your guest.

Offer your guest a drink.

Business attire is appropriate.

Exhibit gracious manners and make sure the guest's needs are met. You are the host and, therefore, in charge.

## Guests:

Do not roam around. Wait for your host in the reception area.

Most areas are off limits except for members.

Wait for your host to take your coat.

Do not introduce yourself to other members.

Do not ask about club fees or offer to pay. Only members can sign the bill.

## Hosts:

Do not brag about your membership.

### WORKING THE COCKTAIL PARTY

Most people have a hard time trying to figure out what they should do at a cocktail party. First, you must ask yourself what your role is at the party. Define whether it is a business or social event and act accordingly. Cocktail parties start between 17:00 and 18:00, and end around 20:30. The host or a representative of the host company is responsible for making introductions.

| Do: | Don't: |
| --- | --- |
| Reply to an invitation that says "RSVP," which means "Repondez s'il vous plait" or respond, please. | Bring a guest if the invitation does not say so. |
| Wear business or cocktail attire. | Wear a tuxedo unless it is specified in the invitation. |
| Eat before you go out so that you do not get too easily intoxicated. | Monopolize the host or celebrity. |
| Arrive on time. Try to be the first person to greet a circle of guests. | Arrive at the end of the party. |
| Make sure your right hand is free and dry in order to do a proper handshake. | Ask boring questions such as "How are you today?" or "What's new?" |
| Introduce people to each other or introduce yourself. | Rush to the buffet and fill your plate, or hover over the hors d'oeuvres. |

## Do:

Be on the move, talk to new people, work the room, have an agenda and keep command of it.

Talk about sports, hobbies, travel, and other non-confrontational topics.

Exchange business cards. Think "potential clients." They can help increase your business and income.

Search out a lunch date if you can profit from an individual's business. Follow up that contact.

Respect and trust people. Listen to what people say.

Make eye contact, maintain pleasant facial expressions, and use body language that is open and receptive.

Thank the host or the organizers before you leave.

Leave at the time stated on the invitation.

Be responsible if you are the host — make arrangements with a cab or bus company to transport intoxicated guests.

## Don't:

Complain about the food, the room, or other attendees.

Put a toothpick back on the plate on which the food was served.

Get into a business discussion or try to sell something.

Drink too much; two drinks are enough.

Flirt or come on to the women at the party.

Hesitate to cut off a colleague who is getting out of control.

Be loud and aggressive or use humour that puts someone down.

Go around telling everyone that you are leaving.

## THE ART OF TOASTING

Toasting can be traced back to the ancient world. Ulysses drank to the health of Achilles in the Odyssey. Augustus, the first Roman emperor, passed a decree in the senate that all diners must drink to his health at every meal.

Every man or woman will eventually have to make a toast. Occasions are endless — at the wedding of a son or daughter, at the retirement party of a friend, when someone has been promoted or graduates, or when a special guest is present.

### Do:

Make the first toast if you are the host. The speech should be brief, from one to four minutes, and to the point.

Practice before a mirror. Try memorizing the main points. If you are afraid of forgetting, bring a small note.

Understand the purpose of your toast. Begin with a goal-oriented sentence.

Speak clearly to everyone in the room; breathe, pause, and be enthusiastic.

Maintain good eye contact with the whole group.

### Don't:

Make a toast if you have drunk too much. Ask someone else to do it for you.

Read a toast; it must come from the heart.

Make fun of someone or put someone down.

Mention sex, money, or religion; or give an off-colour toast.

Give the first toast if you are not the host.

# Do:

Give the toast after dessert is served. Make sure people have wine or champagne in their glasses. If you decide to give a toast during the meal, tap on your glass gently to get everyone's attention first.

Indicate that you are coming to the end of your toast.

# Don't:

Take a drink if you are the one being toasted, just say "thank you." Drinking to yourself is akin to patting yourself on the back.

# Business Travel

**Business**Travel

## TRAVELLING BY COMMERCIAL JET

Find the best travel agent that you can get, especially for business trips. For leisure travel you can do a lot of the research on the Internet and book your flight for a lower cost.

The most comfortable way to travel on business is in the business-class section of a commercial jet. Business class offers many advantages. The first is the larger seats, which are deeper and recline further than those in the economy section. There is also more breathing space around you and a significant storage area.

Many airlines now have seats that transform into beds. In first class some airlines provide writing paper with designer pens, massages, pajamas to wear and later take home. Expect pre-flight premium champagne, vintage wines, gourmet meals, duvets or blankets, luxury amenity kits, individual entertainment screens, and great service. Many airlines offer computers and software to use. Others give a free rental car for a week.

If you cannot justify the expense of business class, economy is the only choice. Ask for a free upgrade to business class. You stand a chance of getting an upgrade if you are a frequent flier, have paid full fare, or are travelling with someone who already has a first or business class ticket. Airlines sometimes upgrade people who are celebrating their honeymoon or have an injured leg that must be kept elongated.

Find out early what kind of plane it is and which seat is best for you. One must always book a seat in advance so as not to end up in a non-reclining, middle seat, or near washrooms. Choose an aisle seat with an empty seat between you and the window. An aisle seat is preferable because it has a little extra space and is easily reached. The best possible situation is a seat in a row of empty seats: put up the armrests and spread out.

The most requested seats are in the front six rows because they are the easiest to board and exit. They are also quieter because they are ahead of the engines. The seats behind the bulkhead and the ones next to the emergency exits have the most leg room. There is responsibility attached to seating in the latter area; in the case of an emergency, you would have to open the hatch door and assist the others. These seats cannot be assigned over the phone.

If you want to enjoy a film on board, always ask when you book your seat whether you are well positioned for the screen. Some seats do not have a good view of the screen, especially on wide-bodied planes. If you are not interested in the movie, respect the other people who are. Leave the window shutters down, as requested by the flight attendants. Use your overhead light if you wish to read.

Consider joining the airport club of the airline you use. It will provide you with a nice, quiet place to rest before takeoff. You can use the telephone and fax machine while enjoying free drinks. It certainly beats the crowds if there is a delay or a long stopover.

Travel with grace no matter what way you choose to go.

## TRAVELLING BY CORPORATE JET

Corporate jets save time and money. They are like flying offices. It is an honour to be invited to travel on the company's jet. The advantage of not having to wait in line or for your baggage is a real treat. If you travel regularly on a corporate jet, buy gifts for the crew at Christmastime.

### Do:

Make your own plans for getting to and from the airport. Be on time.

Dress as if you were going to work.

Leave the best seats for senior executives.

Help yourself to the food if there is no steward on board.

### Don't:

Board the plane until your host has arrived.

Dress like someone going on a holiday.

Bring five suitcases, and don't expect anyone to carry your suitcases for you.

Ask for alcoholic drinks.

BusinessTravel

**Do:**

Clean up your own mess.

Find out the pilot's and co-pilot's names and thank them.

Compliment the crew for a lovely flight.

Write a thank-you card to the person who arranged your flight.

**Don't:**

Ask for reading material; bring your own.

Expect the crew to pick up after you.

## TRAVELLING BY HELICOPTER

Helicopters are popular in large cities where buildings have landing pads. It is a pricey, glamorous, and quick way to get to work in the morning. Only presidents, high-powered executives, and famous people can afford this extravagance. Never ask your boss if you can get a lift with him.

## AIR TRAVEL VOCABULARY

*Non-stop:*

The aircraft flies from one destination to another without stopping.

*Direct flight:*

Has the same flight number throughout the trip. However, the plane will stop once and maybe more times.

*Connecting flight:*

You have a guaranteed connection on another plane, but it does mean you'll have to change aircraft.

*Ground stop:*

A ground stop happens when there is a large reduction in capacity at the airport, such as when a runway or entire airport has been closed due to a big thunderstorm or localized fog.

*Gate hold:*

Sometimes an aircraft stays at the gate rather than taxiing out to the runway, which usually means there has been a delay somewhere. The airline may decide to leave its passengers waiting on the plane so that the plane can leave quickly once it gets the go-ahead.

*In trail:*

This refers to the amount of space between the planes at takeoff. There has to be a minimum gap of eight kilometres between aircraft. Air-traffic controllers sometimes increase the in-trail spacing. In stormy weather, for example, outgoing traffic may be spaced out by 32 kilometres.

*Airborne holding:*

Sometimes a number of planes approach the airport at the same time, so they are held back and asked to follow a racetrack pattern in the sky. This helps air-traffic control to maintain the appropriate distance between aircraft.

*Wait for connecting passengers:*

If it is the last flight of the evening, airlines usually wait for connecting passengers. But if there is a flight later in the day to put them on, the airline will leave these passengers behind.

## TRAVEL TIPS

Find out through your travel agent whether there are any fare reductions or special corporate rates. Take advantage of frequent-flyer programs.

Find out what travel benefits your credit card might offer.

If you are travelling on business, use the company's travel agency, or ask friends or colleagues if they know of a good agent or travel agency.

There are discounts for booking 7 days, 14 days, and 21 days in advance. Buy airline tickets when the fares are lowest, which is usually three times a year: late May or early June, late August, and between Thanksgiving and Christmas.

The Internet is a great way to get deals on hotels, flights, and vacation packages. Take nonstop flights, which are less likely to be delayed. If you cannot fly nonstop, find a connecting flight through an airport with the least chance of bad weather.

Get a paper airline ticket rather than use an e-ticket when travelling abroad. Paper is better when you are using more than one airline, if you need to switch airlines at the last minute, or when you travel through airports in places where the computer infrastructure is unreliable.

Make sure your travel insurance policy covers all aspects of your trip: life, medical, cancellation, travel delay, defaults by an airline, auto accidents, terrorism, hijacking, and hotel overbooking.

Arrange in advance how you will get to and from the airport. In some countries it is very difficult to communicate and you could get stuck if you have not arranged to be picked up.

Check the statutory holidays of the country you are going to. Learn and respect the customs of your host.

Be aware of the travel regulations and baggage restrictions of the airline and country to which you are travelling. In some countries, religious items may be confiscated. Pornography can get you in trouble. Prescription drugs without the original bottle and doctor's name can land you in jail.

Reduce the chance that the airline will lose your luggage. Remove all luggage tags from past trips and put on new ones with the address and phone number for both your home and destination. If the airline has another flight to the same place that leaves before yours, either switch to the earlier flight or wait until after it leaves to check in your luggage.

Double-check your reservation. Shorten plane delays by calling your airline's toll-free number or your travel agent and book a seat on the next flight.

Telephone the airport before you leave to make sure your flight is on schedule.

Take only a carry-on piece of luggage if you can. You will not have to worry about losing your suitcase and it gets you out of airports quickly.

Use an airline club — it has advantages. It ensures that you will not be bumped from an overbooked flight, you get upgraded, and you'll be processed faster at the ticket counter because you have access to the business-class line-up.

Make sure you are properly compensated for being bumped off an oversold flight. The airline may offer you a free future flight, but you can insist on a cheque instead. If the delay costs you more than what you are offered, demand a higher settlement. Remember, once you take your free trip or cash your cheque, you waive your right to ask for anything else.

If your flight is delayed and another airline has a flight that arrives at your destination earlier, a major airline should put you on the competitor's flight.

If you are in an over booked position do not volunteer to take a later flight until you know whether you will be confirmed on the next flight or just have standby status. Ask whether the airline will provide meals and phone calls while you wait, or a hotel room if you are stuck overnight. Check to see if the free ticket has an expiration date or blackout period, and whether you must wait until 48 hours before departure to make your reservation.

On your return home, have all the sales slips of your purchases ready for customs.

## AIRLINE / AIRPORT TIPS

Find out whether your flight is likely to take off on schedule by calling the airline's 1-800 number. Tell them what flight number you are on and ask what the aircraft number is and its status.

You may also call the airport to find out more information or check their web site. Flight arrivals and departures are also available through your cable television network.

When a delay is announced, immediately call your airline's 1-800 number. If you go to the ticket counter, you will only encounter dozens of other passengers trying to get help from a few frazzled agents. You can also find out about delays using your pager, phone, or palmtop. Check your airlines' web site to get instructions on how to do it.

If you are delayed while travelling in the U.S., ask to be "240'd." This refers to *Rule 240*, which stipulates that if a cancellation or delay is the airline's fault (e.g., is not caused by bad weather or a labour dispute), the carrier must ensure that you leave for your destination within two hours of the originally scheduled departure. That might even mean it has to put you on another carrier, in first class, at no extra charge to you.

Keep your cool with airline personnel — shouting will not get you anywhere. Better to commiserate than get arrested.

## COPING WITH THE EFFECTS OF AIR TRAVEL

Air travel is hard on the body. Learn to prepare your body for a long haul.

### Before you leave

**Do:**

Several days before leaving, have high-protein breakfasts and lunches and high-carbohydrate dinners.

Change your sleeping patterns. When going east, go to bed one or two hours earlier the night before departure. When going west, stay up one to two hours later. Have a body massage a day or two before departure. It helps to get rid of stress and tiredness.

Do a workout the day you leave. This releases potassium in the body, a small way to prevent jet lag.

Eliminate any caffeine three days before your flight.

### On the plane

**Do:**

Immediately set your watch to the time of your destination.

Ask for vegetarian food. It is light and healthy.

Drink eight ounces of water or fruit juice every hour.

## Do:

Change into comfortable clothes to aid relaxation. Take off your shoes. Bring extra socks to keep your feet warm or put on the pair of slippers that most airlines offer in business class on international flights.

Try to sleep as you would at home, according to the time zone. Use an inflatable neck pillow, eye mask, and earplugs if needed.

Apply moisturizer and spray facial water on your face to prevent dryness.

Move around and do a little exercise to keep your circulation going.

Bring a game or book for mental stimulation.

Put on the headset if the person seated next to you insists on conversation and you want to read or relax.

## Don't:

Drink alcoholic beverages, tea, and coffee if at all possible; they act as diuretics, and dehydrate the body. Getting drunk is something from the past and it is not healthy.

Eat heavy or fatty meals. They are hard to digest when you are inactive.

Eat just for the sake of eating.

Cross your legs; it interferes with blood circulation.

Wear your contact lenses on a flight. The air is too dry.

Fully recline your seat when the person in the back of you is still eating.

Use the washrooms during meal time.

Floss your teeth or do your nails; respect others and do personal hygiene in private.

Chat or complain about the flight to the person next to you.

BusinessTravel

### When you arrive

## Do:

Change back into your suit before landing, especially if you are meeting associates at the airport.

Adapt right away to the time zone of your destination. Eat at the same time as the locals even if you are not hungry. It is a great way to get your body back in order.

Take a shower, and if it is daytime, go out for a walk. Try to stay in the sunlight in order to reset your body clock. Never go to bed if you arrive in the middle of the day.

## JET LAG & MELATONIN

Jet lag occurs when you change time zones during travel and your biological, or circadian, clock is disrupted. Our bodies get disoriented on long flights that cross time zones, so we feel like sleeping when we arrive at our destination, even though the local clock reads noon.

Some experts say that it takes 24 hours to recover for every two to three time zones we have crossed. Some symptoms of jet lag are loss of appetite, weariness, fatigue, and a decrease in physical performance and mental capability.

There's scientific evidence that a natural hormone called melatonin regulates our biological clock. At night, melatonin is secreted in large amounts by our pineal gland to help us sleep. During the day, melatonin is repressed by light. A number of people use synthetic melatonin to help their body get over jet lag.

It is extremely important, however, to take synthetic melatonin at the right time and at the right dosage. When travelling west (ex. Vancouver to Hong Kong), it helps to take one 10 mg. tablet every night for three nights before travelling. On the day of travel, take one tablet at night on the plane and continue for another three nights upon arrival.

Always take the pill one or two hours before going to sleep. When travelling east (ex. Vancouver to London), take 10 mg. on the day of departure and another upon arrival at bedtime, and continue for three more nights.

One can find melatonin in health food stores.

## HEALTH

Get medical insurance before you leave. Being physically sound before a trip is quite important: you do not want to get sick in a Third World country, or anywhere, for that matter. Medical costs can be exorbitant. Before you leave, get a complete body and blood examination, and a dental checkup. Make sure that you have received the required immunizations against disease. Some countries require a certificate of inoculation.

Call your local clinic or ask your doctor for advice. What you need depends on where you are going and the length of your stay. Bring some medication with you in case of emergency (malaria, diarrhea, etc.).

Here is a list of recommended inoculations compiled with the help of Health & Welfare Canada and IAMAT (International Association for Medical Assistance to Travellers):

## INOCULATIONS

| Destination | Recommended | Hazards |
| --- | --- | --- |
| Africa | Ro, Ma*, Y, HA*, Mg*, C*, TF*, HB*, PL*, RA*, PO*, M* | Watch what you eat. Drink bottled water. |
| Asia Pacific | Ro, HA*, Mg*, Ma*, C*, PO*, TF*, Y*, HB*, JE*, RA* | Watch what you eat. Drink bottled water. |
| Australia & New Zealand | Ro, HB*, Y* | Always check whether the water is potable. |
| Canada | Ro, HB* | None. |

| Destination | Recommended | Hazards |
|---|---|---|
| Caribbean Islands | Ro, Y*, PO*, HA*, HB*, TF*, RA* | Always check whether the water is potable. |
| Central America | Ro, C*, HA*, TF*, Y*, PO*, RA*, T* | Watch what you eat. Drink bottled water. |
| Russian Federation (CIS) | Ro, C*, Ha, TF, JE*, PL*, TBE* | Giardia (intestinal parasite) Watch what you eat, drink bottled water. |
| China Mainland | Ro, JE*, HA, PO*, C*, TF*, HB, PL*, Y*, PO* | Watch what you eat. Drink bottled water. |
| Eastern & Central Europe | Ro, TBE*, HB*, Y* | Watch what you eat. Drink bottled water. |
| Western Europe | Ro, HB* | None. |
| Hong Kong | Ro, HA, JE*, TF, HB* | Tap water may be contaminated. |
| India | Ro, HA, Ma, Mg*, JE*, PL*, Y*, PO*, C*, TF, HB*, RA* | Dysentery. Watch what you eat. Drink bottled water. |
| Japan | Ro, JE* | None. |
| Mexico | Ro, Ma*, Y*, PO*, C*, HA*, TF*, RA* | Diarrhoea/upset stomach. Watch what you eat. Drink bottled water. |
| Middle East | Ro, Mg*, HA, TF, HB*, Y*, PO*, RA*, M*, PL* | Watch what you eat. Drink bottled water. |

| Destination | Recommended | Hazards |
|---|---|---|
| South America | Ro, HA, Ma*, PO*, C*, TF, PL*, RA*, T*, Y*, C*, M* | Diarrhoea/upset stomach. Watch what you eat. Drink bottled water. |
| South Korea | Ro, JE* | Watch what you eat. Drink bottled water. |
| Taiwan | Ro, HA, TF*, HB, JE*, Y* | Watch what you eat. Drink bottled water. |
| United States | Ro, HB* | None. |

## IMMUNIZATION CODE:

Ro: tetanus, diphtheria, poliomyelitis, typhoid
HA: viral hepatitis A
HB: viral hepatitis B
Mg: meningitis
JE: Japanese encephalitis
Y: yellow fever (a certificate of immunization may be required for travellers arriving from infected areas)
M : meningococcal meningitis
Ma: malaria
C : cholera
Pl: plague
TF: typhoid fever
PO: poliomyelitis
TBE: tick-borne encephalitis
T: louse-borne typhus
Ra: rabies
*: only required for travellers to rural areas



BusinessTravel

## FOOD TO AVOID WHEN WATER IS NOT POTABLE:

- Raw fish, shellfish, salads (fresh vegetables and fruit that are not peeled), mayonnaise, and cold desserts.
- Tap water; drink bottled water from a reliable source.
- Ice in drinks.

## PACKING TIPS

Minimalism is the name of today's packing game. Limit your luggage to a carry-on suitcase or garment bag whenever possible. This will reduce security checks, lengthy waits around the baggage carousel, and the risk of ending up somewhere without any clothes. Bring a briefcase and computer tote if needed. Most airlines will let you carry all these items on board, but they have the right to refuse during peak seasons and holidays if the plane is full.

Phone the airline to find out the size and weight of both carry-on and check-in luggage before you even start packing.

If you can't carry everything on the plane with you, always bring a change of clothes and toiletries on board in case your bags get lost or stolen.

Bring valuables on board, such as your camera, lap top, cellular phone, traveller's cheques, credit cards, cash, and passport.

Carry your prescription pills with you on the plane. All medication should be in its original container. Travellers with HIV may want to ask their doctor to label their medication in a way that does not reveal their illness.

Bring a pocket calculator for converting currency and mileage.

Bring light, easy-to-carry, and damage-resistant luggage. Shop around and look at different styles before purchasing. Ask the store clerk about the features of the bag and its warranty. Ask yourself how often you will travel and for how long a period you will be away. This will help you decide which features to choose and which product line to buy.

Organize your packing by listing the items you plan to take on your trip. Make a list of your luggage contents for insurance purposes in case of theft.

Consider the length of the trip and the reason for taking it: is it business only or pleasure as well? Plan your wardrobe accordingly.

To avoid back strain, pack your bag standing up — put your suitcase on a desk.

Carry toiletries in unbreakable plastic containers. About all you'll need are a body and face moisturizer, sunblock, toothbrush, toothpaste, dental floss, a little shaver, and a manicure set. If you are not booked at a quality hotel, you'll also need a body soap, shampoo, conditioner, and a hair dryer.

Resealable plastic bags are a must when travelling. Use them to hold anything from wet bathing suits, dirty socks, bars of soap to seashells, brochures and film.

Take an empty carry-bag that can be folded up and put in your suitcase. Use it for souvenirs and other purchases that you accumulate on your trip.

Leave business cards inside all of your bags in case the outside tags are lost en route.

Photocopy all travel documents and credit cards and keep a copy in a separate place.

Duplicate suitcase keys.

Do not put your home address on the tag. Use your business address instead. Never leave your luggage unattended at any time.

## PACKING A WARDROBE FOR BUSINESS TRAVEL

The clothing you wear on a business trip is very important. Whether you are representing yourself or your company, you must always look impeccable. You want to look conservative but also approachable. Think carefully about your clothing choices to be sure they create the correct image for you.

Colour-coordinate your clothing and stick to two colour schemes in cool or warm tones. Try not to take any white clothes. Darker colours will hide dirt, while neutrals are the most flexible because you can mix and match several pieces. Pack the best fabrics for travel: crepes, gabardines, and high-twist wrinkle-resistant wools. Avoid bulky garments, they take too much space in your suitcase.

Check the weather forecast for the next four days to help you determine your wardrobe choices.

Take an all-weather trench coat and boots, if needed. Carry or wear them onto the aircraft. Make sure to take comfortable shoes. Pack them in old socks, or plastic bags to protect your clothes from dirt.

Try your clothes on before packing them. An impeccable fit is essential.

Dress in businesslike garments to ensure better treatment at customs checks.

Many surveys have made the point that a man with a tie is treated better than a man without one. Wear a tie with a blazer, a casual shirt, cotton or light wool trousers, and a pair of slip-on shoes or loafers.

For women, it is appropriate to wear a knit suit or a wool pant suit of good quality with sweater or blouse. Wear flat shoes and nice accessories.

To assure a comfortable voyage, change into a sweatsuit or other stretch clothing after boarding, and return to your more serious look before landing.

If you are a frequent flyer, invest in a ballistic-nylon garment bag. If you spend more money on your bag it can last 10 to 15 years.

Here is a list of garments required for a ten-day business trip with some casual outings:

**Men**

Take two business suits with pants that can be mixed and matched, or one business suit and one sports jacket or blazer

One extra pair of dress pants (if you are bringing a sports jacket)

One pair of jeans or casual cotton/wool trousers (optional)

Four dress shirts, four ties

One casual shirt

One sweater (optional)

One pair of sweatpants or sports shorts, two T-shirts, and one swimsuit (for exercise)

One pair of business shoes and one pair of suede loafers or casual shoes that can be used for both business and casual events

One pair of running shoes

Four pairs of business socks, two pairs of sports socks

Five sets of underwear (you can wash them with shampoo, if needed)

One all-weather trench coat, if needed (wear it onto the plane)

One pair of boots, if travelling in winter (wear them onto the plane)

A briefcase

**Women**

One three-piece business suit (cool wool/gabardine/crepe), a jacket, pants, skirt or dress

One two- or three-piece knit suit (Chanel-style sweater or tunic) with trousers, a long or short skirt or dress

One blouse, a jersey top, one light sweater (cotton or wool) optional, one camisole, one shell

One black evening dress (optional)

Two nightgowns

Four sets of underwear – bras, panties, thong or bodysuit (you can use shampoo to wash them in your room)

Three pairs of pantyhose, knee socks, and short socks

One pair of leggings, a sweatsuit or shorts, a T-shirt and a swimsuit (for exercise)

One pair of jeans or stretch pants for casual events (optional)

Three pairs of shoes: one pair of low- or mid-heel pumps, one pair of flat or slip-on shoes, and runners for exercise or walks

One all-weather trench coat, if needed (wear it onto the plane)

One pair of boots, if travelling in winter (wear them onto the plane)

Accessories: purse, jewellery, scarves, shawl (optional), and a briefcase

BusinessTravel

## HOW TO PACK A GARMENT BAG

To avoid wrinkles on hanging garments, cover individual hangers with plastic dry-cleaning bags. Always hang the items that wrinkle the most in the back of the bag. There will be less creasing when the bag is folded in half.

On the first hanger place one pant suit, two ties or scarves, and one sweater. Hang the trousers first, then the accessories over the pants. Next put your sweater on the hanger, and the jacket over that. For less wrinkling, stuff the sleeves of jackets with socks or underwear.

When hanging two pairs of trousers or skirts, make sure the waistbands hang on opposite sides of the hanger. Repeat this process until all of your clothes are packed.

There should be at least two big pockets at the top of the garment bag. Stuff the shoes with socks and put one pair of shoes or one shoe in each pocket.

At the top left side of your garment bag you should have enough space to pack four items — your folded blouses or shirts. Shirts and blouses should be folded the same way they were when you bought them. You can ask your dry cleaner to do it for you, and to wrap your shirts in plastic as well. You will be pleasantly surprised by the result. Pack two shirts or blouses at a time, face to face, to avoid the collars from getting crushed.

In the middle of the bag, put your toiletries kit, and use the bottom compartment to hold more casual items and underwear.

In the outside pockets, place the remaining shirts, your jogging suit, two sports shorts, and two T-shirts.

## HOW TO PACK A SUITCASE

If you use a suitcase, buy the style with large swivel wheels, a combination lock, and a built-in retractable bar handle for pulling the suitcase along.

This style has the advantage of making you self-sufficient when there are no porters or carts around, and it's easy on the body during the tiring commute.

"Interfolding" is the most efficient way to pack a suitcase. To pack trousers, place the waistband against one side of the suitcase and allow the legs to hang over the other side. Place another pair of pants on top of the first with the waistband up against the opposite edge of the case. Repeat with all of your trousers, and skirts for ladies. Do not worry, you'll be folding the pant legs in later.

Roll up your ties or scarves and put them in jacket pockets or fold them in two and place them between garments. Lay your jackets flat. Do not button them. Fold one sleeve across the lapel then fold the other sleeve. Fold the jackets in half lengthwise and put them on top of the trousers or skirts. Place folded shirts and blouses face down on top of the jackets.

Sweaters should be folded like the jackets, and packed on top of them or rolled and tucked into the sides of the case. Cover all these items with the pant legs so that it makes a nice little bundle.

Belts can be interlocked around the inside of the suitcase, or rolled and put inside shoes or wherever space is still available. Fill the shoes with socks, then put them in shoe bags and place them against the sides of the suitcase soles down. Fill empty space with folded or rolled underwear. Pack clothes tightly.

## TRAVELLING WITH YOUR LAPTOP

Leave your laptop at home when going to major cities in Europe; top hotels there will provide you with one. North American hotels here are more concerned with supplying access to the Web at high speed, so you'll need your laptop.

At many hotels in the U.S. you can use your laptop to link up to the Internet using the high-speed access provided by companies such as CAIS Internet. CAIS has a system that uses the hotel's existing telephone wires so that you can talk on the phone and surf the Net at the same time. All you need is a laptop with an Ethernet card. Most hotels charge about $10 a day for the connection. To find out if your hotel has such a system, call ahead and ask, or go to www.cais.com/mu/hotel.htm to get a listing of equipped hotels.

Call or fax to find out if your hotel room is equipped with the latest technology.

## Do:

Call the airline and find out if you can use a laptop on the flight. Advise them when you book a seat that you will be using it.

Make back-up copies of all the data on your laptop and leave copies at home or the office.

Bring along back-up disks of data files and the software operating system. Bring an adapter and extra batteries.

Keep all of your disks with you in a special bag.

Before boarding, show the customs officer that your laptop doesn't contain anything illegal by simply putting the power on.

Put notebook computers, cellphones, and the like under the seat in your carry-on bag, wrapped with soft cloth for protection.

Use your laptop only when you are at over 3000 meters in altitude.

## Don't:

Let your laptop be x- rayed or passed through a metal detector.

Leave your computer on when boarding the plane.

Use a computer on an aircraft during take off and landing.

Pack your disks in luggage that is put in the cold storage area.

Use a printer. It interferes with the plane's communication system.

### TRAVELLING WITH YOUR PC-CARD MODEM

PC cards are the newest thing on the block, and if you are willing to pay the price you can get a notebook computer that will do as much as a desktop system can. They are ideal for business travellers because they allow you to communicate with head office online.

**Do:**

Always use your PC cards in the same order. Be careful how you insert and remove them.

Be careful with the connectors that fit between the card and the network, they are not very sturdy.

Use the right card-specific software drivers.

**Don't:**

Carry your PC cards in your jacket or in your trouser pockets.

Move around or lift your notebook while it's plugged into the computer network.

Force a PC card into a slot.

## PREPAID MOBILE-PHONE KITS

Advances in phone technology have made travelling a lot easier. But mobility does not come cheap. The roaming charges for cellphones are often not clearly spelled out by phone companies.

As the market for roaming services grows, however, the rates will likely fall. In the meantime, prepaid mobile-phone kits are a relatively cheap alternative. Card kits come in denominations of $25 or $50.

These kits are especially useful if you are staying in a foreign country for more than a few days, or if you visit the same place often. They also allow you to receive calls from people in the country that you are visiting.

(see Cellphones p. 46)

## MOBILE TRIP MANAGER

With an Internet-enabled cellphone or personal digital assistant, you can rebook flights, change hotel reservations, and reschedule the drop-off and pickup times of rental cars. By booking your trip through Trip.com (*www.trip.com)* or any of the other travel agencies that use the Galileo reservations system (*www.travelgalileo.com*), you can access your personal trip itinerary with your own PIN code. The service gives you access to the central reservations systems of more than 500 airlines and 45,000 hotels, and you can check flight times for more than 40 airlines, which are displayed in real time and based on FAA data. That means you get the same information as the gate agent.



BusinessTravel

The Galileo system will also e-mail you two hours before departure to confirm your flight time and updates the information every 15 minutes. If anything changes, you receive another notice, and if the departure is delayed, another e-mail will tell you the cause and estimate how long it will be.

## CAR RENTAL TIPS

Shop around for the best deal.

Do not buy all of the insurance offered; the most important one is the liability insurance for passengers and property. Your credit card should cover damages in case of a collision. Call your credit card company for all of the details. Ask if there is a deductible and what the policy is in case of an accident: does one need a police report? Do you have to report the accident to the company right away? Be aware that some insurance companies do not cover speciality vehicles.

At the rental lot, examine your car inside and outside, check for dents and nicks. Ask for another car if you see any damage or get the rental agent to put the information in the contract and put your signature beside it. Make sure there's a spare tire and check whether the gas tank is full. If the car rental employee suggests you pay for a full tank of gas on return, do not take the offer unless you know how much mileage you will do. There will be no refund on unused fuel.

## LIMOUSINE TRAVEL

When you travel by limousine, it unquestionably defines your status. You are in a power position. Whether the limousine is rented, yours or a company's, there are some rules to follow:

### Do:

Expect the limo to be equipped with state-of-the-art systems (TV, CD player, fax machine, and computer).

### Don't:

Shake the hand of your chauffeur, or ask him how he is doing. Do not keep the glass partition open.

## Do:

Wait for the chauffeur to open the door before you get in.

Choose to open your own door when you exit if you wish; whether in a group or alone.

Let the newcomer or young executive sit on the jump seat or in the middle of the back seat when travelling with company members.

## Don't:

Chat with your chauffeur or let him give you his personal opinion on things when sitting in the back. On the other hand if you are in the front seat and are new to the area it is fine to ask the driver some questions.

Let the driver address you by your first name.



### HOTEL LANGUAGE

The language of hotel personnel and what it means:

*Confirmed reservation:*
The hotel has accepted your booking for a specific time and will keep the room until 18:00 that day. No prepayment or credit card number is required.

*Guaranteed room:*
A room reserved and prepaid with a credit card. The room is held and you will be charged whether you show up or not.

*Double room:*
A room for two people. Always ask for the type of bed that you like. Your choices are one double/queen or king-sized bed, or two single beds.

*Meal Plans:*
The American plan includes a room and three meals from a limited menu.

A modified American plan includes a room and two meals from a limited menu.

A full American plan is the same as above except that it allows unlimited menu choices.

A Continental plan includes a light breakfast — normally a basket of rolls and croissants with juice and coffee.

A European plan in the **U.S.** means a room only. In **Europe** it means a room and a buffet breakfast.

## HOW TO GET THE BEST HOTEL RATE

You don't have to accept the first price that hotels quote you over the phone. That price is often the "rack rate" (the rate listed in brochures).

The "fallback rate" or "corporate rate" is the minimum that hotels are willing to accept. Respond to hotel's first quote by saying, "That's a little high for me. Do you have something less expensive?"

Online travel agencies and discount Web sites are good places to search for bargains. Start your search at a major Internet site, then look for deals at a discount site. When you find what you are looking for, call the hotels to ask for rates using their 1-800 number.

Remember to inquire about whether you qualify for a special discount.

Consider calling consolidators. Only try those that focus on your planned destination.

## HOTEL TIPS

Choose hotels that are easy to check in and out of. Call the hotel directly and ask for an upgrade when making the reservation; if you call an 800 number (central reservations), they will not give you one.

Choose a hotel that has consistent, reliable service.

Book a hotel in the area where you will be doing business.

Ask to see the room before you take it.

Make sure your room is not dark or located near the elevators.

Avoid a room on street level. Go for a top-floor room with a view.

BusinessTravel

Business travellers should expect or look for these types of services from their hotel: complimentary newspapers, a one-hour pressing service, terry cloth bathrobes and slippers, good quality vanity products, 24-hour room service, VIP care, a modern fitness centre, and a full business facility.

Hotels are now luring business travellers by providing the best in computer and high-tech equipment. In most hotels around the globe one can use fax machines, laptop computers, electronic voice mail, and in some you can check your hotel bill and order food from a television screen. Boardrooms and meeting rooms with audio visual devices can be used for a fee.

Unpack when you arrive in your hotel room. Press or steam items as required. Use the free pressing service if the hotel offers it; if not, pay for it.

You are better off using the hotel safe for big amounts of money or jewels. A room safe can be opened easily by a thief. Hotels will not compensate you for your loss unless you can prove negligence.

Prepare for your trip by doing research on the best places to eat. Find out what sporting events and plays are on, and which museums to visit. Make your business trip memorable.

Keep fit on the road.

When lonely, call home before going to bed.

Know the currency and recalculate all bills. Carry a pocket calculator with you. Get your value-added tax (VAT) back.

## HOTEL GRATUITIES

Always ask if there is a daily service charge. Some hotels may take as much as US$15 a day (more common a practice in **Europe** than **North America**). Many others add a 15 percent service charge to restaurant and hotel bills and, even then, there are times when additional gratuities are expected. In a five-star hotel you are expected to tip more than usual; in a Third World country, tip hotel staff less.

When in doubt about the gratuity ask the concierge at your hotel; in some countries tipping is humiliating and hotel staff won't accept any money.



BusinessTravel

Always take a pile of American one-dollar bills when travelling around the world — it is the most accepted currency. If there are no service charges, tip in **U.S.** dollars as follows:

| | |
|---|---|
| Taxi: | when picked up at the airport, 15 - 20 percent of the fee, otherwise 10 percent is fine. |
| Parking attendant: | $2 each time the car is returned to you; give more if your car is worth $90,000+. |
| Doorman: | depending on the length of your stay, $5 - $20 upon arrival or $1 - $2 for opening a door or for hailing a cab. |
| Bellhop/bellmen: | $2 - $3 a suitcase or $5 in all. If you have a carry-on bag on wheels, you may decline this service and do it yourself. |
| Room service: | $2 - $5 depending on how much service you receive; if the bill is high, tip 20 percent of the amount excluding taxes. |
| Laundry or package delivery: | $2 |
| Housekeeping/chambermaids: | $2 per day left at the end of your stay. |
| Concierge: | If you have used the service daily, $10 - $30 left at the end of your stay. |
| Massage/spa: | 15 - 20 percent for each treatment. |
| Bus tour drivers and guides: | Tip $1 - $2 a person per day. Present the total at the end of the trip. |
| Shoe shine: | $1 |
| Coatroom attendants: | $1 per article of clothing. |
| Hair stylist: | Tip 10 - 15 percent of the cost; give $2 to the hair washer. |

## GLOBAL GRATUITIES

| | |
|---|---|
| **Australia & New Zealand:** | Tips are the exception rather than the rule. If you want to give a tip, round up taxi fares and restaurant bills to the nearest dollar. |
| **Austria:** | Service charges are usually added to the bill. |
| **Barbados:** | Tip people in the hospitality industry 10 - 15 percent. |
| **Canada:** | Tip 15 - 20 percent. |
| **Caribbean in general:** | Give maids and cabbies generous tips. |
| **China:** | The government use to prohibit tipping. Tip discreetly 10 - 15 percent. |
| **Czech Republic:** | Round up to the nearest Koruna. |
| **France:** | Service charges are added to the bill, but you should leave a 5 percent tip on the table. |
| **Germany:** | Service charges are added to the bill, but you should leave a 5 percent tip on the table. |
| **Hong Kong:** | Tip 10 percent for most services. |
| **Hungary:** | Just about everyone gets a tip here — even doctors and dentists. In restaurants, give a 10 percent tip directly to the server. |
| **India:** | Tipping 10 percent is the norm. |
| **Israel:** | Restaurants and hotels will add a 10 percent service charge to your bill. |
| **Italy:** | Tip 10 percent — even if service charges have been included on the bill. |
| **Japan:** | The Japanese think tipping is unnecessary. It is up to you. |
| **Korea:** | Tip 10 percent in restaurants and hotels. |

| | |
|---|---|
| **Malaysia:** | A service charge is already added to bills; extra tipping is up to you. |
| **Mexico:** | People commonly tip 10 - 15 percent. |
| **Philippines:** | Tip 10 percent for most services. |
| **Russian Federation:** | Westerners are expected to tip generously — no matter how bad the service. To ensure good service, tip in advance. |
| **Saudi Arabia:** | A 10 percent service charge is added to bills. Tip another 10 percent for special services. |
| **Spain:** | Leave a tip even though service charges are included on the bill. |
| **St. Vincent:** | Service charges are included on the bill. |
| **United Kingdom:** | Service charges are included on the bill. If not, tip 15 percent. |
| **United States:** | Tip 15 - 20 percent. |

## HOTEL COMPLAINTS

If there is a problem with your room, whether it's that your bed is not comfortable or the service is poor, do not hesitate to complain. Speak with someone face to face and stick to the specifics of what is upsetting you.

**Complaints that may warrant a free night's stay:**

- Someone is trying to get a hold of you and the staff at the front desk tells the person that you are not at that hotel. You find out later that you were not registered properly and under someone else's name.
- The pool is closed.
- There is no beach but there is a picture of one on the hotel brochure.
- The sound of a jackhammer before 8:00 a.m.
- The hotel is under construction or renovation.
- There's a false fire alarm while you are sleeping.
- There is no hot water or the heating system does not work.

- You have reserved a king-sized bed and they only have twin beds.
- You have reserved the honeymoon suite and it was given away to another couple.
- You have a reservation and indicated a late arrival but there are no rooms available.
- A prostitute propositions you in the elevator or lobby.

**Complaints that may warrant a free meal or lower room rate:**

- You have to wait two hours for a room when arriving in the early afternoon.
- No one is there to help with your suitcases; the bellhop is nowhere to be seen.
- You have asked for a non-smoking room and it reeks of cigarette smoke.
- The next-door guests are extremely loud.
- A hotel staff is discourteous or plain rude.
- The spa is closed but it was a big feature in the brochure.
- The bed is really uncomfortable and they cannot give you another room.
- Your room is near an elevator and the noise is unbearable.

## Do:

Go to the front desk and talk to someone. If it is a big problem, ask for the general manager or property manager.

Be personal in your approach by using the person's name. They should be wearing a name tag; if not, ask for their name.

Talk calmly and ask for someone to come and look at the problem.

Express your displeasure and ask for compensation.

## Don't:

Demand an explanation — it is usually irrelevant and will not solve anything.

Try to solve the problem yourself; let them do it.

Scream or swear at the front desk staff.



BusinessTravel

## Don't:

Allow people to interrupt you while you are explaining the problem.

Accept any postponement; insist that the problem be corrected immediately.

Let the person taking care of your case help another client or disappear, otherwise you will have to repeat your entire story to someone else.

Feel embarrassed about complaining.

### COMMUNICATING WITH FOREIGNERS

When you travel in another country you are representing not only yourself but your company and your country. Politeness and good form go a long way.

Understand and respect the culture and customs of others. Know the geography, history, and the economic and political situation.

Learn a few courtesy words in the native language such as please and thank-you, excuse me, good morning, and good evening.

Avoid being met at the airport by the people you are about to do business with. You will be tired and not in a mood to socialize. Have the hotel pick you up instead.

Practice the right pronunciation of the names of the people that you are dealing with abroad. Any effort on your part will be greatly appreciated.

Be cautious about what you eat, drink, and say when you are in another country. Be a good guest.

Do not complain to your host if the food makes you sick, the toilets are disgusting, and the heat unbearable. Understand that in some underdeveloped countries doing business can be extremely difficult on the body and emotionally. Be prepared.

When entertaining, keep in mind what kind of cuisine and outings your guests would like. When in doubt, ask your contact.

Alter your expectations. Do not expect things to happen as in your country. Be patient.

## PREPARING FOR YOUR FIRST MEETING

Never rush your first meeting. Ideally, you will do your homework and communicate with the company in writing before your trip. Make the appointment with the right person ahead of time — you must know who calls the shots in the company before you go.

Never book meetings for the first day you arrive. Allow yourself time to rest. Do not schedule big receptions every night.

If you need a local representative, make sure he or she is the right contact for your needs. However, do not count on him or her for everything.

Greet your host in his native tongue, but do not try to make sentences if you are not proficient in the language. It is critical that your counterparts understand exactly what you are saying. The same word can have different meanings in different countries. Talk slowly, use uncomplicated syntax, and enunciate.

Use an interpreter who knows the technical terms of the business that you are in. Call the embassy for referrals. Always check credentials.

Remember that interpreters are not always 100 percent correct in their translation. Beforehand, advise your interpreter how you want him or her to act and proceed. Specify the dress code for meetings and negotiations.

When speaking through an interpreter, make sure that you look at the executives with whom you are dealing. Your conversation is with them, not with the interpreter. Never say a negative comment about your host's company to your interpreter.

Keep in mind that in some countries a foreigner will initially be more curious about you as an individual than in your venture. You must establish a relationship first. Without one you will never be able to conclude a deal.

Always write and make a report of what was said during a meeting and, if they want one, give a copy to your counterparts.

If you use someone's office during your stay in another country, leave a thank-you note and gift before leaving.

BusinessTravel

## NEGOTIATING ABROAD

The art of negotiating is a skill that can generate impressive results. Negotiating is a fact of life and is done every day on a personal and professional level. When negotiating the price on the purchase of a new home or going abroad to close a major deal, there will always be two different points of view.

The key to a successful negotiation is to bring out the differences and integrate them in a way that pleases both parties. Satisfying everyone's needs is the main purpose of negotiating.

There are distinctive approaches and different types of negotiators. Some individuals rely solely on intuition, some play hard ball as if it were a battle to win, and others constantly seek a compromise. The ideal negotiator manages the whole procedure with the aim of seeking mutual gain on both sides.

| Do: | Don't: |
| --- | --- |
| Look at negotiations as an opportunity for everybody to win something. | Come into a negotiation ill-prepared or rushed. |
| Think of all possibilities. Establish your objective. Use a strategy to reach your goals. | Argue: it is unwise, inefficient, and it endangers your position. |
| Make sure that you have all the information you need and are well prepared. Have a list of what you would like to achieve and anticipate what your opponent expects to gain. | Procrastinate, overreact, criticize, be abusive, or react with an emotional outburst. |
| Figure out what the other side finds appealing about your proposal. | Accept unreasonable agreements or demands. |

## Do:

Make your proposal consistent with their values.

Give a slick presentation, use video, slides, and graphics if needed.

Maintain a diplomatic approach. Be sincere and consistent. Discuss each other's perception of what's going on.

Separate the people from the problem — be hard on the problem and soft on the people.

Focus on interests not positions.

Assess the opposition and anticipate their plans. Know their strengths and weaknesses. Let them present their case first.

Get others to listen and accept your ideas by persuading them that the decision you want was their idea.

Know when to back off and when to put on the pressure. Know which participant is the most important.

Think twice before saying anything. Talk less, learn more.

Learn to walk away from a deal if it is no longer a benefit to you.

## Don't:

Let people know that you have a deadline.

Let ultimatums stop you. Just disregard them.

Bluff too much or take things for granted.

Look upon negotiating as jungle warfare.

Trust negotiations to luck.

Reveal your own views too early, give too much information out, or share it too casually.

"Go in for the kill."

Try to catch your opponent off guard.

Use too many big words to confuse.

Blame them for your problems.

BusinessTravel

## Do:

When reaching a deadlock, postpone discussions until everyone is ready to deal again.

Keep negotiations confidential. Honour all commitments made during negotiations.

## Don't:

Show anger or walk out of the room when reaching an impasse or deadlock.

Be a victim.

**Observe non-verbal signs:**

Be aware of your own and your counterpart's gestures, posture, and facial expressions. One must be able to read the non-verbal signs to understand what the other person is really saying.

Remember that in some countries the same gesture can have a different interpretation.

Negotiate if the person looks at your eyes for a while and has a one-sided smile; it means that he is looking at your proposal in a favourable way. Negotiate when seated individuals unbutton their coats, uncross their legs, and move up toward the edge of their chair. They could be displaying a desire to reach an agreement.

Do not try to negotiate if the prospect's eyes are downcast or his or her face is turned away — there is no interest.

## MORE NEGOTIATING TIPS

Seating arrangements have an impact on negotiations. The head of the table is a power position. This person is in charge. To sit opposite each other is confrontational. To sit on the same side of the opposite team (if they let you), may lead them to think you are part of their team.

Your business cards should be translated with your host's native language on one side and **English** on the other. Always handle business cards with respect. When addressing your hosts, use the title that's on their business cards. Be aware of rank.

When negotiating with a group, a good way to remember the names of the people you are talking to is to put each person's card in order of where they are sitting at the table.

Let the host handle the pace during negotiations.

It is always better to have more than one person do the negotiating. Most companies send a group of people with some of them specially trained in negotiations. If you do not speak the language, hire your own interpreter. Do not use their interpreter — he or she works for them.

Be thoroughly prepared. Do your homework, find out how people bargain in the country that you are going to and what the market facts are. To compromise or make a concession in a deal is positive in some countries while it is totally negative in others.

Discuss all of the elements that will affect the deal (cost, quality, payments, and what role each person has in the project). Business practices are different everywhere.

Many times it is better to listen than to speak. If you hit an impasse don't capitulate, it may be simply a lack of comprehension or a misunderstanding of the language or term used.

You must have a signed agreement before you leave. The final contract will not necessarily reflect what you are used to in your country.

A short contract that everyone understands is better than a long one full of big words that arouse distrust. In many countries a contract is only a sign of good faith and is not legally binding.

(See chapters 5 to 12 for negotiating in different parts of the world.)

## GETTING THE MONEY OUT

Be aware that there are very few dependable sources of credit information available in many foreign countries.

The only way to ensure good business and reliability is to trust your foreign partner and to be part of the ongoing process.

Work out all the financial terms of payment before signing the deal.

Make it part of the negotiation to get your returns early. Try to arrange for a local bank to be part of the deal.

Find out all of the restrictions or laws on currency. How much money you can take out at a time? Always demand to be paid in hard currency.

In some countries you have to barter to get your money.

Another way to get your money out is to invest in a product that has to be exported to a another country. Or you could bring in funds on the basis of a loan that must be paid back with hard currency such as the **American** dollar. Sometimes, however, even if the local currency is readily convertible, high domestic inflation can destroy any profit. So make sure the rate of return reflects that fact or there will be no profit when funds are converted into your currency.

# Africa General Etiquette

Below are the common business practices and traditions of **Africa.**

## GREETINGS & FORMS OF ADDRESS

A light warm handshake is the acceptable form of greeting when you meet and when you leave. Wait for a woman to extend her hand first. Close friends may kiss each other on both cheeks.

In **Arab Africa**, the traditional salaam greeting is in order (see Chapter 9: **Middle East & Gulf States**). Women do not shake hands. You may acknowledge them with a nod.

Guests should rise when an esteemed or senior person enters the room. Inquire after the person's health and compliment him or her. Greet everyone with a handshake.

Titles are important. Address your associates with Mr., Mrs., or Miss and the family name. Avoid using first names until you have been invited to do so.

In **French**-speaking **Africa**, kissing a friend on both cheeks is common. **French** etiquette is followed, especially amongst the upper middle-class.

## APPOINTMENTS & PUNCTUALITY

Make appointments a few weeks in advance and reconfirm them when you arrive in the country. Changes are not uncommon.

A contact is an important asset for conducting business.

In **Nigeria**, it is essential to have an associate with a very strong connection to influential people. There is a general distrust of white business people so your reputation must be impeccable. Keep your actions and words in check as news travels quickly.

It is helpful to know whether you are dealing with Christians or Muslims because they have different ways of doing business (see Chapter 9: **Middle East & Gulf States** for more information on Muslim society).

You are expected to be punctual, but it is not unusual for **African** business people to be late. Do not appear agitated if your associates are late. When they arrive, be the first to hold out your hand.

## BUSINESS CARDS

Exchange business cards during introductions. They should be printed in the local language on one side and **English** on the other. If your name is hard to pronounce, provide a phonetic translation below it.

Present the card with your right hand. It is disrespectful to use the left hand or to casually throw a business card on the table. Have promotional material available in both languages.

You may not receive a card in return, as not everyone has business cards. Senior executives will often exchange cards.

## MEETINGS & PRESENTATIONS

Meetings are conducted in **English** in **Kenya, Nigeria**, and **South Africa. Morocco** uses **French** or **Arabic**; some countries use the local language to converse. Seek out an interpreter if necessary.

Tea and coffee will be served prior to the meeting. As a courtesy you should accept all offers, but make a lukewarm refusal before accepting.

Small talk takes place before and during the meeting. **Africans** like to get to know you better before entering into a business or personal relationship.

Presentations should be clear, concise, and not too flashy. Stay friendly and low-key. You are expected to know your product inside out.

If you host is **Muslim**, he may excuse himself abruptly and leave; he is likely attending to his prayer duties and will return in about twenty minutes.

Intermittent eye contact is a sign of politeness, except in **Morocco** and **South Africa** where direct eye contact is important to business people.

Be prepared for a large number of people at meetings and during negotiations.

## NEGOTIATIONS

Always send the same people to negotiate. **Africans** dislike a change of representatives before a business venture is completed. Executives like to do business with someone of equal status.

Do not be pushy, the "hard sell" is not a suitable approach and will be met with resistance. Instead, stress the positive aspects that the venture will generate. Be discreet in your approach and encourage group discussions.

Negotiations will take longer than in the West, business people dislike rushing into anything. Trust must be established first. You should adjust yourself to the pace.

Avoid questions that require a "yes" or "no" answer. Many business people, out of politeness, dislike saying "no" and instead prefer to give a vague answer. Avoid raising your voice in anger. If you must criticize someone, do so diplomatically in private, otherwise you will lose face in front of your counterparts rather than the person being admonished. Patience and a calm exterior go a long way.

Success involves sustaining good relations. If you lose the friendship, you will lose the deal, so take care not to offend someone. Nurture trust in the relationship through frequent, short visits. Telephone calls and correspondence are not enough.

Book open flights to allow for changing deadlines and to avoid pressured decisions.

Expect to bargain, so allow room for concessions. Anticipate numerous delays and adjustments before a deal is closed. Patience is in order and so is the ability to "stick to your guns" when ready to conclude. Be decisive and firm; it will pay off.

Business transactions require a great deal of bargaining and it is advisable to be fluent in one of the local languages or have an interpreter with you.

**Nigerian** negotiators are highly educated and usually middle-aged. You should be polite and well mannered; listen and talk very little. Never interrupt. Exercise your patience during negotiations. Be well prepared, make your presentation brief and to the point. Trust is of great importance and it does not take much for a **Nigerian** to lose confidence in you.

In **Morocco,** you will likely be negotiating with a large group of people. Conduct yourself in a formal manner. Bargaining takes time and will require patience. When it is time to conclude, be firm. Your decisiveness will pay off.

In **Algeria**, business negotiations are a low-key affair. Don't try to rush things. Keep in mind that if you refuse a request you will be considered impolite.

In **Kenya**, if you lose your temper during negotiations, your counterparts will probably just laugh at you.

**South African** business people are formal and conservative in their approach. They are a proud group who values success.

Business practices are similar to those in the **United Kingdom** and the **Netherlands** (see Chapter 8: **Europe**).

Business transactions will require a great deal of bargaining and will take time due to bureaucratic constraint.

Decision making takes more time than in the West. Top executives make the final decisions in private companies. Companies owned by a group of people, decide collectively.

Suggest a written contract to avoid any misunderstandings. Words can be spoken out of politeness without serious intentions.

## WOMEN

Most **African** countries are in a political crisis and ruled by dictators. In these countries, neither gender has rights, and there is little if any opportunity to participate in the political process. Much of **Africa** cannot feed itself. In most rural areas, the labour is still done by women.

**Nigeria** has the highest rate of literacy in **West Africa**, but women are not equal to men in politics or business. In 2000, Northern Nigeria's most populous and wealthiest state, **Kano**, imposed full *sharia* (Islamic) law. Domestic violence is not uncommon in **Nigeria**, and disciplining a child, a servant, or a wife is legal. Women are now allowed to inherit property from their husbands, however.

Class distinction is predominant in **Morocco**. The elite and the most educated control the country. Women are not treated equally. In **Morocco**, a husband may commit murder, injure, or beat his wife if she commits adultery (article 418 of the Penal Code). He may do likewise to the accomplice at the moment he catches the two in the act of adultery.

The **South African** economy is the most developed in **Africa**. In 1999 the female representation in Parliament ranked seventh worldwide. **South Africa** has revised its system of land distribution so that an individual, rather than a household, can own land. The change now makes it is easier for a woman to be economically self-sufficient in **South Africa.**

In **Egypt**, a law that let rapists go free if they marry their victims has been revoked and a new law allows women to divorce their husband without his consent.

**Ethiopian** law still protects a rapist if he marries his victim.

In **Lesotho,** women are not allowed to own property.

In **Bangladesh** penalties have been extended to protect women from abuse and in the **Ivory Coast** forced marriages and sexual harassment have been prohibited.

In **Algeria**, **Mali,** and other **Muslim** countries, men can be married to more than one woman at a time and generally have four wives. A wife is required to obey her husband.

The law in **Algeria** and **Sudan** obligates that women still obey their husbands.

In **Cameroon**, women can be prevented from working outside the home legally by their husband.

Female genital mutilation is now illegal in **Senegal**, the **Ivory Coast** and **Egypt**.

## CORPORATE GIFTS

Corporate gifts should be given on subsequent visits and after a deal is closed. They should be presented in a social setting.

Appropriate gifts include quality pens, electronic diaries, pocket calculators, CDs, and famous movies on VCRs. You may give a picture book or a regional souvenir from your country.

On a subsequent visit you may bring your hosts' children clothing (t-shirts, caps, jackets) from a renowned **African-American** sports team.

Fine liqueurs and champagne for a **non-Muslim** host is also acceptable.

Avoid opulent gifts as they may be misinterpreted as bribes. Handkerchiefs indicate sadness and parting.

To be on the safe side, do not accept or give gifts with your left hand — use the right hand only.

## BUSINESS ENTERTAINING

Entertaining is often done in hotels, clubs, and restaurants. Men customarily gather without their wives.

Business and social entertaining begins later in the evening and continues well into the night. The inviter pays for the whole group. Reciprocate any invitation.

Business lunches are popular in **South Africa** and **Nigeria**.

## HOME INVITATIONS & GIFTS

When you enter someone's home, follow your host's lead — you may have to take off your shoes. If so, you will be offered a pair of slippers.

Although it is rare, you may be invited to dine in a home. You may arrive up to half an hour late. Gifts are not necessary, but you may bring some flowers, candies, a basket of fruit, or a dessert. Gourmet food is always welcome.

Avoid giving flowers as a gift in **Kenya**, as they symbolize sorrow and condolence.

With a **Muslim** host, avoid gifts of alcohol and sculptures or photographs with images of women or dogs.

A thank-you note afterwards is greatly appreciated.

## TABLE MANNERS

Table manners vary greatly from country to country. Generally, dinner begins much later than in the **West** and lasts longer. Allow your host to seat you, whether at a table or on the floor. Bring a good appetite, it shows the hostess that you are enjoying yourself.

Sample a bit of every dish; you may request seconds of the dishes you particularly liked. Use your right hand only if there are no utensils, otherwise eating continental style is appropriate. Leave a token amount of food on your plate — it indicates that there was enough food to go around. When you are finished, place your utensils parallel and vertically on your plate. Tea or coffee and desserts will be served. You may stay to converse for a short while.

In the **North**, you may be presented with a water basin to wash your hands before the meal.

Always eat with your right hand in a **Muslim's** home.

## GOOD TOPICS OF CONVERSATION

Discuss culture, history, and sports. Positive changes in the economy, accomplishments, the wildlife and tourism are welcome subjects.

## TOPICS TO AVOID

Avoid talking about religion (fundamentalism), politics, economic problems, women's role in society, and **British, Dutch**, and **French** colonialism.

Do not make any off-colour jokes.

Refer to people as **Africans** not blacks.

It is an invasion of privacy to inquire about your host's family life. However, you may be questioned about your personal life.

## CUSTOMS & TRADITIONS

Do not admire your host's possessions with excessive compliments or he or she may feel obligated to give the object to you and be offended if you refuse.

Some of the social customs in **South Africa** are very much in the **Dutch** and **British** tradition (see Chapter 8: **Europe**).

**Morocco, Algeria**, and most of **North Africa** is **Muslim**. During Ramadan, most offices and shops will be closed or have reduced hours. This is a time of fasting between sunrise and sunset.

Foreigners should not eat, drink, or smoke in front of **Muslims** during the day or at any time in public. In some places it is illegal and carries a stiff fine (see Chapter 9: **Middle East & Gulf States** for more information).

In **Senegal** and the **Ivory Coast**, many of the social customs and language are **French.**

Worry beads are common in **North Africa** and the **Muslim** population — they have no religious significance.

Many people often say "Inshallah," which translates as "God willing" and is used the same way Westerners use "I hope so."

Men can be seen publicly walking hand in hand. This is a sign of friendship and has no sexual connotations. Do not draw back if your elbow or hand is being clasped and held. However, public displays of affection between the sexes is forbidden. Stand farther away from women and do not converse with them unless you have been introduced.

Homosexuality is prohibited under the law in **Botswana** and **Somalia**.

## GESTURES

People have a smaller personal space and so stand closer together when they converse. Do not step back or you may offend them.

To show respect for your associates, keep your body language in check. Sit and stand with good posture, and maintain good eye contact.

In **Kenya**, most **British** gestures are understood and used. Stand in silence when the national anthem is played at the theatre or cinema.

A gesture that is recognized all over the globe is the raised right fist, which symbolizes "Black Power."

Cover your mouth when you yawn.

## GESTURES TO AVOID

In **Nigeria**, use only intermittent eye contact. To stare or look directly at someone is considered rude, even a challenge.

To point or beckon with your finger is rude and used only for animals, use your full hand instead.

The "hand push" where the arm is extended and the hand held forward with fingers spread is considered offensive, it symbolizes smearing dung in one's face.

A level, splayed hand with palm downward and a bent middle finger is vulgar.

Never swear, even mild oaths can elicit offense.

Keep both feet on the floor. To expose the bottoms of your shoes or feet is offensive. It is an insult that implies that you are placing someone under your feet, thus equating him with dirt. Never use your feet to point, move objects, or place them on furniture.

In rural areas, avoid strong eye contact.

## DRESS CODE

In general, men and women should wear conservative business suits for all meetings. Cotton and linen suits are suggested for summer's extreme heat. Women should dress modestly. Loose garments (blouse should be untucked) and a shawl are recommended. Don't wear tight, stretchy clothes — and definitely not shorts. A swimsuit should be worn in bathhouses.

Dark suits/silk dresses are required for formal events except in **South Africa** where formal events call for black-tie/long gowns.

In **South Africa**, business people dress as in the **West**. Safari suits are also popular.

In **Kenya**, lightweight cottons and linens are advised. Wear a lightweight suit for all business occasions especially when meeting an official for the first time. **Kenyans** generally dress informally.

Casual garments are appropriate for social occasions everywhere (see Chapter 8: **Europe**).

In **Nigeria**, a lightweight business suit is recommended for visits to government offices. For regular business, a long-sleeved shirt and tie is acceptable. A jacket is not needed. Foreign women should dress in **European** style. Modest attire and scarves are recommended where Islamic laws are practiced.

In **Morocco** and **Algeria**, most men wear a long robe called fokia, made of cotton, or a silk caftan. Jellabas are made of wool and worn on top of a robe or business suit when it is cold. Women follow a strict dress code and the head must be covered.

## PHOTOGRAPHY

Ask permission before you photograph people. If they refuse, respect their wishes and do not press. Most will allow you for a fee, especially performers.

In **Kenya**, a photography permit may be necessary, there are wonderful opportunities to capture photographs of animals in the wild.

Avoid taking pictures near airports, train stations, or military sites, as these are security sensitive and may result in the confiscation of your film or even your camera. If you are at all in doubt, ask first.

# Asia General Etiquette

Below are the common business practices and traditions of **Asia**. For general etiquette in **Australia and New Zealand**, see Chapter 7.

## GREETINGS & FORMS OF ADDRESS

Handshakes vary from country to country, however a **Westerner** should wait for a woman to extend her hand first — if she does not, one should nod.

Respect for seniority, status, and age is remarkably important in **East Asian** culture. Guests should rise when an esteemed person enters a room and allow him or her to sit down first. You should inquire about his or her health and compliment them. Always defer to the most senior person present. Elders are never interrupted when they speak. To show respect, stoop as you pass by them.

Greetings vary from country to country. In general, address **Asian** business colleagues by their title (Doctor, President) and family name. Acquaintances are addressed Mr., Mrs., or Miss and their last name. Wait until you are invited to use first names.

In **Chinese-speaking** countries, address people by their professional title and family name; or Mr., Mrs., or Miss with their family name. When you address a woman, use Mrs. and her husband's last name. Remember that the **Chinese** place their last name first. **Wong Kam To** is **Mr. Wong**. First names (such as **Kam To**) are used only between family members and friends. The **Chinese** shake hands and it is very important to them that you remember their name.

**Indians** and **Malays** often do not use surnames, so address them by their title and first name.

Most East **Asians** (people from **Japan, Korea, Thailand, Brunei, Malaysia, Myanmar** (**Burma**), and **Vietnam**) bow to each other.

In **Japan**, how one bows — the length and depth — depends on the status of the person. The more senior the person the deeper the bow. Foreigners are not expected to understand the complexity of these rules and a basic nod of the head will suffice.

**Malays** bow slightly or do the salaam, which is a traditional greeting similar to a handshake without the grip.

One or both hands are held outwards to lightly touch the other person's fingers, then brought back towards the chest to express "I greet you from my heart." Unless a cloth is used to prevent skin-to-skin contact, this greeting is only done between people of the same sex.

**Indians** may welcome you with the namaste; palms pressed together in prayer with a nod.

It will be appreciated if you take the time to pronounce names as correctly as possible.

## APPOINTMENTS & PUNCTUALITY

Appointments should be made about a month or two in advance and reconfirmed when you arrive in the country.

A contact or letter of introduction is an asset and sometimes very necessary for conducting business. A cold call will only result in meetings with people who are low on the ladder. To familiarize your counterparts with your company, send pertinent information in advance.

Networking with the right people will put you ahead of the game. Due to the high volume of red tape and bureaucracy, a contact can help tremendously. A government official or a local agent can help achieve your goals more rapidly. Be ready to spend extra money for a good connection. A joint venture with a local company is the most advantageous situation to be in.

To do business in **China** you will need a contact and a letter of introduction. Be prepared to spend extra money for a *guanxi* (good connection). Business is based on the give and take of favours and services, and a *guanxi* will increase your chances of success. You should develop friendships with these contacts — shared interests will foster better relations.

Be prepared for **East Asian** hospitality especially in **China** and **Malaysia**. You may be picked up at the airport and driven to your hotel. A designated person or a group of people will take you to the office, eat, and socialize with you. Their services will be available at your request until you board the plane home.

To show respect, you should be on time for all appointments. Allow yourself extra travelling time as traffic can be heavy. Do not be surprised and do not show impatience if in some countries (**India, Indonesia, Philippines, Pakistan, Malaysia, Thailand, Taiwan**, and **Brunei**) business people are late for a meeting. When they arrive, extend your hand first in greeting.

Avoid crowding your schedule, as meetings can take longer than anticipated.

Keep in mind that **Islamic** establishments treat Thursday afternoons and Fridays as days of rest.

## BUSINESS CARDS

Have your business cards printed in English on one side and the local language on the other. However, cards printed only in English are acceptable in **Hong Kong, Brunei, Myanmar** (**Burma**), **South Korea, India, Pakistan, Indonesia, Philippines, Malaysia**, and **Singapore.**

Business cards are taken seriously, so make sure your title and position are listed on it. Extending your business card is a polite way of getting acquainted after a greeting or introduction, however you may not necessarily receive one in return. Present your card with the lettering facing the recipient for easier reading. Begin with senior members.

Offer your card and important papers to the **Chinese, South Koreans**, and **Japanese** with both hands, and accept theirs the same way.

The **Chinese** list their achievements and important associations or affiliations on fold-open cards.

Use the right hand only when you present business cards, promotional material, or money to a **Thai, Malay, Indian,** or **Indonesian**. The left hand is considered dirty and unlucky.

Treat the business cards you receive with respect. A card should be kept in a respectful place. A breast pocket or wallet is appropriate; a back pocket is not. Never write on a card you just received, as this would be impolite. Never fold them or crumple them in your pocket. Look at them and memorize the person's name and title. Place them in front of you on the table during a meeting. This will enable you to personally address everyone by his or her name and title.

Colours have specific meanings in different **Asian** countries. To avoid misunderstandings, use black and white instead of colours in your promotional material.

Do not sign or write anything with a red pen, as it transmits a message of unfriendliness.

When dealing with the **Chinese**, avoid blue or blue/white combinations for business cards, pamphlets, or promotional items, as this colour represents grief. Gold ink is the most prestigious colour for the **Chinese** characters on your business cards.

## MEETINGS & PRESENTATIONS

Learn some of the language. **Asians** are pleasantly surprised when foreigners acknowledge and observe their customs. Take time to learn their history and respect their ways. Your efforts to understand their country will be greatly appreciated.

Gather technical information about the **Asian** firm's products before you go: research patents and go to trade shows.

Decide beforehand what technical information you are willing to share with your **Asian** counterparts, and be sure everyone on your team knows.

First meetings are very important and will set the tone of a future alliance. Small talk for 10 to 20 minutes is the norm. Topics will mostly revolve around your itinerary, the hotel, sightseeing, and questions about you and your family. At subsequent meetings this time will be spent catching up on the latest news.

The first meeting may also include a short introduction to the company. When you talk about your company, do as the **Asians** do and refer to "our" company, and use "we" rather than "I."

Always accept refreshments that are served during meetings. To refuse a drink is a breach of etiquette. It is considered an insult and indicates that you are not really interested in doing business. Allow your host to reach for his drink first.

If you are the host, always provide refreshments. Meet your **Asian** colleagues at the elevator or front door, and say good-bye to them there too.

At the beginning, relationship building is more important than business.

Establish a good personal working relationship before moving on to business matters. Sell yourself first, then move on to your product.

Know your product inside out, as well as your competitor's. You must have a solid market presence to hold any credibility in most parts of **Asia**. Be very well prepared. Your expertise is important, and your merchandise must be of high quality and competitively priced.

The older the company spokesperson the better. Age carries the weight of experience and respect. Determine who will be present at the initial meeting and send someone of equal status to avoid any embarrassment. Show respect by addressing an elder first. Make eye contact when you explain your proposal, even if the elder does not speak **English.**

Have audiovisual and promotional material translated into the country's language. Make one copy available for each member at the meeting. Send written material two weeks ahead of time to avoid surprises and confrontations in discussions. It will show respect and help speed up negotiations.

Your presentation style is important. You should not appear to be overly aggressive, pretentious, or flamboyant. Avoid the hard-sell approach. Instead, aim to be low-key, honest, and sympathetic.

Speak slowly, clearly, and avoid colloquialisms such as sports metaphors, which will only confuse your **Asian** colleagues.

If you are having trouble getting information from the **Asian** side, ask the same question in a different way at different times.

To elicit a response from your **Asian** counterparts, ask them to "please" add their ideas, rather than simply signal with your hands or eyes. Give them time to respond.

The element of "face" is very important in **Asia**. Giving face means showing respect and honour. To lose face means to lose the respect of those around you. This can happen by public humiliation or an affront to one's dignity. The loss of face of an **Asian** colleague can ultimately lead to the loss of the deal.

Explain your proposal clearly from all angles. Present it in a relaxed manner without being excessively enthusiastic. If need be, explain specific points as many times as is required. **Asians** would rather disregard your offer than say they did not understand, for fear of losing face.

Never discuss embarrassing issues, or argue or criticize a person in public. It is a breach of etiquette that will be long remembered and can jeopardize a business deal. Never interrupt a speaker. Do not make negative comments about your competition, your company, or your country. If you must criticize, do so quietly and tactfully in private using the utmost diplomacy.

Social harmony is greatly valued. Refrain from displays of emotion, such as anger. Your associates will have greater respect for you if you can keep your cool and present everyone in the best possible light. Practise patience and perseverance.

Hire an interpreter if needed. Don't speak too quickly, as he or she may be able to handle only a few sentences at a time.

Interpreters play a minor role during meetings but should be consulted afterwards to determine the subtle nuances of what transpired.

A good interpreter will smooth things over or change phrases that seem threatening to the **Asians**, e.g., negative comments like "absolutely not," "you must be joking," or any sentences with no in it.

Be careful of what you say in **English**; some business people may understand but not admit it. Periods of silence are common during meetings. Time is taken for contemplation of new material.

**Asians** don't like to say no. They will try to convey it in a different manner. If you are too pushy, you will get the answer you want to hear, but with no intention on their part to follow through. Conversely, you should also avoid answering with a no. Instead, imply that you will consider the request.

Negative questions or comments will only confuse the issue for your hosts.

Ask subtle questions to determine their position. Always give **Asian** business people a way out, and you will all save face.

If a **Japanese** person sucks in his breath through the teeth with a "sah" sound, it could mean he is upset and becoming impatient.

If a **Chinese** person waves his hand in front of his face like a fan, it could mean a negative response or anger.

Yes does not always mean yes — it can mean that they are only listening. A yes response could be an acknowledgement of understanding but not necessarily mean an agreement has been reached.

**Malays** signify yes by quickly shaking their heads side to side, which looks like the Western "no" and can be easily misunderstood.

**Indians** express agreement by tossing their head side to side, which may also be interpreted as meaning "no," although the gesture is rather different if carefully observed.

Harmony and atmosphere are very important and highly valued. Do not use pressure or hard-sell tactics. Try to persuade them diplomatically instead. Promise only what you can deliver. **Asians** will hold you to your word. If **Asian** business people become loud or forceful in conversation, avoid returning the gesture. Remain calm and find a different way to express your concern.

You will know that your **Asian** counterparts are feeling uncomfortable, losing interest, or even angry if: they lack all expression, smile or nod impatiently, glance at a clock or watch repeatedly, stop making eye contact or asking questions, ask the interpreter or an assistant how long the presentation is going to last, or there is a long silence in response to a request.

If you see these signs, call for a break in the meeting and do not bring up the issue again. Take up the issue later on, informally, through an intermediary.

After every formal meeting, meet with your team. Refer to the notes you should be keeping.

## NEGOTIATIONS

**Asian** business people prefer to deal with individuals they know. The purpose of negotiations is to establish a business relationship built on trust and compatibility. For **Asians**, business relationships are ties based first on obligation and reciprocity, and then profit.

Long-term goals are more important than short-term gains. **Asians** want to know that you are in this for the long haul. Joint ventures are common.

Relentless information gathering is a common feature of preliminary negotiations in **Asia**, often to the chagrin of **Westerners**.

Your **Asian** counterparts will ask many sensitive questions, some of them repeatedly.

Once they have gathered information, **Asians** will look for ways to cooperate. Unfortunately, it is not so easy for **Western** business people to get detailed information from the **Asian** side.

Always keep in mind that in **Asia** your product or technological know-how could be counterfeited. Don't assume that your **Asian** partner will protect you; you'll have to do that yourself.

Don't rely on what **Asian** firms tell you about the local market. Verify what you have been told, and do your own feasibility studies.

**Asians** are very cautious in business matters and need ample time to make business decisions. They like to consider all aspects before making a commitment. Every point and detail will be discussed. Decisions are given proper deliberation and all implications will be considered. Be patient and prepared for lengthy business negotiations, as there is always room for more discussion.

Negotiations are used as a forum to continue developing the working relationship and a stronger commitment to the venture. Expect delays on deadlines and negotiations to continue even after the deal is done.

Save the real negotiating for informal meetings after business hours with the **Asian** team's senior person.

**Asians** employ markedly different negotiating strategies than their **Western** counterparts.

While propriety characterizes **Asian** negotiations, they also use methods based on military tactics. In fact, these war-inspired strategies are passed on from mentor to apprentice, thus preparing new generations specifically for negotiations with foreign companies.

Be prepared for the delaying tactics of **Asian** negotiators. **Westerners** sometimes give in to the **Asian** side simply because delays are costly. To avoid the pitfalls of negotiating in **Asia**, keep an open time frame and don't offer concessions just to speed up the process. It takes time to wear down your "opponent," which is the key to a successful deal in **Asia**.

The **Asian** side will be operating out of self-interest — try to figure out what your counterparts really want.

Stand by your position and don't lower your price by any more than a token amount. When a deadlock occurs, make your demands with passion, as if it were vitally important. Let them know that you are not going to back down.

Don't get too personally involved with your counterparts. Keep some distance.

The **Asians** will respect you more if you are a little aloof.

Companies that are government owned can generate a great deal of bureaucracy and red tape. Find out who makes the real decisions within the government.

**Westerners** should never directly pay any commissions; this should be handled by an **Asian** partner in a joint venture or by a distributor.

Ask someone on the **Asian** side to provide organizational charts of the company as well as the industry as a whole. Keep a list of the decision-makers, so you can figure out how all the players are associated. That way, you should avoid dealing with a competitor of your business partner.

Be prepared to travel many times before any deal is concluded. It is best to book open tickets. It will allow for last minute changes and emergencies, and you will avoid pressure from **Asian** associates to make hasty decisions. Try to deal with top executives because they have the final say. Never send a young person to negotiate a deal.

Do not use anyone in your business dealings who is intolerant of different races, religions, or cultures.

**Asians** dislike a change of representatives in mid-negotiations. It does not present a stable view of your company. They prefer to deal with people rather than faceless corporations.

Negotiate only with your counterparts or superiors and make sure your team is appropriately matched with theirs. In some countries (**Hong Kong, China, Japan, Malaysia, Thailand, South Korea**), negotiating teams usually sit according to rank.

At a conference table, the leader sits in the middle, the second in command to his right, and the third to his left. Your team should sit opposite them the same way.

In some **Asian** countries it is not customary to pay for professional services separately (they may be added to a project for a hidden fee), so providers of these services may be faced with unexpected demands and haggling over fees.

Take notes and send a typewritten copy to your **Asian** colleagues so that everything is agreed upon and on paper.

However, keep in mind that in **Asia** nothing is written in stone and everything is open to negotiation. Bargaining is the norm, so leave room for concessions.

**Asians** will negotiate holistically, moving from one point to the next without making a commitment. Expect your counterparts to discuss a contract two or three times — and not make concessions until the very end.

For **Asians**, a business agreement is more about the relationship between the two parties than about price. It is based on such things as trust, accountability, and respect.

**China**, for example, still has an economy based on relationships, not contracts. Business transactions are personal agreements that are negotiated privately and cannot be verified or enforced by an outside body.

Some questionable business practices in **China** may influence the progress of your deal. Deadlines will likely be changed and the terms may have to be renegotiated. Watch out for *hei shehui* — the problem of favours. Most companies in **China** are government owned, so you can expect a lot of red tape.

A written contract is a must in **Asia**. Make sure it is short, readable, and clear. Be sure there are no ambiguities. Even so, you may find that your **Asian** counterparts raise many issues you thought were solved after the contract is signed. The **Japanese** refer to this as *jijo henko*, which means "changed circumstances."

In **Japan**, you may find you are dealing with a number of people from the same family. That's because positions in both business and politics are still passed on to family members. Achievement is not as important as who you are in the hierarchy.

Keep in mind that it is the relationship that will keep the enterprise going, not the signed document.

When dealing with a firm for the first time, agree only to an "organic contract." In other words, insist that a number of performance clauses must be met on both sides for the partnership to grow. This will reduce the risks at the same time that it ensures both sides get something out of the deal.

Expect a photographer to take pictures of the group when contracts are signed.

Should serious problems arise later on, solve them face-to-face, not by fax or letter. Problems left unsolved will probably still be there when you return to the country.

Respect local traditions and superstitions for bringing luck to business dealings.

Before beginning new ventures or signing contracts, they may wish to conduct ceremonies for lucky omens, consult oracles or the stars, and choose lucky numbers or days.

If you are setting up a branch in a **Chinese-speaking** country, consult and show respect for feng shui, which is a method of geomancy. Before buying land or a home, or changing offices, a consultant is called in for guidance. He will determine the best location for your house or office, as well as choose the structure and furniture. Feng Shui means wind and water — elements that are believed to affect people positively or negatively. A hill behind and water in front of the property is the best choice. Doors and windows are aligned so that good spirits come in and bad ones stay out.

## WOMEN

Many women hold responsible positions in businesses in America and Europe, but few women hold similar jobs in other parts of the world. At the same time, some employers in the West don't offer women foreign posts in the mistaken belief that the women won't be taken as seriously as the men.

On the contrary, foreign women in the **Asia-Pacific** region can expect to get as much respect as foreign men do. They may even be at an advantage because Asians appreciate that foreign businesswomen are less confrontational than their male counterparts. They are usually more willing to build business relationships and save someone's face — factors that contribute to success in **Asia**.

Before you take a post abroad you may want to read the latest United Nations report on the status of women.

Working in some parts of **Asia** means that you often have to disregard the way local women are treated. In the **Muslim** culture, traditional men will often ignore a woman outside of his family. (This is deemed polite behaviour.) **Malays** may have more than one wife and laws still allow for marital rape.

The Progressive Women's Association (PWA) in **Pakistan** is pressuring the military government there to introduce legislation that recognizes domestic violence as a crime. Many women in **India** and **Pakistan** have been killed by their husband and in-laws in what are known as "stove-burst" attacks. It's the easiest way for a husband to get rid of a wife he no longer wants. There are no gunshots; no fingerprints. All the husband has to say is that the wife was cooking in the kitchen when the edge of her dupatta [scarf] fell in the stove and caught fire.

Marital rape is still legal in **India** and in **Pakistan**. A rape charge will not stand up in court unless there are four male eyewitnesses to prove that the rape occurred. In **India** children are also still illegally wed. The *Globe and Mail* reported in September 2001 that 80 children had been wed in a mass wedding ceremony in the state of **Rajasthan**. Some of the children were less than a year old.

In **Afghanistan**, women cannot leave their home unless covered from head to toe and are denied equal access to education, employment, and health care. They have no right to activities outside the house, including employment and education. Both native and foreign women are not allowed to drive in **Afghanistan**.

There have been some positive changes in **Bangladesh**. There is now a law that increases the penalties for abusing women.

In **Japan**, a woman with a graduate degree from a big-name university might have trouble getting a job — a man will be considered first. If she gets the job, she will be asked to serve tea and coffee as well.

In **Korea**, you are in a man's world and one must be ready to talk business in a bar after working hours.

Women in countries such as the **Philippines, Thailand, Taiwan**, and **China** are well represented in the work force. Until recently, a woman held the post of Foreign Trade Minister in **China**.

Business people always have to adapt to the cultural conditions that surround them and, ultimately, foreign women will be judged by their skills, knowledge, and the position they hold.

Consider getting an **Asian** mentor (perhaps a retired businessman) to help pave the way. Your interpreter (often a woman) may also be of assistance at meetings. Get together with her beforehand to discuss what you want to get across. It is also advantageous to earn the trust of local women.

The names and experience of the members of the negotiating team should be sent in advance. Make sure that your expertise and status are emphasized. Your company should also make the proper introductions. Your home office must be seen to endorse your authority.

Handle sexual advances the same way you would in your own country. Maintain control of the situation; tell your **Asian** colleagues or customers that you are there for business only. Try not to get overly emotional or angry.

Follow the behaviour of the **Asian** women present at social gatherings. Don't smoke or drink alcohol unless they do. Never drink excessively, even if the men do.

Your performance abroad will pave the way for other women who come after you. Believe in your abilities. It is up to you to create the professional trust that is necessary to succeed in **Asia**.

## CORPORATE GIFTS

In general, always pack three kinds of gifts: expensive items for top executives, food gifts and mid-range consumer gifts for managers, and inexpensive (but **Western**-made) novelty items for factory workers or the children of your **Asian** friends.

Corporate gifts should be presented after a deal is closed. They should be wrapped and accompanied by a card (but never use red ink).

Gifts are not opened immediately or in front of the giver. This is done to avoid any embarrassment for anyone who may feel his or her gift was not good enough. Similarly, if you receive a gift, do not open it immediately; simply thank the giver and put it to one side. But if you are asked to open it, first read the card, then delicately unwrap the gift. Refer to the gift later on to demonstrate continuity in the relationship.

Always send a thank-you note to everyone who gives you a gift (even though it is not expected in **Indonesia**). You should even send thank-you notes to **Koreans**, but do not expect them to send you one.

Let your host decide when and where to exchange gifts, and do not give a gift without letting your host or the group know beforehand. Give gifts to individuals only in private, and gifts to a group only at scheduled gatherings, so everyone will be there.

Whatever you do, do not forget anyone in the group; to do so is to make him or her lose face.

Offer gifts with both hands to the **Chinese, Japanese**, and **Koreans**, and use the right hand when presenting it to a **Thai, Malay, Indonesian**, or **Indian.**

Don't give gifts that are "**Made in Taiwan**" or the like, nor **Asian** items such as lacquerware, porcelain china, statues of Buddha, or jade jewellery. Buy items with recognizable labels that you purchased in the **West**.

Suitable gifts include imported liquor (not for **Muslims**) such as cognac, bourbon, scotch, champagne and wine.

Any good quality items for the office (paper weights, high quality calendars, calculators, CDs, computer software, paintings, framed pictures, lithographs, bound diaries, (magazine subscriptions) are suitable.

You could give a handicraft, a ceramic vase, or a sculpture made by an artist from your country.- A picture book of your home region, golf-related equipment and sports memorabilia are also acceptable.

Packaged speciality foods are appropriate in certain countries only (**Taiwan, Japan, China, Hong Kong**, and to the **Chinese** in **Singapore** and **Indonesia)**, but do not give the food at a dinner party.

Lower-range gifts include books, T-shirts, notebooks, toys, and games. Famous label accessories (ties, an attaché case, cufflinks, designer pen sets) are appropriate personal gifts.

Numbers are important in gift giving. Three is a lucky number in **Thailand** and **Hong Kong** (where the word for "three" sounds like "life"), so you could give three of something. The number eight (which sounds like "prosperity") and nine (a homonym for "eternity") are also lucky in **Hong Kong** and **China**. Business people in Hong Kong pay thousands of dollars for license plates with eights and nines in them.

The word for "four" is a homonym for death and mistake in **Taiwan, Japan**, and **Korea** (where some older hotels don't have a "fourth floor"), so in these two countries, give odd numbers of things.

In **Muslim Asia, Westerners** are likely not only to receive many gifts, but often. Expect to receive rather extravagant gifts at your first meeting. You may also be expected to open a gift after a business meeting or speech. Your gift to them will probably not be opened in front of you, nor are you likely to get a formal thank-you.

Don't give **Muslims** gifts of alcohol, pork and pigskin by-products (all of which **Islam** forbids), ashtrays, knives, pictures or sculptures of women, or toy dogs — **Muslims** consider dogs unclean.

**Hindus** hold cows sacred, so avoid leather items. Any time you give money to an Indian it should be an odd number, such as $11 rather than $10.

**Buddhists** are vegetarians, so do not offer animal-based foods or by-products.

Do not give gifts to the **Chinese** wrapped in black or blue with white ribbons, as they are the **Chinese** colours of mourning.

Consider wrapping gifts with red paper, which is the colour of good luck. (Again, the exception is red ink.) Gold signifies riches and is often combined with red.

At **Chinese New Year,** give children and service workers (outside of government) with whom you deal regularly a gift of money in a red envelope (hong bao). The bills must be new, in even numbers, and in even amounts.

Scissors, letter openers, and other sharp objects portend the rupture of a relationship or are an omen of disagreement. Do not give an **Asian** a knife, as it will indicate that you want to sever the relationship.

The gifts to avoid may depend on your associates' background. Generally, avoid giving items that are opulent or have your company logo on them. Don't give anything that represents division or conflict.

## BUSINESS ENTERTAINING

Business entertaining is an important part of a deal. However, it is not always easy to know when it is appropriate to bring up business matters.

For example, a **Thai** will not appreciate attempts to talk business over lunch, but a Filipino will expect it. **Filipinos** and **Muslim Asians** would be horrified by business discussions at dinner, but the **Chinese** won't mind so long as it is brought up indirectly. A good rule of thumb, therefore, is not to talk about business during a meal unless your host initiates it.

After-hours socializing is very popular and takes place in hotels, restaurants, or clubs, and often involves business associates only. Spouses are not invited. Hostesses may join you at the table to serve you drinks and sing with you. The host usually pays for the bill.

Alcohol will flow freely at such gatherings (except among **Muslims**). If you do not wish to drink much, sip slowly and keep the glass fairly full. An empty glass is often a request for another drink. If you do not wish to drink at all, explain that it is for health reasons. Another way to avoid overdrinking is to act drunk, then no one will insist that you drink more. This lessens the impact of a refusal.

If you want concessions on your contract, try to get them over drinks. This is the setting where you might just get them.

Except for functions in **Muslim** countries, you'll probably have to perform for others.

Consider bringing a harmonica (if you know how to play), do card tricks, juggle, draw caricatures, even take Polaroids and pass them around. Only sing if you are asked, and be humble.

Take a cue from your **Asian** colleagues and politely decline invitations before finally accepting them. Dinners are strictly social occasions. The inviter pays for the group; there is no "splitting the bill." You are expected to reciprocate dinner invitations that are equal in stature but never more lavish. Allow your guests to choose the restaurant. Extend the invitation to spouses.

You may be invited to a banquet, especially after a deal is completed.

Formal dinners in all of **Asia** are common. Classical **Chinese** banquets are mostly in **Hong Kong, China**, and **Taiwan**, as well as any place where there are **Chinese** business people. Everyone involved in the deal will be present. Formal dinners or banquets begin at 21:00, and usually take place in a restaurant, the company dining room, or a hotel dining room.

If you are the guest of honour at a banquet, arrive after your hosts; and be the first to leave, because no one can depart before you do. Wait until you are told where to sit. The guest of honour sits facing the entrance to the dining room on the host's right side, which is the honoured position. **Asians** and **Westerners** are usually seated alternately around the table. If the host's wife is present, she will sit opposite her husband. Foreign wives usually sit next to their husbands.

Don't smoke at the table unless your hosts do.

Compliment the centre display. If your host takes off a piece of the display and eats it, follow his lead.

You will be served alcoholic beverages, soft drinks, and tea. The host proposes the first toast, after which toasting is common. If you are the one being toasted, respond with a short speech. If you do not wish to drink alcohol, you may toast with a soft drink or tea.

Never begin to eat before your host. Eat sparingly; as many as twelve courses may be served and sometimes more. The most important guests are served first. If you are the guest, the host will order and serve you throughout the meal. Do not be offended if he uses his own chopsticks to do this. It is an honour if the host takes a small piece of food from his own plate and puts it in yours, but do not reciprocate. Rice is not always served at big banquets, so do not ask for it. Soup comes near the end of the meal.

It is polite to sample every dish, but you are not expected to finish everything on your plate.

To leave food on your plate shows that there was enough food served. Be prepared for some unusual foods.

Countries in **Asia** that do not use chopsticks, use a fork and a spoon to eat. The spoon goes in the right hand and is used to eat while the fork in the left hand pushes the food into the spoon.

The arrival of fruit signals the end of the meal. When you are finished, place your chopsticks or utensils parallel across your plate. **Asian** banquets and dinners end promptly once the guests receive hot towels, if not, they end after desert.

If you are in **Asia** for a while, you may want to hold a banquet comparable to the one your hosts provided. If so, get the help of an **Asian** facilitator who knows the restaurants.

Banquets in **Muslim Asia** (including **Malaysia, Indonesia**, and **Singapore**) will likely be attended by many ethnic groups, so you can expect a wide variety of food. Never ask to drink alcohol or smoke when you are among Muslim people.

If you have to decline an invitation, it is more acceptable to cite work than fatigue or jet lag as the reason.

## HOME INVITATIONS & GIFTS

It is an honour to be invited to an **Asian** home; therefore, be sure to send a thank-you note afterwards.

Remember to remove your shoes before entering a **Thai, Korean, Indonesian, Indian, Taiwanese, Vietnamese**, or **Japanese** home. Take cues from your hosts. Sunglasses and hat are removed as well. Always step over the door's threshold, not on it. Some people believe that a deity resides there.

Always bring a gift, such as **Western** gourmet foods. Fresh fruit is a good choice in the **Philippines**. Smoked salmon is popular with **Asians**.

Avoid bringing gifts of food to a dinner or party if your hosts are **Chinese** — unless it was discussed beforehand. Although the **Chinese** appreciate gifts of food, it may suggest that your hosts cannot provide enough. Consider sending food later on as a thank-you gift.

A gift of food wrapped in white paper will be appreciated in a **Malay** home. Try not to show admiration for something, as your **Malay** host might want you to accept it as a gift.

Do not give white flowers in either **China** or **Japan**, as they are associated with mourning. In **China**, flowers are primarily given to people in hospital or brought to funerals. If a **Japanese** person is in hospital, do not bring a potted plant — it signifies that he or she is "rooted in illness."

## TABLE MANNERS

Meals begin later in the evening. They are large and lengthy. You may be treated to a traditional meal. Adapt yourself to the local customs and follow your host's lead.

If serving dishes are distributed, pass them with your right hand only. You should sample a bit of every dish and return for seconds of those you enjoyed. Eating large quantities shows appreciation.

Cover your mouth with your hand when you use toothpicks.

Never rest your chopsticks upright in the rice bowl since it mocks a religious funeral ceremony and will offend your hosts. Never cross your chopsticks when you put them down, as it is a sign of bad luck for the host.

Place them on the porcelain holder beside your bowl. You may raise the rice bowl close to your mouth when you eat (except in **South Korea**).

## GOOD TOPICS OF CONVERSATION

Suitable issues include sports, cultural heritage, history, art, sightseeing, the country's cuisine, goods to buy, families, hobbies, mutual interests, movies, books, achievements, aspirations, your home region and travel.

## TOPICS TO AVOID

Stay away from discussing religion, politics, personal wealth, crime, and sex; and do not pry into personal relationships — even if they do. You are the stranger who everyone is trying to get to know.

It is common for relative strangers to ask fairly personal questions regarding your age, marital status, and earnings, or how much you paid for certain items. Do not be offended because it is an acceptable show of interest.

Do not tell them that it is personal or none of their concern because you will offend them. It is best to smile and answer lightheartedly.

If you do not wish to elaborate, say something like "I wish I would make more money, that's why I'm here, so we can make a lot of money together," or "I am buying this item for a friend and he is paying for it."

Do not compare your host's country to your own.

Do not call **Muslims "Mohammedans"** — they think it makes them sound like cult-followers. Avoid any discussions of the Taliban, the repressive government of Afghanistan.

To avoid any misunderstandings, refrain from humorous remarks, jokes, sarcasm, or satire until you get to know someone very well.

## CUSTOMS & TRADITIONS

**East Asian** society has existed for thousands of years. From birth, **Asians** are taught values such as paternalism, loyalty to family and organization, national pride, conformity, obedience to authority, and respect for elders.

Avoid admiring your host's possessions excessively or he may feel obligated to give you the object and be offended if you refuse.

To enter a **Muslim** mosque, you must first get permission. Remove your shoes and do not walk in front of a **Muslim** while he is praying, and never step on a prayer mat. Avoid touching the Koran holy book. During **Ramadan, Islamic** offices and shops will either be closed or open with reduced hours. Fasting takes place between sunrise and sunset. It is rude to eat, smoke, or drink in front of a **Muslim** during the day, especially in public.

When you visit a **Hindu** temple, do not touch the statues or smoke.

**Chinese** temples require that you remove your hat. Shoes can be worn in some temples but avoid stepping on the doorframe.

In some remote regions, a curious crowd may suddenly follow you. Do not be offended or frightened, just smile.

Close friends of the same sex can be seen holding hands.

This is a show of friendship and has no sexual connotations. Do not draw back if your elbow or hand is clasped, but do not initiate the physical contact yourself.

Public displays of affection between the sexes are heavily frowned upon. Stand farther apart from women and do not converse with them unless you have been introduced or are in a group.

Homosexuality is prohibited in **Myanmar** (**Burma**), **India**, **Malaysia**, and **Sri Lanka**.

While there is no law against homosexual sex in **Indonesia,** gay men and lesbians suffer from a policy of official silence and religious intolerance.

It is not illegal to be gay or lesbian in **Singapore**, but homosexual sex acts are illegal and can land people in jail — even if they take place in private.

In **Afghanistan**, the Taliban bans the following: use of the Internet, television, cinema, music, alcohol, pork, shorts, all sports except soccer, shaving, bare ankles, Western clothes, and statues. There can be no inappropriate contact between members of the opposite sex. Men and women are not allowed to eat in the same room, and men are banned from looking at any woman to whom he is not related.

Since the Taliban is no longer in power in **Afghanistan**, only Taliban followers will most likely adhere to these rules.

Modesty is important, so remember to deny or downplay compliments directed toward you while generously complimenting your hosts and associates.

When you are complimented, you are expected to deny it out of politeness rather than accept it with a thank you. The latter expresses arrogance. Humility is a virtue; don't blow your own horn. **Asians** do not easily accept compliments.

Keep your body language in check. Stand with good posture and do not lean against furniture. Slouching in your chair signifies poor upbringing. When you are seated it is polite to keep your hands on your lap. Do not cross your legs; keep them flat on the floor during the meeting. Avoid fidgeting and unnecessary hand or leg movements.

Excessive activity distracts from your message.

**Asians** tend to control their facial expressions, making them difficult to read.

Laughter expresses many emotions besides amusement or happiness. It can be used to convey anguish, disbelief, anger, or may be a cover for an embarrassing or frustrating situation.

Although others may laugh at someone's mistake or misfortune, you should refrain from doing so. **Asians** may make a serious point with a smile or short laugh to soften the message and reduce the potential for disagreement.

Avoid smiling too often. You may be indicating uneasiness. (And be careful that your laughter doesn't make them feel uneasy.)

To indicate obedience and subordination, an **Asian** won't look a superior in the eye. However, **Asian** children are disciplined with a hard stare. As a result, direct eye contact tends to signify condemnation even for adults.

The **Japanese** are very uncomfortable with prolonged eye contact, and **Thais** think it is rude to stare into another person's face because it feels threatening. The **Chinese** and **Koreans**, on the other hand, use more direct eye contact than other **Asians**. In fact, **Chinese** people in **Hong Kong, Singapore**, and **Taiwan** make eye contact about as much as **Westerners**.

## GESTURES

People may stand closer to each other while conversing than in **North America**. Do not step back or you may offend them. To point, **Asians** use the whole hand, palm up, or they curl their fingers and extend the right thumb in the right direction.

To beckon, stretch out your hand palm down and make scratching motions with your fingers or wave the **North American** good-bye.

It is polite to remove your sunglasses and keep your hands out of your pockets when conversing with people.

## GESTURES TO AVOID

Avoid any physical contact in public. It is offensive to pat a colleague on the back or any other form of backslapping, touch his shoulder, or squeeze his arm. This is reserved for family or close friends.

Never use the index finger to point because this is used only for animals.

Do not beckon people with the palm up.

Never swear; even mild oaths can offend.

It is rude to wink.

Refrain from smoking when you speak to anyone.

As the highest part of the body, the head is regarded as the seat of spirituality in Buddhist culture. To touch someone's head or hair is rude and offensive. Especially avoid patting children on the head. Do not touch the head of a Buddha statue.

By contrast, feet are considered the dirtiest part of the body. Keep both feet on the floor. To expose the bottoms of your shoes or feet is offensive. It is an insult that equates the recipient with dirt, thereby placing him under your feet. Never use your feet to point or move objects, nor place them on furniture.

Avoid stepping over the legs of people seated on the floor. Apologize if you step on someone's foot.

## DRESS CODE

In general, men doing business in **Asia** should wear a dark conservative suit, a white crisp shirt, and a tie, paired with black business shoes (this outfit is also acceptable formal wear). For casual occasions, a lightweight sports jacket, casual trousers, a coloured shirt, and a pair of loafers are appropriate, or bring a safari jacket and wear it with khakis.

When it is very hot, consider a linen or tropical-weight suit.

Women doing business in **Asia** should also dress conservatively and modestly. Avoid wearing low-cut blouses, tight sweaters, tank tops, or sleeveless shirts. For business, wear a lightweight suit in a medium tone, a skirt and blouse or a dress.

Women will find that a designer silk or crepe outfit is fine for evening wear. Bring a low-heeled shoe for business and flat shoes for casual occasions. Shoes should be of good quality and in perfect shape. Wear only real jewellery in **Asia**; less is more except in **Hong Kong, Shanghai,** and **Singapore**.

Both genders should pack comfortable sturdy shoes with good traction for sightseeing. One must often step in and out of boats, climb many steps to see a temple, or walk along a jungle path.

In **Muslim** countries skirts should be knee-length or longer. Do not wear flashy colours. Loose-fitting cottons and raw silk garments are acceptable casual wear.

Women in **Pakistan** don't usually go out alone, but when they do most of them wear a *shalwar-kameez*. This long cotton shirt and pants is often embroidered and tie-dyed. Visitors aren't required to wear these, but you may feel less conspicuous if you do. Buy a *shalwar-kameez* once you're in **Pakistan**, but avoid getting one in blue and white, which are the colours worn by schoolgirls. Pair the outfit with a *dupatta* (a light scarf) for entering religious sites.

**Malaysia** is a culturally diverse nation, so you will see everything from ethnic **Chinese** women wearing miniskirts to **Islamic** women clothed in scarves and brightly coloured dresses. One of the few suggestions for tourists applies to the beach: wear a one-piece suit and keep in mind that topless bathing is forbidden. (**Muslim** women swim fully clothed.) The overall best outfit for a visitor is a sarong, loose shirt, and sandals.

When visiting a temple or mosque in **Asia**, men and women should dress conservatively; women's legs and arms must be covered. Shoes are not allowed in temples. Shorts or culottes are considered resort wear.

Both men and women should avoid "going native" in their clothing choices.

Rainwear and/or an umbrella are a must in some countries because of the monsoons and sudden showers that can occur year-round in some hot countries.

Overall, it is always better to dress in a fashion that does not draw attention to one's self. Good quality garments are a must. Be prepared for high heat and humidity in some **Asian** countries.

In **Kashmir,** a guerilla group has directed **Muslim** women to wear a veil over their faces or use the *burqa*. For **non-Muslim**, it has ordered women to adhere to a dress code distinguishing them from Muslim women. **Hindu** women are asked to cover their heads with a saffron cloth, and colour their forehead with the *bindi* mark (circle, or dot - red for married women).

## PHOTOGRAPHY

Ask permission before you photograph people; some may request a donation. Respect their wishes and do not push if they refuse. Religious buildings and museums may levy fees for taking photographs or forbid it altogether. Avoid themes that depict poverty or crime, as this will upset the locals.

For security reasons, do not use your camera at airports, train stations, or official buildings. You may risk having your camera and film confiscated. Ask first if you are at all in doubt.

In most **Muslim** countries such as **Afghanistan** and **Pakistan**, you are not allowed to photograph men, women, and animals.

# Australia & New Zealand
## General Etiquette

Below are the common business practices and traditions of **Australia** and **New Zealand**. See Chapter 6: **Asia** for more information.

## GREETINGS & FORMS OF ADDRESS

A firm handshake with direct eye contact is customary when you meet and when you part. **Australians** and **New Zealanders** will usually reply with "G'day." Men should wait for a woman to extend her hand first. If you see someone often, a simple nod and "Hi" or "Hello" will suffice.

At parties, your host will introduce you to the other guests. It is also acceptable to introduce yourself if you wish.

Initially, address your associates by their professional title or sir, and social acquaintances with Mr., Mrs., Miss, or Ms. and surnames until you are invited to use first names. As in Europe and **North America**, the surname follows the first name.

Expect to quickly be on a first-name basis with the **Australians**; they have a relaxed attitude and the word "mate" is often used as an informal address.

In **Australia** a title does not dictate respect; one has to gain the esteem of his or her peers.

For traditional greetings with the **Maoris**, rub noses.

## APPOINTMENTS & PUNCTUALITY

Make appointments by phone or fax about three weeks ahead, and reconfirm when you arrive in the country.

Face-to-face communication is preferred to written correspondence and telephone calls. Punctuality is important. In **New Zealand**, arrive five minutes early, which is better than being on time.

In **Australia**, use any connections and introductions you have, as there is an old boy network of senior executives and major players.

Appointments are simple to arrange with executives; they are easy to approach and are more than willing to discuss business.

The best time of the year for trips is between March and November.

## BUSINESS CARDS

Present your business card during introductions or at the beginning of a meeting. Do not expect to get cards from everyone in return.

## MEETINGS & PRESENTATIONS

Tea may be served during a meeting. It is acceptable to refuse the offer if you do not wish to drink.

Business practices are similar to those in **North America**. Eye contact is important to build trust in a working relationship.

Small talk is the norm at the beginning of meetings. **Australians** and **New Zealanders** like to develop a friendship before getting into business matters.

Do not get too personal or discuss your private life at business meetings. Instead, pick neutral subjects for small talk.

**New Zealanders** have a tendency to be more constrained and placid than **Australians**. The business mood is also more solemn than in **Australia**.

Do not try to make a big splash or appear too confident in your presentation. A low-key approach is best. **Australians** and **New Zealanders** are not easily impressed.

Be simple and minimize your expertise. Let your knowledge and skills speak for themselves.

## NEGOTIATIONS

Following the excesses of the 1980s, international investors are now more cautious about investing in **Australia**. When considering acquisitions, investors look at the strength of the balance sheets.

Reflecting that caution, **Australia** has a new corporations law that covers everything from directors' responsibilities to prospectus information.

Present your offer in a concise and clear manner. Major issues should be outlined first, with an emphasis on long-term goals and benefits. Facts are important but details should be discussed later.

Never use high-pressure tactics, give orders, or patronize. Be direct and sincere; present the pro's and con's of the deal.

People in these two countries value equality and will resent any attempts to pull rank or treat subordinates unequally. Manual labour enjoys higher prestige in **Australia** and **New Zealand** than in **America**.

Even though individualism is highly rated, in the end, corporate policy comes first.

Negotiations are straightforward and firm. **Australians** and **New Zealanders** do not have a problem saying no to any offer that won't make a good profit. Earnings take precedence over market shares.

Be prepared for different people showing up at the negotiating table. Bargaining is not the norm.

Never get angry or let emotions get in the way while negotiating — you will be judged untrustworthy. **Australians** and **New Zealanders** are averse to displays of emotions.

Be patient, decision making takes time. The top management will make the final approval.

When negotiations are finished, do not expect compliments on a job well done.

**Australians** usually distrust authority and people who act as if they are better than others. Modesty is the best policy at all times. In conversation, don't dwell on your education, professional success, or related achievements.

Cynicism is part of the **Australian** character, particularly in regard to the wealthy or powerful. There is greater respect for the underdog.

**Australian** business culture is modest, casual, and has an air of nonchalance.

**Australians** are receptive to sports analogies in presentations and conversation.

If you are teased, take it in the good-natured way it was intended. It is okay to tease right back, but refrain from being mean-spirited.

## WOMEN

In **Australia**, men like to chat amongst themselves after dinner; it would not be appropriate for a woman to tag along. Stay with the women present or return to your hotel.

Equality in gender is accepted, but women are still battling for equality in earnings and high postings.

(See "Women" in **Asia** and **Europe** for more information on women working abroad.)

## CORPORATE GIFTS

**Australians** and **New Zealanders** do not expect gifts from foreigners doing business with them. If it is your custom, you may do so on special occasions or when a deal has been sealed.

Appropriate gifts are quality office items, computer software, a CD-ROM, coffee-table book, or an artwork or handicraft by an artist of your country. Speciality food or liquor from your home region is also a good choice. Sports memorabilia are acceptable.

Gifts are normally opened in front of the giver, a thank-you note should follow. Do not expect gifts in return.

## BUSINESS ENTERTAINING

In **Australia**, power breakfasts and luncheons are very popular. Business entertaining often involves attending a sporting event. Accept social invitations.

Power breakfasts are gaining in popularity in **New Zealand**. Lunch appointments are for discussing business.

Business and social entertainment is largely informal, but they start on time. Dinners are social occasions that include spouses. Avoid talking business at dinner, which may take place at a restaurant or a barbecue. It is fairly easy to develop friendly relations.

A lot of business is conducted over drinks. Let the host bring up the subject. It is customary at a pub on social occasions for members of a group to take turns buying "rounds" of drinks for everyone. When it is your turn say, "I'll shout this round." Accept a drink when one is offered to you. It is rude to refuse. However, if you do not wish to drink, explain that it is for health reasons.

When you dine out, keep in mind that entrées are appetizers, not the main course.

Before you host a dinner at a restaurant, find out whether it sells alcohol. You may have to bring your own supply because some establishments don't have a liquor license. Your **Australian** guests may be put off if alcohol is not served with their meal. Beer is usually the preferred drink.

## HOME INVITATIONS & GIFTS

Never go to an **Australian** home unannounced. Wait for an invitation. **New Zealanders** love to entertain and are quick to invite people to their home.

Barbecues are the most popular gatherings.

When you visit someone's home, remember the terms and times: "afternoon tea" is at 04:00. What people call supper in **America** and dinner in **Europe** is called "tea" in these two countries, which is the evening meal served between 18:00-20:00. The term "supper" is a late-night snack.

When you are invited to dine in a home, bring a gift for your hosts. Flowers, liquor, wine or chocolates are acceptable. Gifts should be unpretentious. A simple thank-you when you leave is all that is expected.

Be on time for dinner; it is an insult to be late. Beer and wine with snacks are served prior to dinner. The meal begins around 18:00-19:00, soon after everyone arrives.

## TABLE MANNERS

The guest sits to the right of the host.

**Australians** and **New Zealanders** eat Continental-style: the fork is always held in the left hand and the knife in the right hand. When eating soup, fill the spoon by moving it away from you.

Keep your wrists on the table and do not rest your hands in your lap.

Try to finish everything on your plate. It is acceptable, however, to leave something you don't like. Your hosts will not be offended. When you are finished eating, place your utensils together and across your plate diagonally.

Little conversation takes place during a meal. When the meal is finished and everyone is relaxing over dessert and coffee, the conversation resumes.

## GOOD TOPICS OF CONVERSATION

Discuss current affairs in world politics, sports (such as football, rugby, cricket, and horse racing), cuisine, wine, jobs, hobbies, interests, sightseeing, and the beauty of **Australia** and **New Zealand**.

## TOPICS TO AVOID

Refrain from asking questions about religion, internal politics, unions, nuclear arms, racial problems, native tensions, and personal questions regarding jobs, schooling, and salaries.

Do not comment on accents. Avoid making comparisons between your country and theirs, or remarks suggesting that your country is superior. When you speak about yourself or your country, sincerity and modesty will impress them much more than boasting.

Do not compare the similarities between **New Zealand** and **Australia**, and never mistake a **New Zealander** for an **Australian**.

Do not discuss the aborigines with your **Australian** associates; it is a touchy subject, better to be left alone.

It is best not to discuss the **Maori** people with your **New Zealander** hosts.

## CUSTOMS & TRADITIONS

The British have influenced many customs and habits.

As in **Britain**, respect queues for buses and taxis.

Good sportsmanship is highly valued in business and social situations.

Aussies have a good sense of humour — it can be quite dry and they like to chide each other. Try to respond with directness and good humour to any pointed comments or teasing. To argue a subject is considered entertaining.

Once approached, **New Zealanders** are reserved but friendly. They have a calm, peaceful disposition.

Do not praise something too much or your **New Zealand** host will feel obliged to give it to you.

## GESTURES

As a reminder of what not to do, one should keep in mind former U.S. president George Bush's faux pas at the end of a trip to **Australia**. Walking up the stairs to his aircraft, he turned around and gave the crowd a thumbs-up sign. In **Australia**, this sign is the equivalent of giving someone the finger in **America**. A mistake both he and Aussies will always remember.

Watch your posture. Stand and sit straight, do not lean against the wall or furniture. Use hand gestures only when necessary, as excessive fidgeting will distract from your message.

**British** gestures are understood and used.

To beckon, stretch out your hand palm down and make scratching motions with your fingers.

## GESTURES TO AVOID

In a pub, never place an empty glass upside down with a thump — it will signify a challenge to a drinking or fighting match.

The two-finger victory salute has a rude connotation.

If you see friends from afar, you may wave to them, but avoid yelling.

Always cover your mouth when you yawn, and excuse yourself.

Avoid chewing gum or using toothpicks in public.

Environmental concerns are important. It is insensitive to litter.

It is considered unmanly to express any type of emotion.

Refrain from winking at women.

Avoid hugs or pats on the back, which are reserved for very close friends.

To make public displays of loud speech or aggression is unacceptable.

## DRESS CODE

A dark, lightweight suit or sports jacket and tie are recommended for men going to business meetings in **Australia**. It's acceptable to take your jacket off in the summer.

Items made of tropical wool, linen, or cotton can be worn year-round in **Sydney** and **Melbourne**. Tuxedos are appropriate formal wear for special events.

**New Zealand** businessmen tend to be conservative and wear tailored suits. A dark business suit worn with a tie is appropriate for all occasions. Formal business occasions in the evening require that you wear a different business suit than the one you wore during the day.

Some fine restaurants require a tie and jacket, but most social situations are less formal and a tie is unnecessary.

It is not uncommon in summer to see businessmen wear short-sleeve shirts, ties, shorts, and knee-length wool socks called stubbies.

When invited to a home for the first time, wear a suit unless otherwise advised. For relaxed afternoon social gatherings, jeans, and even shorts, are acceptable.

Businesswomen should wear a dress, a suit, a blouse and skirt, or a pantsuit. **Australian** women wear skirts more often than slacks. For a dinner in someone's home, a skirt or dress is appropriate. For casual wear, women may wear jeans or shorts. For a golf game, skirts are more popular than shorts.

For a meal in someone's home or at a restaurant, wear a dress, skirt and blouse, or dressy pants and blouse.

A cocktail dress is recommended for formal receptions or dinner dances. Jeans, a T-shirt, running shoes, a hat, and a handkerchief to brush off the flies are recommended for trips to the outback.

Beach wear is very liberal for both men and women, but bring a hat for the heat.

Bring warmer clothes and rain gear if you are visiting during the winter or if you are going to **New Zealand** where the climate is temperate year-round.

## PHOTOGRAPHY

Ask permission before you photograph people. Respect their wishes and do not push if they refuse. The native population resents being photographed as a tourist attraction. For security reasons, do not photograph airports or official buildings.

# Europe (Eastern & Western)
General Etiquette

Below are the common business practices and traditions of **Europe**. Learn the geography of **Europe**, and read newspapers to get an understanding of current affairs and the political climate.

## GREETINGS & FORMS OF ADDRESS

Shake hands with a firm grip when you meet and when you depart. If you meet the same person more than once in a day, shake hands each time. Always shake hands with the more senior person first, then shake hands with everyone else.

Women shake hands with each other as well as with men, but wait for a woman to extend her hand first. Frequent handshaking is the norm.

In **Greece**, **Portugal**, **Spain**, and **Italy**, handshakes last a long time, five to seven strokes is common. In the **United Kingdom**, **France**, **Monaco**, **Luxembourg**, **Belgium**, and **Iceland**, the handshake is quick and light. In **Ireland**, handshakes are quick, short, and firm.

Do not address **Europeans** by their first names unless you are invited to do so. Do not invite **Europeans** to call you by your first name until you have known each other for some time; they will not feel comfortable doing so.

**Europeans** may work together for many years and never be on a first-name basis.

Address your associates by their professional title and their last name. For social acquaintances, use Mr., Mrs., or Miss with the person's last name.

In **Eastern Europe**, **Germany**, **Austria**, and **Finland**, if someone has a title such as "economist" on his or her card, address that person as Economist Schwartz, not Mr. or Mrs. Schwartz. If he or she is the president of the company, address him or her as Economist President Schwartz. Academic titles are more important than corporate ones.

**Latin Europeans** may have two family names. Address someone using the first of the two surnames on his or her business card. E.g., Gabriel Garcia Lopez is Mr. Gabriel Garcia. In **Spain**, use only the person's last name, so that Garcia Hernandez is Senior Hernandez.

In **France**, if you are not sure whether a woman is married, address her with madame, instead of mademoiselle. In **Germany**, use frau instead of fraulein; and in **Spain** or **Italy**, use senora instead senorita.

In **France**, always use the formal "vous," when you address someone in French. The familiar "tu" is for family and friends only.

At small gatherings, wait for your host to introduce you. At large parties you should introduce yourself. Rise when you are introduced to an older, senior person or the guest of honour.

**Europeans** stand closer to each other in conversation than **Asians** and **North Americans**, so do not back away. Eye contact is important.

(For more information on Personal Space see p. 76.)

## APPOINTMENTS & PUNCTUALITY

Appointments are essential and should be made in writing several weeks ahead and followed up by fax a week in advance. Reconfirm when you arrive in the country. Earlier appointments in the day are preferable.

In **France** and **Britain**, the "old boy" network still exists. The proper connection will assist you tremendously in business transactions. Always be formal in your dealings.

In **Germany**, **Spain**, **Portugal**, **Greece**, and **Turkey**, a contact or a letter of introduction will help to open the doors to smoother business proceedings.

In **Belgium**, business people discuss trade issues every week on "Bourse Day." This is on Wednesdays in Brussels and Mondays in Antwerp. Saturdays are for conferences.

Never try to make a cold call to get an appointment; it is just not done. **Europeans** do not like to conduct business on the phone. Once you have established a relationship, ask if you can call.

Weekends are reserved for leisure and family activities. Avoid calling a colleague at home regarding a business matter.

Punctuality is important and a sign of respect on your part. Avoid showing impatience if your colleague arrives late. Always be on time for your first appointment, then take cues from your hosts.

In the **Baltics**, keep your schedule flexible, punctuality is rare. To avoid red tape you will need a local partner.

Generally, **Northern Europeans** are more concerned with punctuality and you would do well to arrive earlier than the scheduled time. **North of the Alps**, people show up exactly on time, not one minute earlier or later. The **Swiss** start work around 07:30 or 08:00.

As you move **South** and **East**, timing is more lax. In **Latin Europe**, you may be kept waiting up to an hour. The **Spaniards** begin at 10:00 and work late into the evening.

**Italians** are usually on time for business meetings. **Greek** business people can be late by as much as 30 minutes. If your host does show up late, you probably could also be a little late on subsequent meetings.

The after-lunch siesta has been replaced by the power nap. The competitive pace of business in **Spain** means siestas are now the privilege of the older generation only.

Don't make appointments for weekends or Wednesday afternoons. **Greek** businesses are closed for personal or family time.

In **Greece**, a personal contact is a big advantage in business proceedings. Your contact will consider it hospitable to pick you up at the airport and will probably be with you the entire time of your stay.

## BUSINESS CARDS

Bring an ample supply of business cards. Present one to the secretary when you first arrive in the office. In general, exchange business cards with your colleagues at the beginning of a meeting. In London, however, cards are exchanged at the end of a meeting, and in **Belgium** cards are exchanged either at the beginning or at the end.

Your position and university degree(s) should be indicated on the card. It will give you more credibility. In **Europe**, experience and tradition carry clout. Companies that have been in business for a long time will earn more respect. Indicate the year the company was founded on your card.

In **Germany**, business cards indicate someone's importance by the initials following the person's name. The initials "ppa" (Prokurist) mean that person has signing authority — he or she is a decision-maker. An "i.v." (Vollmacht) can make limited decisions. An "i.a." (ImAuftrag) is someone who represents the company but has little power.

Be sensitive to the language of business used in each country. Although most business people speak **English**, you may need to translate your cards or your promotional materials into the local language. It shows that you are willing to go the extra mile.

## MEETINGS & PRESENTATIONS

Small talk is important in **Europe**. It is the initial groundwork of the business process.

Wait for your associates to raise the subject of business. The first time you meet your colleagues, don't ask questions about personal matters, such as family.

**Europeans** consider it mandatory to build trust first. They like to develop a good, personal working relationship rather than deal with a faceless corporation. Avoid talking too loud or fast, or coming on too strongly.

Beware of trying to break the ice by initially being too friendly. In the **North**, people may get offended and your overtures will be met with resistance. In the **South**, you can expect a more casual approach.

In the **North**, conversation may be kept to a minimum while in the **South** it is extended and not rushed.

In **France**, it is important to speak **French** or at least show that you have studied it and are trying very hard. Do not get upset if you are corrected. The **French** are all teachers at heart.

In **France**, the managing director of a company is the *PDG* (*President Directeur Général*) and he or she gets the job based on merit. The PDG is responsible for making all the major decisions. At meetings, the president or the mediator of the proceedings sits in the centre.

Your first meeting In **Ireland** may be a social affair intended for people to get to know you. Meetings seldom start on time here and often last longer than planned. Business is conducted in English.

In **Ireland**, it is to your advantage to tell a lot of stories in your business presentation.

In **Eastern Europe**, you may find your colleagues cautious. There have been a lot of changes in this part of the world, and people here must abide by a myriad of new rules and bureaucracy in business. Their caution is also a reflection of the business practices of the previous governments rather than any uncertainty about dealing with you. Management and workers respect each other and work as a team. Executives are not paternalistic with their employees.

In **Turkey**, the state is very powerful. The **Turkish** people don't elect the country's president (the parliament does), and no one is allowed to insult the leader.

The **Dutch** and the **Germans** are business-oriented and prefer to talk shop during meetings. They will inquire about your firm and how it fits in with theirs. Time is set aside in the evenings to get better acquainted with you, usually over dinner and drinks.

In **Sweden**, most companies are small, privately owned, and focus on exporting. Investing is open to both foreigners and nationals. Many **Swedes** take long coffee breaks, believing that breaks are important to performance and well-being.

Always accept drinks that are offered to you at a meeting. In **Eastern** and **Latin Europe**, you may be offered an alcoholic drink as a sign of friendship — accept it and sip it.

In **Greece**, expect business meetings to run long. Details are important in **Greek** business culture. If you try to impose a deadline, however, you will probably be snubbed. **Greeks** also like to express their opinion, sometimes quite forcefully. You don't have to agree, but avoid getting into an argument, as it will affect your business relationship.

Your presentation should be impeccable and without error. Give precise information. Find out about hidden charges and customs duties in the **European** market and include them in your proposal. Be efficient and to the point. To make a good impression, you should be knowledgeable about your product, your competitors, and the industry. Be prepared to field a wide range of questions.

In **Britain**, **Italy**, and **France**, presentations should be factual, direct, clear, and detailed.

The **British** show little facial expression, so it can be difficult to know what they are thinking.

Presentations in **Central** and **Northern Europe** (**Germany**, **Holland**, **Switzerland**, **Austria**, and **Scandinavia**) should be crisp, clean, organized, understated, and conservative — no clutter. Use dark colours in your promotional materials, black and white is fine.

**Germans** are generally orderly, efficient, and reliable in business — and they expect the same from their business associates. Many have strong opinions on many topics. Some **Germans** may appear arrogant, but don't let that put you off. They tend to get straight to the point and are simply stating their beliefs.

In **Latin Europe**, promotional material should be made on quality paper and presented with elegance and good taste. The pace of presentations should be slower.

Trust is very important to **Europeans**. Even if they are interested in your product and its advantages, suspicion can kill a deal. Do not tell jokes, and never criticize your competition or an individual in public. If you must comment, do so diplomatically in private. Public humiliation is an affront.

Good manners are critical and ignorance is no excuse for bad behaviour. **Europeans** are very class conscious. They have a distinct notion of what refined conduct should be. They prefer not to do business with someone who lacks social graces. The way you act can make or break a deal.

Before doing business in the **Russian Federation**, it is important to learn about the political situation. It is not an easy place to do business. As reported in the *Economist*, "**Russia's** government and state have been unstable since independence in 1991." Although the economy has picked up, foreign businesses are largely staying out of **Russia**.

You may want to think twice before doing business in **Ukraine**. Although the country is lobbying the West to be recognized as a candidate for entry into the EU (**European Union**), corruption remains widespread and there's next to no investment.

Most **Swiss** expect business associates to conduct themselves in a responsible and sound manner. Controlling your emotions and leading a disciplined personal life are also qualities valued by the **Swiss**.

## NEGOTIATIONS

Be patient in both your business and personal dealings. It takes time to establish a relationship in **Europe**, but once established, the business relationship will grow. **Europeans** are conservative in their approach. Negotiators are older and experienced. They are careful in decision making and not willing to take too many risks.

Do not try the hard-sell technique, especially in **Austria**, **Belgium**, **Monaco**, **Italy**, **Luxembourg, Switzerland**, **Germany**, **Iceland**, **Finland**, and **France** — people in these countries don't like to be pressured. Many **Europeans** like to give their opinion on various issues, sometimes quite forcefully. Take this in stride, as free expression is afforded to everyone and you need not agree with his or her opinion. Avoid getting into an argument, as it will affect your business relationship.

A verbal agreement is not enough — you are not guaranteed anything until the legal documents are signed. Nevertheless, the details are not always carved in stone. Changes can, and most likely will, be made even after signing.

In **Austria**, the pace of business negotiations is slowed down by the **Austrians'** attention to detail and a great deal of bureaucracy. **Austrian** and **Swiss** negotiators are generally older and experienced. They make decisions carefully and won't take many risks.

The **French** like to negotiate. It gives them a chance to argue and philosophize. Do not press or try to rush the **French**, they need time to be comfortable with a project. He or she will investigate the benefits and losses from all sides. Show that your venture will benefit everyone.

Expect a great deal of red tape and delays in **France** — you must be patient and see the project through before the results become apparent. **French** negotiators are very analytical and logical reasoning prevails. Before decisions are made, much time will be spent debating. Agreements will be approved only after all the top executives have had time to analyze the situation. In **France**, every major settlement must go through a chain of command.

Business people in **France** and **Monaco** tend to view the outcome of a negotiation as having a winner and a loser. Avoid confrontations during bargaining. Direct people's focus toward the mutual benefits the venture would provide for all parties involved rather than as a win/lose situation. Facts will pave the way. Make careful notes to keep track of the proceedings.

In **Luxembourg**, business people are astute and staunch negotiators. Allow them to start negotiating first.

**British** negotiators are formal, older, experienced, and conservative. Do not try to negotiate in a hurry. The **British** like to take their time reviewing a proposal. They tend to base their decisions on established laws and rules, rather than their own personal feelings. Most business people at all levels of an organization consider company policy the final authority.

Allow them to do most of the talking. It will give you a better sense of their needs and concerns. They dislike bargaining. Make some concessions — give them a reason to believe the deal will result in economic gain.

Be aware of government-imposed rules and restrictions.

Never lose your composure during negotiations with the **British**. They are extremely polite even when they are angry. As a nation, they are known for understatement. Subtle humour is appreciated. **British** humour is characterized by not stating the obvious and implying the opposite of what is being said. To appreciate this style of humour, pay attention to what is not being said or done. Be forewarned: the **English** often use humour, especially irony or sarcasm, to ridicule an adversary or show disagreement.

The **British** may utilize an egalitarian or hierarchical tactic to decision making but final decisions are made by the director or president of the company. If there is resistance to a written agreement, insist that although verbal agreements are acceptable in the U.K., a signature is required by the company lawyer in your country.

With the **Irish** and the **Scots**, negotiations take time. A written agreement is in order. The **Irish** tend to consider all aspects of a proposal before making a commitment.

The **Germans**, **Dutch**, **Austrians**, and **Swiss** are conservative and, generally, older negotiators. They are highly disciplined, cautious, and concerned with small details. Once a decision is made, you can count on the **Swiss** to proceed quickly.

**Germans** are very secretive in negotiations, making it difficult to see the big picture. Only top management makes decisions. Rank is important in business dealings. **Germans** are interested in long-term contracts instead of quick deals. They like to deliberate over the pros and cons before committing to a venture. Only the written word is legally binding.

**Belgians** are pragmatic and open to compromise in bargaining and negotiations. They are astute business people and tough negotiators. You won't have to deal with a lot of red tape. Allow your **Belgian** associate to make announcements first.

The **Flemish** live in the north of **Belgium** and speak a language similar to **Dutch**. Do not call them Flems. The **Walloons** live in the south. Be careful not to mistake **Belgians** for the **French** just because they speak the same language.

With **Scandinavians** one must be patient. Take time to socialize, do not rush to close a deal.

With **Icelanders** negotiating takes time but is straightforward.

The **Norwegians** and the **Dutch** have a very formal business culture, while the **Danes**, **Swedish**, and **Fins** are more relaxed in their business dealings.

In **Finland**, **Denmark**, **Norway**, **Sweden**, and the **Netherlands**, decisions are made jointly by executive and staff members. They work as a team rather than as a hierarchy, with each contributing specific skills. Signed agreements are honoured.

In **Denmark**, business people value negotiations. They have an international outlook and tend to focus on the whole picture not just the profit. Once an agreement is made, the **Danes** usually stick to it.

When doing business in the **Netherlands**, be straightforward. If you want to say "No," then refrain from tentative statements such as "I'll consider it," "We'll see," or "Perhaps." The **Dutch** appreciate honesty and would rather you were candid.

**Dutch** society is egalitarian, so don't act superior. Everyone in a **Dutch** company, from the executives to the labourers, is considered worthy of respect.

The **Swedes** do not like to negotiate. They will give you an offer and tell you to take it or leave it. They are not punctual when it comes to deadlines in business matters.

The **Spaniards** and the **Portuguese** are formal and traditional. Personal allegiance to one's family comes before business. Friends take precedence over profit. The fact that your product is good and inexpensive will not necessarily guarantee you a contract. How well you get along, and who you know, will.

In **Spain** and **Portugal**, negotiations require a lot of bargaining. Begin with a more extreme position and then allow for some concessions. Avoid general statements and watch for details.

Refrain from asking your **Spanish** and **Portuguese** colleagues yes or no questions: a yes answer may mean that they understand you rather than agree with you. Don't be offended or concerned if you are interrupted while talking. These interruptions usually mean that your associates are genuinely interested in the discussion.

In **Spain** and **Portugal**, do not assume anything. Always investigate further to figure out your associates' position. Follow their lead in negotiations, be sensitive to their needs, and do not press for a quick decision. Negotiations are conducted with middle managers; however, top executives make the final decisions. A written contract is in order.

**Italians** are sophisticated business people. Negotiators are older and experienced. They may demand drastic changes at the last minute to unsettle the other side. They are not willing to take too many risks. Final decisions are made privately by the company's partners.

With the **Greeks**, negotiations will take time. There is a great deal of red tape. Bargaining is an accepted course of action. Businesses are family-owned and run; the owner will make the final decision. **Greeks** see a contract as an intention to do something — in their eyes, negotiations are finished only when the work is completed.

**Turkish** business people take their time in negotiations, and there will be a lot of bargaining. Begin with an extreme position, then make concessions. Your associates will test you on many details. Emphasize the positive benefits of the venture for both sides and encourage group discussion. The president or the owner makes the final decision.

In the **Czech Republic**, **Bulgaria**, **Romania**, **Poland**, **Hungary**, the **Baltics**, and the **Russian Federation**, negotiations take time. When negotiating, do not ask questions that require a one-word answer. Be prepared and well organized.

People in these countries may respond with "yes" or "no" just to please you and, therefore, not lose face. Decisions are made at the top. Try to negotiate with the most important person in the company. Ask for a written contract.

As **Hungarians** are known to avoid making decisions, patience is required. Do not let the momentum stall. Be insistent and encourage them to conclude the deal.

**Russian** negotiators are experts who specialize in negotiations only. Teams of business people are seated across from one another, with the negotiators in the middle. Your team should consist of senior executives only.

Keep your cool. **Russians** are very expressive. They may explode in anger or threaten to walk out. They like to play hardball. Be patient and persevere. A hard-sell approach may work to your advantage. The **Russians** have time on their side. Negotiate for the final draft, rather than a rough estimate. Delay your acceptance if it is not to your liking.

Although **Russian** negotiators do not like to give concessions or compromise, their offer may change. Do not expect things to be ready on time. Once a contract is signed, do not expect to renegotiate later for a better agreement.

## WOMEN

Times are changing in Western Europe, but most women still play an inferior role in business. Women are still fighting for equal pay and the right to hold positions of power, especially in **Belgium**, **Italy**, **Switzerland**, and **Germany**. It was only in March 2001 that **Switzerland's** parliament voted to legalize abortion.

In **Switzerland**, female business travellers should always dress and behave in a highly professional manner. Your **Swiss** associate will happily accept an invitation to lunch, but be sure to include his or her spouse when extending a dinner invitation.

In **England**, women have a strong presence in political and business life.

In **France**, status is more important then gender. A new law adopted by the **French** senate in the fall of '99 promises women an equal place alongside men in government and other institutions.

Machismo is very strong in **Greece** and **Portugal**. The difference between the rich and the poor is huge.

In **Spain**, women are now getting better posts in education and politics. Few **Spanish** women are in management positions, but visiting businesswomen will be treated with respect. Dress and behave professionally at all times.

Machismo is very important to **Spanish** men and they can be very charming, but some people may feel uncomfortable with their approach to women. For example, Spanish men will sometimes whistle at an attractive woman on the street to signal their approval.

Some **Spanish** women still face problems of domestic violence. *The Economist* reported in August 2001 that violence against women was higher than in previous years.

**Spanish** men will usually accept a lunch or dinner invitation from a businesswoman. As in most countries, whoever extends the invitation pays the bill.

In **Denmark**, **Sweden**, **Finland**, and **Norway** there is a very strong middle class, and business positions are held by both genders. These **Northern** countries have the highest representation of women in parliament in the world. The **Netherlands**, on the other hand, has the least advanced women's movement in **Europe**.

In 1999, **Swedish** women topped an international list for political equality with 40 percent of their parliament's seats. **Denmark** came in second at 37.4 percent, followed by **Norway** at 36.4 percent.

In the **Czech Republic**, women hold many important positions in judicial, political, and social occupations. Women in the **Russian Federation** continue to strive for equality — besides corruption, there is a lot of sexual harassment in business and government.

**Yugoslavia** and **Serbia** still have laws that allow marital rape.

In 2000, **Turkey** passed a law criminalizing spousal abuse. **Turkey** is also updating its civil code giving married women the right to work without spousal consent and divorced women an equal share of assets accumulated during marriage.

To root out **Islamic** extremists, **Turkey** has banned head scarves. In 2000, up to 30,000 female students were expelled from university for wearing a head scarf.

## CORPORATE GIFTS

In **Western Europe**, appropriate gifts include an electronic gadget for the office, a computer program, a first-edition book, a hard-to-get CD, a subscription to a prestigious magazine, an art print, a picture book or video, a food package, or a special item from your home region.

A gift of expensive cognac or champagne is always appreciated, except in **France**.

Gifts should be wrapped. Gifts are opened immediately except in **Turkey**, where they are opened later.

Avoid giving items that have your company logo when in **Germany** and **France**, and refrain from food as a gift in **Sweden**.

Giving presents is not common business practice in the **United Kingdom**. Business and pleasure are kept separate.

Wait for your host to give you a present before offering one.

Never give an **Englishman** a striped tie; he wears his own school tie.

The **French** are slow to cultivate personal relationships. Refrain from offering gifts until you have developed a friendship or until the deal has been closed.

Gifts are exchanged often in **Italy** — give small items to anyone that helps you in the office.

In **Ireland**, corporate gifts are not common.

In **Portugal**, **Spain**, and the **Netherlands** (the **Dutch** do not usually give business gifts), an invitation to a restaurant of your associates' choice is a nice gesture.

In **Eastern Europe**, gifts should not be extravagant and are given to celebrate the closing of a new venture. Appropriate choices include a bottle of fine Cognac or whisky, an electronic notebook or daytimer, a special pen set inscribed with your company logo or a designer pen, a CD, picture book, craft, or something regional from your country. Gifts should be presented at banquets or formal functions.

## BUSINESS ENTERTAINING

Although power breakfasts are becoming more popular (in **France**, **Switzerland**, **Ireland, Monaco**, and **England**), business lunches are far more common and may take place in a café. Reciprocate all invitations to dine. When inviting your colleagues to lunch, allow them to choose the restaurant. Include only those involved in the project.

Dinners are reserved for social occasions to which spouses are often invited. Business is not discussed at dinner. If you invite executives for dinner, order a local wine. It is a faux pas to ask for another country's wine. The person who invites pays for the bill. In **France**, **Greece**, **Britain**, **Spain**, **Belgium**, and **Italy**, restaurants are often the focus of meetings. Lunches can last many hours, and wine or beer is served.

In **Italy**, it is ungracious to refuse a dinner invitation.

In **Britain** and **Spain**, discuss business only after the meal is finished. The most important guest will be seated next to the head of the company.

Good food and wine are part of doing business in **France**. When you invite someone out for lunch be sure to choose an excellent restaurant, and prepare for it to be expensive. Let your guest choose the wine.

In **Germany**, if you invite the executives out for dinner, be sure to order a German wine. It is tactless to choose wine from another country.

Golf is popular in **Ireland**, and is often a way of fostering business relationships.

In **Portugal**, it is considered rude to discuss business at dinner.

In **Germany**, business is mostly conducted in the office and rarely over meals. Business lunches last 30 minutes to one hour, and discussions take place before rather than during the meal. Many companies enforce an alcohol ban at lunchtime.

In **Finland,** many large companies have their own saunas, and it is a compliment to be invited to one. You may discuss business during or after the sauna provided your hosts bring it up first.

**Finns** often take their sauna naked, but you won't cause offense by wearing a bathing suit. There are separate saunas for men and women. Non-alcoholic beer and snacks may be offered afterwards.

In **Eastern Europe**, dinners are the most popular form of business entertaining. In general, lunches must be pre-arranged and approved by the company. Spouses are invited to some social dinners.

In the **Russian Federation**, you may be invited to a theatre or ballet performance instead of a restaurant. However, business dinners (seated) or banquets (non-seated) start around 18:00 and include spouses.

A senior executive from each side of the negotiations is expected to make a small speech. You should host a meal after a deal is concluded.

## HOME INVITATIONS & GIFTS

If you receive an invitation to dine in a home, arrive on time but never late — except in **Spain**, **Italy**, and **Greece**, where it is better to be a little late than early.

Avoid bringing items of a personal nature unless your host made a specific request. Do not give too much of anything. It is considered gauche. Gifts should be wrapped. Send a thank-you note the next day.

In **Western Europe**, it is more common to be invited to your host's home. You may bring wine, champagne, fine chocolates, or flowers.

Do not bring wine to homes in **Portugal**, **Spain**, and **France**, unless requested. Never give perfume — it is too personal. In **France**, it is an honour to be invited to your associate's cottage for the weekend. It means you are very highly thought of.

In **Italy**, refrain from giving a brooch, a set of knives, or a handkerchief, as these items are associated with sorrow. In most of **Western Europe**, bring flowers — and be sure to unwrap them first. Avoid giving red carnations or romantically suggestive red roses — except in **Turkey** where it is acceptable. White flowers such as lilies or chrysanthemums are associated with mourning.

Do not bring twelve flowers, as it implies stinginess ("cheaper by the dozen"); thirteen flowers, which is bad luck; or an even number, which is considered in bad taste.

In the **South**, cut flowers are so plentiful that giving them will make you look cheap.

In **Eastern Europe** and the **Baltics**, it is rare to be invited to someone's home for dinner. If you are, bring chocolates, candies, imported liquor, books, or flowers for your host. Gifts should not be extravagant.

Make sure you unwrap any flowers that you give to hosts in **Bulgaria**. Flowers should be wrapped in the other countries of **Eastern Europe**. In **Bulgaria**, do not bring gladioli or calla lilies, as they are associated with weddings and funerals. Also avoid giving yellow flowers, for they symbolize hatred. In **Romania** and **Turkey** you may bring roses and carnations.

## TABLE MANNERS

Aperitifs may be served first. Dinner begins between 17:00 and 20:00. In the **South**, dinner begins later than in the **North**.

If you are the guest of honour, allow your host to seat you. Wait for the host to make the first toast to the guests before you sip your wine. Wine will be served throughout the meal.

If you do not wish to drink, take small sips and keep your glass fairly full to avoid a refill. Always wait for your host to begin eating or urge you to start.

Never ask for or use salt or pepper at the table — it implies that the food was not properly spiced.

**Europeans** use the continental style of eating. Use your knife to push food onto the back of your fork. Rest your wrists (but not elbows) on the table, and do not put your hands on your lap. Tear, do not cut, your rolls and place them on the table (bread plates are rarely provided). Try a bit of each dish offered; to decline an offer is considered discourteous. Take small portions at first.

You are expected to finish everything on your plate except in the **Baltics**, **Poland**, and the **Russian Federation**, where you should leave a token amount. In these places, an empty plate is a request for more food.

To compliment the hostess, you may take seconds of a dish you particularly enjoyed.

In **Western Europe**, use your knife and fork to eat everything, including sandwiches and fruits.

When you are finished, place your knife and fork (tines up) parallel to each other on the top right of your plate. However in **Denmark**, the tines should be placed facing down; to leave them up suggests that you want more. In **Spain**, leaving your fork and knife on opposite sides of the plate will also indicate that you want more.

Meals often end with a dessert of fruits and cheeses or cakes. Coffee and after-dinner drinks may be served. You can stay for a while after the meal to converse. Shake hands with all those present when you leave.

## GOOD TOPICS OF CONVERSATION

Business in general, technology, professions, art and music, architecture, hobbies, sports, famous artists, travel, and local cuisine. You may also discuss current affairs and world events in general terms.

Humour is often a big part of doing business in **England**. It is to your advantage to have a repertoire of jokes and anecdotes. People who are naturally good at telling jokes and stories should make the most of these abilities.

## TOPICS TO AVOID

It is in poor taste to brag about your personal achievements or wealth. Do not discuss income or private family matters. Never talk against your own country or compare your country to that of your hosts.

Stay away from politics and religion. In **Latin Europe**, do not swear or take the Lord's name in vain.

Refrain from telling off-colour jokes unless you know your host well.

Never refer to the **Irish** as "English." In **Ireland**, don't praise the **English** or express pro-British sentiments. Never discuss the problems of **Northern Ireland,** the IRA, or England's history in the country.

It is bad manners to ask a **Scot** what he wears under his kilt.

In **Spain**, be sensitive to regional differences. Your ignorance of these differences could lead you to make an insult (e.g., mistaking a **Catalonian** for a **Basque**). **Spaniards** get their sense of identity from their region of origin rather than the country as a whole.

Do not talk shop at social gatherings in **Spain** unless your host wants to.

In **Italy**, do not mention the Mafia or taxes.

If you are an **American** in **France**, do not praise California wines.

In **Greece** or **Turkey**, do not bring up their conflict over **Cypress**.

In **Turkey**, do not discuss the country's internal problems with the Kurds and Armenians. Do not refer to **Turkey** as part of the **Middle East** and never call a **Turk** an **Arab**.

## CUSTOMS & TRADITIONS

**Europeans** take great pride in their countries, so be careful not to litter.

Pets are very important to **Europeans** — never make fun of their passion for animals.

When you are walking with older people or women, you should walk beside the curb, between them and the traffic. Always help the elderly, and give them your seat on public transportation.

At the theatre, face the people in your row when you pass them to get to your seat.

**Europeans** do not like to be teased and will be offended if you do so.

To avoid misunderstandings that could have far-reaching effects, do not use sarcasm.

In **Ireland**, being called "plain" is a compliment. It means a person is sincere.

A custom unique to **Norway** is to spit when a fisherman passes you by. It is said to bring him good luck.

In **Norway**, if you see someone you know in public, nod or raise your hand.

Avoid casual compliments about dress or style, some **Europeans** may be embarrassed by such remarks. Compliments should be directed toward virtuous acts rather than appearances.

In **Italian** culture, people are traditionally expected to behave with a sense of decorum at all times. It is called *bella figura* (beautiful figure) and refers to the ability to put on a good show or at least to present oneself well. One's actions must always appear to be the "right" thing to do. **Italians** believe that behaving appropriately, especially out of loyalty to family, friends, and neighbours, contributes to the beauty and sense of order in the world. The further south you travel in **Italy**, the more pronounced is this idea.

In **Europe**, women walk arm in arm and men often embrace each other. This is a show of friendship. However, a public display of affection towards the opposite sex is frowned upon.

In **Latin Europe**, the Roman Catholic Church still has a strong influence in people's lives.

Refer to people by their correct nationality. The English are **British**. People from **Scotland** are called Scots or Scotsmen, not Scotch or Scotchmen. Do not refer to the people of **Wales**, **Scotland**, or **Northern Ireland** as English.

Show respect for royalty. In particular, never joke to **Brits** about the **British** royal family. If you should meet a person of royalty, men should bow and women should curtsy. Do not touch them or shake hands unless they make the first gesture.

Try not to mistake an **Austrian** for a **German**. They are neighbours with a similar culture, but their identity and values are different.

**Eastern Europeans** may ask fairly personal questions. Do not be put off by it. It is their way of showing interest.

Regarding homosexuality, the British government is expected to soon issue an order that will legalize consensual gay sex between adults in the territories of **Anguilla**, the **British Virgin Islands**, the **Cayman Islands**, **Montserrat**, and the **Turks** and **Caicos Islands**.

Homosexuality is still banned in **Romania** and **Armenia**.

## GESTURES

Take off your hat and sunglasses when you enter a home or establishment to speak with people.

To beckon, stretch out your hand palm down and make a scratching motion. To beckon a waiter in a restaurant, simply raise your hand.

To suggest that someone is a bit crazy, the **Dutch** tap the centre of their forehead or pretend to be catching a fly in front of their face. The **North American** gesture for crazy, circling one's index finger next to one's temple, is the way **Dutch** people indicate that there is a phone call for you.

The "thumbs up" gesture is a sign of approval only in **Ukraine**, the **Russian Federation**, **Portugal**, and **Greece**.

When you compliment someone in **Greece**, he or she may blow a puff of air through pursed lips to ward off the jealous "evil eye." Men may finger worry beads, though it is merely for its calming effect and has no religious significance. **Greeks** generally do not respect lineups.

A "V" sign made with one's index and middle finger is a symbol of a political party in **Bulgaria** — the Union of Democratic Forces.

In the **Netherlands**, tapping your forehead with the tip of your fingers expresses "you are insane." In **Bulgaria**, circling your forefinger at one's temple indicates someone is crazy.

The way **Bulgarians** express "yes" and "no" is the opposite way to North Americans. In **Bulgaria**, people shake their head from side to side to indicate "yes," and nod to indicate "no."

**Greeks** express "no" by tipping their heads slightly or raising their eyebrows. They indicate "yes" by tilting their head to one side.

Always sit up straight in public. **Europeans** consider sloppy posture to be rude.

In **Ireland**, wave your hand to someone you know in the same way that you would in North America.

Many **Swiss** do not respect queues because they don't like waiting. **Russians** and **Swedes**, on the other hand, usually do respect lineups.

To wish a person good luck, **Austrians** pound gently on a table or counter with both fists.

In **Austria**, rubbing an imaginary beard expresses that you think someone's remarks are old hat. Drivers indicate that they think another driver is crazy and dangerous by rotating the forefinger at the temple.

In **Germany**, some people express thanks by latching their hands together and raising them fully extended above the head. **Germans** hold their thumb erect to express the number one. To express good luck, **Germans** will make two fists with their thumbs tucked inside and pound softly on something. A form of greeting between acquaintances and between students and professors is to tap their knuckles gently on a table or desk.

In **Italy**, you might see a "cheek screw" — that's when the index finger is twirled into the cheek. It indicates that something is good or attractive; for example, a man may do it when he sees a beautiful woman. To show indifference, **Italians** raise their shoulders. A "nose tap" is a warning to be careful or aware of what is going on. Italians say good bye with their hand up and fingers moving up and down. Expect people to push and shove in crowds.

In **France**, people indicate that they are tired of somebody talking too much by playing an imaginary wind instrument.

## GESTURES TO AVOID

Boisterous or loud behaviour is frowned upon; however, as you move **south**, people are more expressive.

Conversing or standing with your hands in your pockets, pointing with your index finger, back-slapping, snapping your fingers, scratching, yawning, using a toothpick, blowing your nose, and chewing gum in public are all considered vulgar.

It is impolite to cross your legs with your ankle resting on top of your knee.

It is offensive to put your feet on the furniture or use them to push objects.

Knock and wait for a door to be opened, don't just walk in. Close all doors behind you. Men should hold a door open and allow women to precede them into a room. However, men should walk into restaurants first.

One should sit and walk to the left of business people of senior rank.

In the **United Kingdom**, don't make the victory gesture with your index finger and middle finger turned backwards. This gesture means "up yours" and is considered offensive.

Don't "jump the queue" in the **United Kingdom** — lineups are respected here.

In **Britain**, do not put pens or other items in your shirt pockets, it is déclassé. **Brits** do not talk with their hands, so refrain from large, expressive gestures.

In **Eastern Europe** and **Turkey**, the "fig" gesture, clenching your fist with the thumb poking out between the knuckles of the index and middle finger, is an insult. It has two meanings: "you won't get what you want," or is a phallic symbol.

In **Spain**, don't use the "thumbs up" gesture; it symbolizes loyalty to the **Basque** separatist cause.

The **North American** OK sign, with the thumb and forefinger joined in a circle, is comparable to giving "the finger" and is considered an obscene gesture in **Germany**, **Spain, Greece**, and the **Russian Federation**. President Bill Clinton made this sign during a televised program in **Moscow** in 1994, a faux pas that left many heads shaking. The same sign in **France** means "zero" or "worthless."

Avoid excessive gesturing in the **Northern Europe**, as they are not overly demonstrative and will find your motions distracting.

In **Italy**, if you place your hand on your stomach you will express dislike, usually for another person. Rubbing your chin with your fingertips, then pushing them forward, is a gesture of contempt. Pointing with your forefinger and little finger indicates that you wish someone bad luck. It is extremely rude to slap your raised arm above the elbow or thumb your nose.

Try not to yawn in public in **Italy**. If you tap your forehead with your hand you are saying someone is crazy. The "forearm jerk" and the "finger" are insults. It is offensive to pretend to be taking something out of your mouth and throwing it on the ground.

In **France**, you will offend people if you slap your open palm over a closed fist or snap your fingers.

## DRESS CODE

**Europeans** dress well and expect others to do the same. Their first impression of your appearance, good or bad, will often help form a lasting opinion of your character. Finely tailored clothing of classic cut and style predominate in the business world. Shoes should be polished and of good quality and style.

In **Western Europe**, a single, double-breasted, or a three-piece suit donned with a solid-coloured or patterned shirt and tie is suitable. Less conservative styles of shoes are fine.

For less serious meetings, wear a sports jacket or blazer with dress trousers and tie.

In **Eastern Europe** and **Turkey**, dress conservatively for business. A medium to dark suit, white shirt, tie, and black shoes should be worn throughout the year.

In **Latin Europe**, a good-quality suit in a conservative colour, a white shirt and tie, and black lace-up shoes are the proper attire for business meetings.

In **Britain**, do not put pens or other items in your shirt pockets, it is déclassé. **Brits** do not talk with their hands, so refrain from large, expressive gestures.

**European** businesswomen wear the best quality suit they can afford. You will do fine with a stylishly cut suit made of wool in a classic colour. Before showing up in a pantsuit take a cue from your host. In major cities designer clothes are popular amongst successful women. For casual meetings a skirt with a cashmere or light wool sweater is suitable.

A jacket or a sweater, such as a cardigan/twin set, with a shirt/blouse and smart-looking trousers/skirt is acceptable casual wear. It is also appropriate when invited to a home for dinner.

The **French** established *haute couture* (high fashion) and dress with flair. Businessmen and businesswomen are very stylish. In a business setting, do not take off your jacket until your colleague suggests you do. If an invitation says smoking *exigé* or *tenure de soirée*, then it is a black tie affair.

Except for **Latin Europe**, social occasions such as dinner invitations call for a jacket and tie for men and a dress for women. **Northern Europeans** are smart dressers and wear high-quality garments even for casual occasions.

Casual wear is acceptable for outings and shopping. Stylish sportswear is adequate for informal occasions. Cotton pants are acceptable as casual wear for both genders, but shorts belong at resorts.

An evening at the theatre calls for a dark suit/elegant dress, while a tuxedo/evening gown is in order when the invitation reads black-tie, which is mostly for formal events such as openings and gala dinners. Formal clothing is obligatory at some private clubs, exclusive restaurants, and casinos.

In **Eastern Europe**, a dark suit rather than a tuxedo is the usual form of dress for black-tie events and gala dinners. However, tuxedos are worn at formal occasions in the **Czech Republic**, **Hungary**, **Turkey**, and **Poland**.

## PHOTOGRAPHY

Ask permission before taking pictures of people, and respect requests for privacy. Look for signs forbidding photography in churches, museums, and galleries. For security reasons, avoid taking pictures of military sites, airports, official buildings, and personnel. You may risk losing your camera and your film.

# Middle East & Gulf States
## General Etiquette

Below are the common business practices and traditions of the **Middle East & Gulf States**. Learn the geography of the area, and read newspapers to get an understanding of current affairs and the political climate. Because of the difference in culture, the state of **Israel** follows in chapter 10.

## GREETINGS & FORMS OF ADDRESS

The acceptable form of greeting when you meet and depart is salaam alykum. A soft lingering handshake is followed by a reply of "kaif halak."

In the traditional salaam greeting, the right hand first touches the heart, then the forehead. Westernized business people just shake hands.

Women are not usually introduced nor do they initiate shaking hands. A businesswoman should wait for a man to shake her hand. In **Egypt**, **Western-educated** women shake hands with both genders.

**Arabs** are elaborate with greetings. In addition to a handshake, they may touch your arm or shoulder, and after several meetings even embrace you. Consider this an honour.

Guests should rise when an esteemed or senior person enters the room. Inquire after his or her health and give a compliment.

When you enter or leave a room be sure to greet everyone, usually with a handshake.

The terms "al" and "bin" (meaning "son of" or "from the town of") are frequently used before a name, as in al-Ahmed or bin-Mubarak. Sometimes "al" and "bin" are used in the same name.

Titles are important. Address your host by his or her academic rank or title and surname.

In **Kuwait**, **Saudi Arabia**, and the **United Arab Emirates** a sheik is part of the royal family. Sheik is also an honorary title that shows respect. Address your associates with Mr. or Sheik (pronounced "shake") and his first name. Government ministers should be addressed as "Your Excellency," and for social acquaintances, use "sayeed" and their first name.

**Egyptians** are addressed by their title and surname, or by Mr., Mrs., or Miss and their family name, just like their Western counterparts. Never use a first name until you are invited to do so.

It is useful to learn the local body language. **Arabs** stand very close when they converse. This close stance evolved over the centuries as a means to evaluate character through eye movement, smell, and thermal qualities. Touching and patting are important steps in this evaluation process.

Maintain good eye contact and do not flinch or step back — it is considered rude and may be taken as a slight, which can jeopardize trust in a personal or working relationship.

## APPOINTMENTS & PUNCTUALITY

Make appointments a few weeks in advance and reconfirm them when you arrive in the country. A mutual contact in the country is an asset for conducting business and a letter of introduction helps cut through bureaucracy.

In **Egypt**, you need an agent in every city in which you plan to do business.

In **Kuwait**, make appointments in the morning, as **Kuwaiti** executives work no more than six hours a day.

In **Saudi Arabia**, if you are a **non-Muslim** you will need a sponsor to enter the country and to conduct business. This person acts as the go-between, making all of the appointments and connecting you to the right people.

Do not forget that once in **Saudi Arabia** you must strictly follow **Saudi Islamic Law**. You will need an exit permit to get out of the country.

Punctuality is less important in the **Middle East** than it is in the West; it won't be unusual for your associates to be late. **Arabs** feel that if someone is late there is a reason for it. Although you should still be on time, avoid showing impatience by looking at your watch or puttering about while you wait for others. When the person arrives, extend your hand first in greeting. **Western-educated** business people will most likely be on time.

Nurture trust in the relationship through frequent, short visits. Telephone calls and correspondence are not enough. Book open flights to allow for changing deadlines and to avoid pressured decisions.

Business is conducted from Saturday through Wednesday. No business is conducted on Friday (the **Muslim holy day**) and many people do not work on Thursday.

## BUSINESS CARDS

Exchange business cards during introductions. They should be printed in **Arabic** on one side and **English** on the other. If your name is hard to pronounce, provide a phonetic translation below it.

Give and receive business cards with your right hand only. It is disrespectful to use the left hand or to casually throw a business card on the table. Have promotional material available in both languages. Keep in mind that **Arabic** is read the opposite of **English**, from right to left. Back covers of brochures or presentation material become front covers.

## MEETINGS & PRESENTATIONS

Business meetings are often conducted in **English**; however, interpreters are available if your associates prefer to speak **Arabic**.

Do not be surprised to find other business people present in the room and several meetings occurring simultaneously. Phone calls are taken; family members may show up. Your host may move from one group to another, or have his business associates sit in on your meeting. Avoid showing anger or disappointment.

If your host excuses himself abruptly and leaves, he is likely attending to his prayer duties and will return in about twenty minutes.

Tea and coffee will be served prior to the meeting. As a courtesy you should accept all offers, but make two or three lukewarm refusals before accepting. To flatly refuse is a criticism of the host's hospitality. When you do not want any more refills, shake the cup from side to side before returning it to the server.

Business people like to assess a person before entering into a business or personal relationship. Small talk takes place before and during the meeting.

Expect to be asked many personal questions about your background, your likes and dislikes. People in the **Middle East** prefer to develop lasting business relationships with a person rather than a faceless corporation. They also dislike a change of representatives before a business venture is completed.

Presentations should be clear, concise, and not too flashy. Executives prefer to get an overall picture and leave the technical staff to handle the details. You are expected to know your product inside out.

To show respect for your associates, keep your body language in check. Sit and stand with good posture, do not lean against furniture or cross your legs. Keep your feet flat on the floor during meetings. Avoid fidgeting and unnecessary hand movements, they distract from your message.

Long looks and staring are acceptable in the **Middle East**. Your associate's eyes may appear half-closed when you are speaking to him — it indicates concentration and should not be interpreted as boredom. Silence is part of the conversation. It is a time used for processing newly acquired information. Avoid interruptions by waiting for them to speak first.

In **Saudi Arabia**, because of the heat, you may be asked to a meeting very late at night.

In **Egypt** it is an indication to leave when coffee is served and incense is lit at the end of a meeting.

## NEGOTIATIONS

If you can negotiate in a souk (a marketplace in a **Muslim** country), you will be able to negotiate with any **Arab** business person.

In Arabic culture, people are more verbose and almost aggressive when making a point. Not only should you say a lot more, but you should do it in a louder voice. Raising one's voice in pitch and tone — even shouting — is considered a sign of sincerity.

**Islamic** religion, family honour, and lineage are prevalent in all decision making.

Nepotism is a traditional practice in the **Gulf**. Qualifications are not the main asset to get a job — being part of the family is. Honesty and loyalty are the most important attributes.

**Western** and **Eastern** attitudes differ toward negotiations. **Westerners** rely on facts, dates, and logic, while in the **Middle East**, friendships, trust, and values are more important.

Business success in the **Middle East** involves sustaining good relations. If you lose the friendship, you will lose the deal, so take care not to offend someone.

**Saudis** often negotiate using personalized arguments, appeals, and persistent persuasion.

Avoid raising your voice in anger. If you must criticize someone, do so diplomatically in private, otherwise you will lose face in front of your counterparts rather than the person being admonished. Patience and a calm exterior go a long way.

Be aware that in the **Middle East**, the head movement for "yes" resembles the **Western** "no" — a shake of the head from side to side. **Arabs** do not like to say "no" or use the phrase, "I don't understand." Instead, this is expressed as a click of the tongue with the head tilted back or a jutted out chin.

**Arabs** use the word "Bukra," which means tomorrow or later, when they do not wish to commit to an exact time or want to change the subject. Taking pains to be polite, they may try to convey the idea through a parable, which appears to foreigners as double talk.

In business, **Arabs** are shrewd, prudent, and uncompromising. Top executives prefer to negotiate with those of equal status. However, do not be pushy, a hard sell is not a suitable approach and will be met with resistance. Instead, stress the positive aspects that the venture will generate.

Be discreet in your approach and encourage group discussions. Expect to bargain, so allow room for concessions. Anticipate numerous delays and adjustments before a deal is closed. Take cues from your hosts, be conservative in your assumptions, and allow them to make public announcements first.

"Saving face" and avoiding shame are an important part of the culture. You should consider making a compromise on an issue if it will protect someone's dignity.

**Jordanians** are regarded as moderates in politics and religion. The business people are friendly, reserved, and patient. They are highly educated and sophisticated in their approach.

**Jordanians** like to have a clear picture of the deal before they agree to sign.

Decision makers in **Iraq** are government officials. There is a lot of bureaucracy and red tape to go through first.

In **Kuwait**, decisions are made by elders who sit at the negotiation table but rarely will they talk or look at you. A **non-Kuwaiti** professional will be doing the talking for them.

In **Iran**, businessmen are generally divided by **pro-West** and **anti-West** sentiments. Those who are **pro-West** have travelled there and are very good negotiators. In general, **Iranian** businessmen are cordial and conservative in manner and expect the same. The top negotiator will be of senior age and connected to the government. Decisions will be made by several senior men.

Private banking is now allowed in **Iran** for the first time since 1979 (though not foreign banks). The decision is part of a five-year program (2000 to 2005) to promote growth and raise private investment. This means foreigners are no longer forced to exchange their money at official rates, which were far below black market prices.

In the **United Arab Emirates**, the decision makers are normally connected with the ruling families. A man with a paternalistic approach will be the chief negotiator. He is part of that extended business family.

**Saudis** are shrewd, prudent, and uncompromising in business. Top executives who are the decision makers prefer to negotiate with those of equal status.

Flattery is an important part of **Saudi** business culture. **Saudis** expect praise for a job well done and can be very sensitive to criticism. Do not hesitate to praise the aspects of **Saudi Arabia** that you like. Praising **Saudi** women, however, is strictly off limits.

The spoken word is highly regarded in the **Middle East**, so diplomatically suggest a written contract to avoid any misunderstandings. Words can be spoken out of politeness without serious intentions.

## WOMEN

Before travelling anywhere for business, you should know the country's laws and how women are treated there. Keep up to date with the latest information by reading newspapers and searching the web.

In **Egypt**, there are the poor and the rich and there is a huge difference between them. The elite and the most educated control the country. Women are not treated equally. They represent 10 percent of the workforce but very few are in the corporate sector or executives. On the positive side, **Egypt** has legally banned female genital mutilation. A new law also now allows women to get divorced from their husbands provided she returns the money or property the husband paid as a bride price.

In **Kuwait**, women are not treated equally to men and do not have the same rights, however educated women are more emancipated. **Kuwaiti** women are still not allowed to vote, but in the small Gulf State of **Qatar**, women can vote and stand in local elections.

**Jordanian** women are the most educated in the **Middle East**. King Hussein bin Talai had placed great importance on education, which has resulted in an 85 percent literacy rate. However, **Jordan** still permits so-called honour killings in cases of adultery committed by a wife or sister. A husband or brother is exempt from a penalty, in effect making it legal to kill women. The same situation exists in **Syria**.

It is a man's world in **Saudi Arabia**. Women get less of an education then men, and very few jobs and responsibilities are given to **Saudi** women. A male relative must accompany women in public. **Saudi** and **United Arab Emirates** women are prohibited from driving. Men and women are totally segregated in restaurants, buses, schools, shops, and even banks have women-only hours. At home, the mother is in charge of the household. Women should think twice before trying to do business in **Saudi Arabia** because there is so very little that women are allowed to do.

A woman's role in **Iran** is also restricted. Women do not have equal rights in travel (they need permission from their husband), divorce, custody of children, or inheritance. However, women are now getting an education and can stand for parliament.

In **Iran**, adultery is punishable by flogging or stoning. By law, a wife in **Yemen** has to obey her husband and cannot leave home without his permission.

In **Lebanon**, rape is not punishable by law if the abductor marries his victim.

## CORPORATE GIFTS

Corporate gifts should be presented publicly to the group after a deal is closed. Wait for your host to present you with a gift first.

Appropriate gifts should pertain to office use such as quality pens (gold), electronic gadgets, diaries, pocket calculators, business card cases, and engraved items are much appreciated.

A fine compass may be given to a devout **Muslim** to help him find his way to Mecca. You may also give a picture book or something regional from your country. Present the gift with your right hand supported by your left, but never with just the left hand, which is an insult.

Keep in mind that government officials cannot accept gifts. Opulent gifts may be misinterpreted as bribery.

Avoid items with your company logo, liquor, and photos or sculptures of women or animals, especially dogs, which are considered unclean. Handkerchiefs imply sadness or parting.

It would be impolite to refuse a gift.

## BUSINESS ENTERTAINING

Business entertainment takes place in coffee houses and hotel restaurants. These functions are extravagant and limited to men only. Do not bring your spouse. The inviter pays for the whole group.

The male guest of honour is seated to the right of the host.

Business and social entertaining begins later in the evening and continues well into the night.

A traditional feast may feature caviar, an open-spit roasted lamb or baby camel as the main dish, and enormous amount of fruit and chocolates for dessert.

In **Jordan**, power breakfasts and business lunches are becoming quite popular. Dinners are social occasions that begin late in the evening. Inquire first if spouses are to be included.

Devout **Muslims** have strict dietary restrictions. Many are vegetarians, so do not expect to be served beef, pork, or alcohol. If you go to a restaurant with **Muslims**, order vegetarian dishes as well.

## HOME INVITATIONS & GIFTS

Although it is rare, you may be invited to dine in a home. You may arrive up to half an hour late.

Gifts are not necessary, but you may bring chocolates or baked goods to an **Egyptian** home or flowers and candy to a **Jordanian** or **Kuwaiti** home. A thank-you note afterwards is greatly appreciated. In general, flowers in the **Arab** world are mostly given at weddings, funerals, or when someone is ill.

## TABLE MANNERS

Accept offers of beverages before the meal, which can begin as late as 23:30.

Meals are large and lengthy, so make sure you have a good appetite; eating large quantities shows your appreciation. It is very common for women to eat separately from men, even in their own homes.

Your hosts may use forks and knives to eat, however, in a traditional household you may have the occasion to sit on cushions and eat with your hands. Always use your right hand to eat, drink, give, or receive objects. Wait for everyone to be served and for your host to begin. Sample a bit of every dish. To ask for salt would be insulting to your host.

Leave a token amount of food on your plate to indicate that there was plenty of food to go around. When you are finished, place your utensils parallel on your plate. Depart soon after you finish your coffee. If your host would like you to stay longer, he will repeatedly urge you to remain.

**Iranians** eat using a fork and spoon. Use the fork in your left hand to push food onto the spoon. **Islam** forbids the consumption of alcohol and pork.

## GOOD TOPICS OF CONVERSATION

In **Egypt**, you can expect to hear a lot of flowery words, emotion, and exaggeration. **Egyptians** love language – the more poetic the better.

Guests are the centre of attention and are expected to be able to converse on many different topics.

Discuss such things as culture, architecture, their country's place in history and achievements, places to visit, and sports: mostly soccer, horses, and falconry.

## TOPICS TO AVOID

It is best to skirt the issues of religion, politics, and women's role in society. Do no make any off-colour jokes.

Avoid talking about **Israel**.

It is considered an invasion of privacy to inquire about your host's wife, daughters, or family life. However, you may be questioned about your personal life.

## CUSTOMS & TRADITIONS

During Ramadan, most offices and shops will be closed or have reduced hours. This is a time of fasting between sunrise and sunset.

Foreigners should not eat, drink, or smoke in front of a **Muslim** during the day or at any time in public. In some places it is illegal and carries a stiff fine.

Worry beads are common in the **Middle East** and have no religious significance. Many people often say "Inshallah," which translates as "God willing" and is used the same way Westerners use "I hope so."

Be prepared to take your shoes off in some buildings; follow your host's lead.

Do not admire your host's possessions with too many compliments or he may feel obligated to give the object to you and be offended if you refuse.

Conservative clerics in **Iran** carry out their justice for social crimes with public lashings and still defend execution by stoning.

In **Egypt** and **United Arab Emirates**, homosexual sex is prohibited under the criminal code.

(See "Customs & Traditions" in **Asia**, p. 166 for information on the Taliban.)

## GESTURES

Men can be seen publicly walking hand in hand. This is a sign of friendship and has no sexual connotations. Do not draw back if your elbow or hand is being clasped and held.

The left hand is considered unclean — use your right hand for everything you do.

The left hand is reserved primarily for hygiene.

To beckon, extend your hand palm down and make scratching motions with your fingers.

Remove your shoes before entering a home or a mosque.

Shake hands with your host's children, it shows respect for the parents.

## GESTURES TO AVOID

Public displays of affection such as kissing between men and women are forbidden. Stand farther apart from women and do not converse with them unless you have been introduced.

To point or beckon with your finger is rude and used only for animals, use your full hand instead.

A level, splayed hand with palm downward and a bent middle finger is vulgar.

To pat an **Arab** on the back or give a backslap is insulting.

Never use a nickname such as "my friend," as is it considered offensive.

The "thumbs up" sign is an affront to **Arab** people.

To glance at a watch indicates that you wish to escape from someone's company.

Never swear or mention God, even mild oaths can elicit offense.

Do not walk in front of an **Arab** while he is praying and never step on a prayer mat.

Keep both feet on the floor. To expose the bottoms of your shoes or feet is offensive. It is an insult that implies that you are placing someone under your feet, thus equating him with dirt.

Never use your feet to point, move objects, or place them on furniture.

## DRESS CODE

In the **Middle East** and **Gulf States** your approach to dressing should be modest. The body must be covered at all times for both genders, even when it is hot. Men should stay away from jewellery except for a watch and wedding band. Jeans and shorts are unacceptable for both.

For men, a dark, conservative business suit, a white shirt, a tie and black lace-up shoes are recommended for meetings and formal events. A suit or jacket and dress pants are fine for social visits unless advised otherwise. Note that wearing a tie may not be appropriate in Iran. Neckties are blacklisted for **Iranian** men and stores face serious consequences for displaying or selling them.

For casual attire, wear a long-sleeved shirt buttoned up to the neck and trousers. Casual wear should be clean and neat.

**Jordanian** men wear a head-dress of a red or black and white check fabric, even with **Western** attire. Many women wear traditional long dresses. In contrast, the younger crowd wears **European**-styled garments.

Women should not wear pantsuits, trousers, or any other garments that are tight or revealing. Skirts should be way below the knee or ankle length; necklines should be high. Always keep a scarf with you and wear it if people stare at you.

It is offensive to bare one's chest, legs, or arms in public. It would be impolite and an insult for you to do so.

Women in **Egypt**, **Jordan**, and **Kuwait** are not obliged to wear the traditional robes and hide their faces. Real jewels and gold watches with diamonds are popular.

In **Iran**, **Saudi Arabia**, and the **United Arab Emirates**, people wear the traditional robes. The men wear a full-length dress and head-dress.

In **Saudi Arabia** and **Iran**, the religious police (matawain) patrol the streets and make sure that people are observing the dress code. In **Saudi Arabia**, men wear a head-dress (ghotra) and a long white robe (thobe); women wear a veil that covers the whole face except for the eyes and a long black dress called abaya. All **Saudi** and **Iranian** women must be covered from head to toe when appearing in public.

In **Iran**, women must wear the traditional dress. A woman who appears in public in anything not prescribed by the **Islamic** dress code (*hejab-e-shar'i*) can be sentenced to prison or fined, though men in urban areas can wear trousers and shirts. **Western** women should wear an *abaya* (similar to a legal gown) on top of their clothes and cover themselves when approached by the police.

## PHOTOGRAPHY

Ask permission before taking pictures in a mosque — there may be fees involved.

Do not use your camera near military sites or personnel, official buildings, airports, or train stations. These are sensitive areas and can result in confiscated film. It is best to ask first if you are at all in doubt.

**Islam** forbids the reproduction of the human image and many believe that it steals the soul. Especially avoid photographing women.

# Israel General Etiquette

Israel

Below are the common business practices and traditions of **Israel**. For more information on Arabic culture, see Chapter 9: **Middle East & Gulf States**.

## GREETINGS & FORMS OF ADDRESS

A warm handshake followed by "Shalom" is the acceptable form of greeting when you meet and depart. "Shalom" means peace and is used to say hello and good-bye. Friends may pat each other's shoulder or back. Only very close friends hug. Wait for a woman to extend her hand first.

**Orthodox Jewish** men rarely introduce their wives or any other women in a group.

Titles are not considered important. Do not be offended when you are called by your first name.

Unless told differently, address **Israelis** by Mr., Mrs., or Miss and their surname.

## APPOINTMENTS & PUNCTUALITY

Make prior appointments for visits to government officials and presidents of companies. Other appointments can be made once you get there.

If you have no other choice, it is not considered impolite to telephone and immediately show up for a meeting.

You are expected to be punctual. However, **Israelis** are casual about time, and it is not unusual for your associates to be up to half an hour late.

Business is conducted from Sunday through Thursday. Friday at sunset until sundown on Saturday is reserved for **Sabbath**.

## BUSINESS CARDS

Exchange business cards during introductions. **English** is used in business circles. In general, business cards and promotional materials do not need to be translated. Out of respect for your host you may have your cards in **Hebrew** on one side and **English** on the other.

To impress your host, have your business cards engraved. It is a sign of status in **Israel**.

**Orthodox Jewish** men do not touch women. A woman's business card should be left on the table for the men to pick it up.

## MEETINGS & PRESENTATIONS

Meetings are less formal in **Israel** than in the **U.S.** and the **U.K.**

Tea and coffee may be served prior to the meeting. Politely accept the offer.

Business is conducted at a similar pace to that of a large **American** city such as **New York**. **Israel** is a very competitive country.

Business is influenced by religious law, but it really depends on how orthodox the government in power is.

**Israeli** business people are aggressive and may appear abrupt. Do not take offense, it is a national mannerism and in no way reflects on you. A **Jewish** person born in **Israel** is called a "sabra" after the cactus, rough on the outside and soft on the inside. In this country the "hard sell" really works.

Presentations should be clear and brief. **Israelis** do not like to deal in large concepts but rather focus on detailed plans and financial printouts.

## NEGOTIATIONS

In business, **Israelis** are shrewd, prudent, and uncompromising. They will begin negotiations from an extreme position to show that they are willing to compromise. You should take an intense position as well in order to find a mutually acceptable middle ground. Expect much bargaining and concern with details. **Israelis** want to be clear on the deal before they agree.

Negotiating in **Israel** can be very disconcerting. As in many situations, it is arduous to get a positive answer to a straight question. However, persistence and patience will go a long way. Stress the positive aspects the venture will generate for both sides. Avoid raising your voice in anger. Never criticize someone publicly.

Fast results are more important to **Israelis** than long-term goals.

Decision making takes more time than in the **West**. Top executives make the final decisions in private companies. Companies owned by a group of people make decisions collectively.

## WOMEN

Equality between men and women exists on the national level; both genders are subject to obligatory military service. But equality doesn't exist in divorce cases. For **Jews** in **Israel**, matters of marriage and divorce are under the exclusive jurisdiction of rabbinical courts. Husbands are granted enormous power under rabbinical law and divorce cases can drag on for decades. If a woman wants to remarry, she needs a "get" — a bill of divorce. If the husband does not want a divorce, the wife cannot remarry within the **Jewish** religion. If she remarries outside the religion, her children are considered bastards and cut off from the **Jewish** faith for 10 generations.

Civil marriages are not performed in **Israel**. Many **Israelis** go to **Cypress** for civil marriage services, but they are still subject to rabbinical law if either spouse demands it.

**Israeli** women are educated and well represented in the workforce.

Some sects of **Orthodox Jewish** women still shave their heads and wear a scarf or a wig.

## CORPORATE GIFTS

Presents should be presented when a deal is closed. Wait for your associates to present you with a gift first. Appropriate gifts are quality items for the office such as pens, electronic diaries or pocket calculators, books, and CDs. You may also give something regional from your country.

## BUSINESS ENTERTAINING

Most business entertaining takes place in coffeehouses, hotel restaurants, and nightclubs. Power breakfasts and business lunches are restricted to associates. Dinners are social occasions, but first inquire if spouses are included.

Business and social entertaining begins later in the evening and continues well into the night. The host pays for everyone.

Government buildings, state-owned hotels, restaurants, and many homes serve only kosher food prepared according to Jewish dietary laws called kashrut. This practice has existed since the time of Moses. One must not mix milk and meat; they are to be eaten separately and cooked in different pots. The animal must be slaughtered a certain way by a licensed shohet and only specific parts can be eaten. Pork and shellfish are forbidden. **Reform Jews** do not insist on practising *kashrut*.

## HOME INVITATIONS & GIFTS

An invitation to lunch is more common than to dinner. When invited to dine in a home, bring chocolates, candies, or flowers for your hosts, and send a thank-you card afterwards.

## TABLE MANNERS

Refreshments are served before the meal. Allow your host to seat you. Wait for everyone to be served and for your host to begin.

The host makes the first toast; you may propose a toast afterwards.

**Israelis** use the continental style of eating. At the end of the meal, leave a bit of food on your plate to show your host that there was plenty to eat. When you are finished, place your utensils parallel on your plate. You should leave soon after the meal.

## GOOD TOPICS OF CONVERSATION

**Israelis** love to argue and may appear opinionated. It is nothing personal. Go with the flow, and don't feel compelled to openly agree with what people say.

Discuss topics such as sports, history, culture, and sightseeing destinations in Israel.

## TOPICS TO AVOID

Do not talk about religion, the government, the **Arabs** in the **West Bank**, political unrest, or **U.S.** aid.

## CUSTOMS & TRADITIONS

**Israel** has a relatively high standard of living. The customs are completely different from the **Arab** countries surrounding it. **Israel** has a huge cultural diversity of **Jewish** people. They come from different parts of the world sharing in common only their religion. Other than that, they do not think, behave or look alike.

More than 2 million **Arabs** live in **Israel**. For centuries the **Palestinians** and the Jews have tried in vain to cohabit. Each group is thoroughly influenced by tradition and religion.

The Sabbath is strictly observed from sundown Friday to sundown Saturday. Religious people do not smoke or drive. If you are a guest or in a kosher restaurant, do not request butter for your bread or milk for your coffee.

(See "Customs & Traditions" in **Asia**, p. 166 for information on the Taliban.)

## GESTURES

Men stand fairly close when they converse. It is customary to see them touch a person on the arm while talking. Some **Israelis** express themselves with excessive hand movements while others are totally reserved and calm.

Many Western gestures and meanings are understood, such as the OK, victory, and thumbs up signs — all of which are acceptable.

## GESTURES TO AVOID

The "hook 'em horns" gesture (fist raised with index finger and little finger extended) implies marital infidelity.

The "fig," with the thumb protruding between the index and middle fingers, is vulgar.

To point a finger at an open upturned palm expresses disbelief and implies that "grass will grow on my palm before your words will ring true."

To point or beckon with your finger is rude and used only for animals — use your full hand instead.

## DRESS CODE

A business suit is necessary for meetings with government officials, otherwise business dress is much less formal.

Jackets and ties are optional and short-sleeved shirts are acceptable.

**Western-style** suits and dresses are fine for women. **Israeli** women dress very well and wear jewellery.

Dark business suits for men and silk outfits for women should be worn at formal events. Tuxedos and long gowns are mostly for black tie functions at embassies.

Shirts/sweaters and trousers/skirts are a good choice for social visits and casual wear. Shorts are considered beach wear for both genders.

**Orthodox Jewish** men are unmistakable in black hats, long black coats and white shirts with no tie. They are bearded and have side curls called payot. Less orthodox but still religious **Jews** wear a skullcap called yarmulka or kippah.

## PHOTOGRAPHY

Ask permission before taking pictures in places of religious worship. Avoid photographing military sites or personnel. **Hasidic Jews** and **Arab** women do not like to have their picture taken. Do not photograph altercations between **Jews** and **Arabs**. The army or police may confiscate your film.

# Chapter 11

# North America (Canada & United States)

North America (Canada & United States)

General Etiquette

Below are the common business practices and traditions of the **United States** and **Canada**. Although **Mexico** is part of **North America**, the way of conducting business and its traditions are **Latin American** (see Chapter 12).

Learn the geography of **North America**, and read newspapers to get an understanding of current affairs and the political climate. It is to your advantage to know something about the culture, language, currency, and measurements.

## GREETINGS & FORMS OF ADDRESS

Greet men with a firm handshake and good eye contact when you first meet or when you are introduced. Shake hands when you depart. Men normally wait for a woman to extend her hand first.

A proper **North American** handshake is a full-hand grip that is firm and warm with an understated downward snap. In **North America**, a person with a poor handshake will be judged immediately by his or her peers.

Address people by using Mr., Mrs., Miss, or Ms. (pronounced "miz") when you are not sure if someone is married — and the person's family name. Use the title and last name of people in authority, such as company presidents and CEOs (chief executive officer).

Until they suggest it, don't use first names with people in high positions, such as company presidents and CEOs. **North Americans** will soon invite you to call them by their first name.

In the **United States** it is common to be named after your father as in John Kennedy Jr. (junior).

In a corporate setting the most important executive is always introduced first, regardless of gender. Allow your host to introduce you at small gatherings. At large parties, introduce yourself to those around you.

It is a common practice for people to say, "How are you?" when they meet. Just say, "Fine, thank you" — they are not inquiring about your health.

## APPOINTMENTS & PUNCTUALITY

Before you go to **Canada** or the **United States**, talk about it with someone from the country or someone who has been there.

Appointments should be made a few weeks in advance. Morning meetings are the most common. Reconfirm your appointment when you arrive in the country.

Be punctual. If you are delayed, call ahead to notify. In any city with huge traffic jams, such as **New York** or **Los Angeles**, a fifteen-minute delay is acceptable.

In **North America**, it is permissible to make a cold call (calling a person without an introduction or appointment).

## BUSINESS CARDS

**North Americans** primarily exchange business cards for further contact or special needs.

When you first arrive at an office, present your business card to the secretary or receptionist.

Exchange your business card when you are introduced to someone or at the beginning of a meeting.

Have your cards translated into **English** if it is not your first language. When doing business with **French** speaking **Canadians**, have all material and cards translated into **French**.

Do not be offended if you present your card and the gesture is not reciprocated.

## MEETINGS & PRESENTATIONS

Meetings begin and end as scheduled.

Beverages may be served during a meeting. Accept them if you wish. You will not offend your host if you refuse his or her offer.

Business meetings are less formal than in other parts of the world. Although casual conversation is commonplace among newly acquainted colleagues, it is reserved mostly for after meetings.

There is very little small talk at meetings. **North Americans** like to get down to business immediately and follow the agenda.

Do not spend a lot of time and money fostering personal alliances with the people behind the deal. Developing a relationship is not as important as getting a deal done. **North Americans** often place profits ahead of business relationships.

When dealing with **North Americans**, be very efficient in your presentation. You must know all the details about how your product or service works. They will ask about the quantity of your product available and precisely when it can be delivered. They may even ask you for a discount on the price. Hesitation or a lack of knowledge can be interpreted as a sign of weakness.

Expect slick presentations from **Americans**. They will use charts, slides, graphics, and a lot of data. Expect **North Americans** to look at you intently while you are speaking and listening. They aim to excite interest in the product they are selling or to make sure you see things their way.

If you need something explained to you, **North Americans** will gladly help by demonstrating the concept in a number of different ways.

Often, parts of a business meeting are conducted over the telephone to save time.

**Americans** prefer innovation to tradition. They tend to be very open communicators.

**Canadians** are schedule-oriented and like to get straight to the point when doing a presentation; details are left until the end to be discussed. Nevertheless, they are quite analytical and will demand a lot of background information and particulars before jumping into a deal.

In **North America**, the promotion of an individual in a company is based on the person's ability to take responsibility, work with a team, and achieve goals. You will not get promoted just because you know someone important in the company. Competition is highly valued — everybody wants to be winner.

## NEGOTIATIONS

**American** business people are confident, resourceful, competitive, ambitious, and direct — they think and speak big.

**North Americans** work hard, move quickly, and like to do business whenever they can. Since they are corporately mobile (frequently changing positions within a company or companies), they rarely devote time to developing long-term friendships at work.

Send a representative that speaks **English** well. He will be judged on his fluency and ability to communicate his ideas.

You may send a single representative to negotiate on your behalf when doing a small deal.

In the **U.S.**, your negotiator may be young. Age does not necessarily carry weight. Youth and ideas often take centre stage. Company procedure is observed regardless of whom is doing the negotiation.

Be prepared for the popular hard-sell technique of the **Americans**, which may appear blunt or even crass to foreigners. **Canadians** are generally more conservative and reserved in their approach. Do not come on too strong or too slick; it will turn people off. They value egalitarianism but expertise is expected, just like the in the **United States**.

**American** business people usually break a deal down into small pieces and solve each issue separately. Many foreigners would rather consider the project as a whole and not one piece at a time.

Negotiations are approached in a problem-solving manner. Decisions are made after requested information has been gathered and pondered over for accuracy and effectiveness.

**North Americans** work quickly. If you need time to think carefully about any aspect of the negotiations, it is perfectly reasonable to ask for a recess.

If the pace slackens or periods of silence occur during negotiations, **North Americans** will attempt to fill it by agreeing or helping you finish your sentences.

Business in **North America** is goal-oriented rather than process-oriented. Interest lies in short-term projects that produce instant returns and numbers that reflect progress. Long-term contracts are viewed as cumbersome. If they do not like what is presented they will not have any trouble saying no.

**North Americans** believe negotiations should be a fair exchange. They are willing to make concessions, but not to bargain or haggle. They do not make outrageous demands, as co-operation is preferable to competition.

Instead, they "lay out their cards" and ask you what they can expect the end result to be. The bottom line (what the end result will be in financial gains or assets) is the most important aspect of negotiations. **North Americans** really mean it when they say, "time is money," so it is important to get to the point.

In the **U.S.**, most business deals are conducted one on one or in a small group. Final decisions are normally made by a group of executives.

**Canadians** negotiate as a team and make decisions in a group.

Legal contracts are binding and expected to be honoured above the spoken word or a handshake. Contracts are governed by civil law in the **U.S.** Likewise in **Canada**, where the civil code is based on the **English** model, except for the province of **Quebec**, where laws are based on the **French** system.

It is customary for independent lawyers to be present at the negotiating table. Deadlines are strictly adhered to and lawyers may be consulted every step of the way. They are involved in drawing up the final draft of the agreement.

Contracts are lengthy documents, often of about a hundred pages, filled with detailed legal jargon. Lawyers, however, can be so immersed in their legal wording that they overlook the human aspect upon which the deal is built. This can put off some investors.

## WOMEN

Women in the corporate world are considered equal with men and you should treat them the same way. **North Americans** are team players who acknowledge individual effort and accomplishment.

Men still dominate the corporate boards of both **Canada** and the **U.S.** Despite gains in equal rights, women are still fighting for positions of power and equal pay in the corporate world.

A 2001 survey carried out by Catalyst, a well-respected non-profit research group in the **U.S.**, found some progress but suggested that most firms do not recognize women in the talent pool for top jobs.

Catalyst surveyed 560 public and private companies in the **U.S.** and **Canada** and found only 7.5 percent of board members were women. While it concluded that women were better represented on the boards of financial institutions and Crown corporations, they were scarce on the company boards of construction, high-tech manufacturing, and import-export companies. The survey also found that women held only 12.5 percent of the top jobs in the largest corporations.

The small percentage of women in positions of power can make it difficult for those few who have made it into the corporate boardroom. Some women find their ideas are given less consideration than those expressed by men — even when the idea is the same. Women would be well advised to observe the men around them to figure out who gets listened to and why. Men can help by treating women the same as they would their male associates.

Women in **Canada** and the **United States** are often overlooked for overseas jobs. The main reason is the stereotype that women are unwilling to move because of family and personal obligations.

The Inter-Parliamentary Union in Geneva reported that **Canada** ranked 20th place and the **United States** 43rd in world standings for legislative gender equality (1999).

(See "Women" in all continents for more information on women working abroad.)

## CORPORATE GIFTS

Corporate gifts are sometimes exchanged when a deal is finalized or when you leave the country. When given a gift, **Americans** do not necessarily reciprocate immediately. They have no set time limit for returning favours and gifts.

In **Canada** gifts should be modest; being pretentious is considered unrefined.

The tax departments in both countries discourage business gifts, as they allow very little money for tax deductions.

At Christmastime, gifts are often exchanged between work associates. All gifts should be wrapped and a card should be included. In **Canada** and the **U.S.** any colour of paper and ribbon is acceptable.

Gifts are opened immediately in front of the giver, except for wedding gifts, which are opened later.

If the gift is small, the recipient will thank you personally. If the gift is lavish, he or she will send a written thank-you note.

Appropriate presents include items from your country, such as a bottle of liquor, artwork, a special book, a handicraft, or food or a picture book from your region. Office items such as a quality pen set, calendars, and paperweights are also acceptable.

Avoid electronic items, as most offices are already fully equipped. Also refrain from giving cheap crafts such as objects emblazoned with your company logo. Do not give personal items such as perfume or clothing to businesswomen.

A common gift is to take someone out to a restaurant or to a special event.

## BUSINESS ENTERTAINING

Corporate entertainment is generally not as elaborate as abroad. Power breakfasts and business lunches are very popular, but business dinners are rare. Dinners are social occasions that include spouses, and business is not discussed.

Business may be conducted over breakfast (known as a power breakfast) or, more commonly, a business lunch. Many business people work on weekends, so you may be invited to a business brunch in either the late morning or early afternoon.

It is not common to have an alcohol drink at lunch. Big businesses and corporations frown upon employees drinking.

It is customary for the host to pay when invited out for business. On social outings people sometimes share the cost of the meal, called "splitting the bill," "getting separate cheques," or "going Dutch." If you wish to take your host out for a meal or drinks, let them know that you are "picking up the tab."

You may be invited to a cocktail hour before dinner. **Americans** put ice cubes in almost all their alcoholic drinks, even in white wine and sometimes champagne; **Canadians** rarely do so.

Be on time for meal invitations, and reciprocate all dinner invitations. The inviter pays for the group. You may be up to half an hour late for other social occasions.

Other types of entertainment include sports events; you may be invited to go see a ball or hockey game. You may also be invited to a game of golf or even to attend a weekend getaway. In the case of the latter, you may offer to reciprocate when they visit your country.

## HOME INVITATIONS & GIFTS

When you are invited to dine in a home, gifts are not necessary. However, you may bring chocolates, a bottle of wine, flowers, or a small potted plant for your hosts. Flowers in an even number are appropriate. Do not bring white lilies, as they are associated with funerals.

Do not make impromptu visits to someone's home without calling first.

## TABLE MANNERS

Arrive on time. Dinner may begin at anywhere from 18:00 to 21:00, but most likely earlier rather than later. Conversations strike up when pre-dinner drinks are served with snacks. It is okay to pass, one is not obliged to drink or eat right away.

The host sits at the head of the table. The guest of honour sits next to him. Wait until the host begins eating, then follow his or her lead.

In **Canada**, both **North American** and **Continental** styles of eating are followed. In the **U.S.**, the **North American** style is mostly used, which consists of switching the fork from the left hand to the right hand after cutting the food.

Begin with the utensils farthest from the plate and work your way in. When you eat, do not make noises while chewing or with your utensils.

Wine is usually served with the meal. Dinner rolls are circulated first. Place them on the bread plate provided on your left. Salad is served next.

Food may be served on platters; do not hesitate to serve yourself. You may not be urged to take seconds.

During the meal, present and translate a toast in your language.

When you are finished, your knife and fork should be parallel and placed diagonally across your plate, pointing to the 10 o'clock position.

Coffee and dessert will be served after dinner. You may stay to chat for a few hours. Thank your hosts for the dinner and the evening, and send a thank-you note afterwards.

## GOOD TOPICS OF CONVERSATION

Discuss sports, types of exercises, food, hobbies and interests, business (when spouses are not included), families, art, movies, and travel.

**Americans** will discuss business at just about any time.

## TOPICS TO AVOID

Avoid discussing religion, and internal and foreign government policies. Stay away from the subject of race, abortion, the homeless, and sex discrimination.

Do not discuss poverty, racism, American foreign policy, gun laws, and the crime problem.

When dealing with **Canadians**, do not discuss the problems between the **French** and the **English**.

Avoid comments on the **French Canadian** accent, it is considered rude.

**Canadians** do not like to be called **Americans**, or for anyone to make comparisons between **Canada** and the **U.S.** They are proud of their country.

**North Americans**, especially women, do not like to be asked personal questions. Do not inquire about marital status or how much money they make.

## CUSTOMS & TRADITIONS

Maintain good eye contact when speaking to someone — it builds trust and affinity. Avoiding eye contact implies you are hiding something. This can have far-reaching effects in both social and business circles.

The politically correct word for **Indian** is **Aboriginal Peoples** or **First Nations** people. The correct word for **Eskimos** is **Inuit**.

In **North America**, the concept of saving face hardly exists. **Canadians** and **Americans** prefer to tell it like it is and do not worry too much about the consequences or feelings getting hurt.

In **North America**, expect to be asked, "what do you do?" meaning, "what kind of work do you do?"

Do not be surprised by compliments on the subjects of attire, work, or how well you play a game (sports); they are given often in conversation — just say, "Thank you."

There is a large movement in **North America** towards creating non-smoking environments both in the workplace and public areas, such as restaurants. Observe the signs; don't light up in non-smoking areas. Smoking is increasingly restricted in public places.

## GESTURES

**English-speaking North Americans** stand at arm's length when they converse. They rarely touch each other unless they are close friends or wish to make a point.

Standing too close to a **North American** may be perceived as an invasion of one's personal space. In some parts of **North America**, business people still use a back slap, but this practice is slowly dying out. To discourage this practice, you may wince slightly to show your dislike of it.

It is polite to stand a few feet behind someone using an Automated Bank Machine (ATM).

Men often rise when a woman enters a room.

To wave hello or good-bye, extend your hand, palm outward, and swing it from side to side or shake the fingers up and down.

To beckon, raise your hand vertically with the fingers pointing upward and the palm facing inward; motion toward yourself. Alternatively, extend your index finger and curl it toward yourself.

To beckon a waiter, raise your hand discreetly. To beckon a waiter for the bill, lift your arm and make a writing motion.

Hold up an imaginary phone to your ear to advise someone of a telephone call.

In a social setting it is perfectly acceptable to sit with your legs crossed either at the ankle or knee, or with your ankle resting over the opposite knee (this last position is for men only).

Do not be offended if a person uses their left hand to write, point, eat, or to give something to you. In **North America**, it makes no difference if one uses the right or left hand.

The OK symbol (the thumb and forefinger touching to make a circle) and the thumbs-up sign show approval. The victory/peace symbol is another positive gesture.

To wish for good luck, cross your index and middle fingers.

## GESTURES TO AVOID

A middle-finger salute is vulgar and can flare tempers. An emphatic jerk of one's forearm has the same meaning.

Never pat anyone on the behind, it could generate a sexual-harassment lawsuit.

Do not jump a queue (lineup), whether you are at a bus stop or a concession line. It is very rude and you will be rebuked. Expect lineups to pay for purchases in stores, buy tickets at movie theatres, and to get on public transportation. Even without a formal line, people are served on a "first come, first served" basis. Be patient while waiting for service.

Do not use toothpicks in public.

In **Canada** it is impolite to exhibit aggressive and loud behaviour.

It is not common for people of the same sex to hold hands. This gesture is perceived as a sign of sexual preference.

## DRESS CODE

In general, a conservative two- or three-piece business suit is required for most business meetings for both genders.

For men, a sports jacket worn with a tie and dress trousers is very popular. A striped shirt is also an extremely fashionable choice for business wear.

Shoes for both genders must be polished, with heels in proper condition, and professional looking. Black is the best choice.

Formal wear for important events is black tie. Otherwise, cocktail wear such as a dark suit or silk dress is fine. Most invitations will indicate the dress code.

To dine, casual dress is often acceptable. For casual outings, the dress code is relaxed and one can don anything from shorts to jeans to chinos and a jacket. If in doubt about appropriate attire, ask your host.

People who work in the entertainment or the fashion industry dress casually chic.

In big cities, older elite businessmen dress fairly conservative, while younger men can be quite flamboyant in bright suspenders and ties. Businesswomen wear designer clothing and the colour black is still quite popular.

In **Texas** and **Calgary, Alberta** men wear cowboy hats and boots even for business.

Jewellery is popular for women.

## PHOTOGRAPHY

**Canada** and the **U.S.** are large countries in which every state and province has something to offer the photographer. People are free to use cameras just about everywhere, and there are minimal restrictions around government buildings and airports.

# Latin America (including Mexico)
## General Etiquette

Latin America (including Mexico)

Chapter 12

Below are the common business practices and traditions of **South America** and **Mexico**. Although **Mexico** is part of **North America**, the way of conducting business and its traditions are **Latin American**.

## GREETINGS & FORMS OF ADDRESS

A prolonged handshake of five to seven strokes, with a loose grip is the customary greeting when you meet and leave. Good eye contact is important during conversations.

Close male friends greet each other by touching the forearm or elbow, or by embracing in a friendly abrazzo.

Men should stand when a woman enters the room. Shake a woman's hand only if she offers it and bow slightly. Women do not usually shake hands with men. They will shake the hand of women friends as well as kiss them on the cheek. Women can be seen walking hand in hand in public. This is a show of friendship and nothing more.

At small gatherings you will be introduced to others by your host, but at large parties you should introduce yourself.

Titles are important. Address your associates by their professional rank and family name. For social acquaintances, use Senor (Mr.), Senora (Mrs.) or Senorita (Miss) and the family name. Avoid using first names until you have been invited to do so. Show deference toward elders and people of high rank.

Most **Hispanics** use a double surname: the first one is the father's followed by the mother's surname. Use only the paternal surname when you address them.

In **Costa Rica** address people by their **Christian** names preceded by Don (for a man) and Donna (for a woman). Use titles if they apply, such as Doctor or Engineer.

## APPOINTMENTS & PUNCTUALITY

Make appointments two to three weeks in advance and reconfirm them when you arrive in the country. It is not uncommon for meetings to be cancelled or changed. Family concerns take precedence so you may be deferred. Do not try to conduct business by telephone.

It is best to schedule your meetings for the morning and do not crowd your schedule, as meetings may last well into lunchtime. Let your host decide whether he or she wants to make appointments during siesta, which is from 13:00 to 15:00.

You are expected to be punctual. Meetings generally begin on time, however, you may be kept waiting if you are dealing with the highest person in the organization.

Businessmen expect to deal with someone of equal status. It is much easier to do business if you have the right contacts.

These introductions are essential for a successful business venture and will help you to accomplish your goals much faster.

Respect and status are gained through credibility and how well your associates are connected. Introductions can be made by banks and consulting firms or personal friends and family.

## BUSINESS CARDS

Exchange business cards during introductions. Include your title and position in the company on your card and present it with the **Spanish** printed material facing the receiver.

Most executives speak good **English**, however, your cards and promotional material should be available in both **Spanish** and **English**. (In **Portuguese** for **Brazil**).

## MEETINGS & PRESENTATIONS

Learn some **Spanish** for your visit and brush up on the local history. A good knowledge of your associates' language would help your business dealings to progress smoothly.

Greet each person present at the meeting. Meetings are conducted in a relaxed manner. They begin and end with small talk (sometimes for fifteen minutes) about your family and social interests. Do not ask personal questions on your first meeting. Let them do the talking. It is very important to cultivate a relationship first. You must sell yourself initially then proceed to sell your product.

Accept the coffee or tea that is served during a meeting. Most often the coffee will be served black with sugar but no milk or cream. Coffee will be served many times — accept it gracefully.

How you present yourself and your material is as important as the content of your presentation. **Latin Americans** respond well to the use of charts and graphics in a presentation.

Business meetings may go well into the evening sometimes as late as 22:00. Wait for the person in charge to leave before you do.

In **Uruguay** business people are well educated, sophisticated, and competent in business procedure. They are attuned to the way **North Americans** do business. Meetings are formal, brisk, and straightforward; however, they don't usually begin on time. Executives work very long days.

Expect meetings to last longer than anticipated and be prepared to make a few trips to complete your goals. Give the appearance of being strong and confident but not aggressive. Avoid making hasty decisions.

**Latin Americans** consider the **North American** approach of getting to the point and leaving the details for later too straightforward.

## NEGOTIATIONS

**Brazil** and **Mexico** are the key markets for international investment in **Latin America**. Increasingly, however, **Chile, Argentina, Venezuela**, and **Peru** are gaining the interest of buyers. These economies are growing quickly, and for investors who are willing to assume a little more risk, they offer diverse opportunities.

There are two types of negotiators in **South America**. The first is the traditionalist, who received his position through family or political connections. He wields power and because of status, his decisions are not questioned. If the deal falls through, it was not meant to be. Faith and destiny have an important role in the unfolding of events.

The other negotiator is modern, cultivated, Western educated, and English speaking. He knows the most recent technology and proceeds much faster in business dealings than his counterpart. Still, if you scratch deep enough, the values of both individuals are the same.

Always send the same negotiators; to change people will sabotage your possibility of a deal. **Latin Americans** like to feel they are negotiating with human beings and not a corporation.

Business dealings move at a slow pace. There is a great deal of red tape and bureaucracy. Several people are consulted before a decision is made. You will have to make numerous trips before the completion of your venture.

**Latin Americans** are more interested in short-term projects. Their focus is on the large picture and general ideas for developing the project and may gloss over details.

Emphasize the benefits both sides will enjoy with the advent of the project. You must present it as a win-win situation or they may be suspicious of your proposal. To **Latin American** business people compromise means giving up something. Do not attach strings to your demands.

The human factor takes precedence over performance. Business people value status, dignity, respect, and integrity above achievement, initiative, or efficiency.

Effort is more rewarded than results. It stems from their fatalistic outlook on life: what is meant to happen will happen.

A person may be promoted because he or she is well liked, not because of qualifications. Loyalty to superiors predominates in **South America**.

**South American** business people do not like to say no, it is considered impolite. To obtain candid answers, avoid yes/no questions or you will be told only what they think you would like to hear rather than lose face. They would rather keep peace and harmony than disagree with you. Stay away from direct questions or any type of confrontation. **South Americans** may not give you a straight answer immediately, so do not expect immediate results, be patient. Deadlines may be moved more than once.

In **Argentina**, make sure you understand every detail of a deal without being overbearing. Tact is important and confrontation will not get you the deal you were hoping for.

In **Bolivia**, high-pressured sales won't necessarily get you the desired results. **Bolivian** negotiators prefer a quieter approach.

**Brazilian** negotiators like to bargain but don't like aggressive tactics. For some, saying "no" is part of their style. You must be able to read the situation and determine whether someone really means business or not. Expect to deal with a lot of bureaucracy, regulatory agencies, and various officials. Doing business here takes patience and a long-term commitment.

**Chileans** and **Paraguayans** tend to be conservative negotiators. You will meet resistance if you try a hard sell approach. Aggressive moves are considered rude. The firm's top executives make the final decisions.

**Colombian** business people are generally polite and helpful. Negotiations are slow and quiet, sometimes taking place over a coffee. **Colombians** do not like to be forced into making quick decisions. Do not attach conditions to your demands because many don't like to feel that they had to give something up.

**Peruvian** business people tend to be conservative, formal, and subtle. Don't pose direct "yes" or "no" questions. When challenged, **Peruvians** will likely tell you what you want to hear rather than lose face.

**Venezuelan** business people tend to be cosmopolitan and well informed. You must be able to speak well in front of a group. Deal with the top executives in a firm because they are the ones who make the important decisions. Let people in high positions speak first and don't interrupt.

In the **Cayman Islands**, negotiations often move quickly. Your business partners will want to know the bottom line for all aspects of the deal. Get a written agreement. Deadlines are usually met and adhered to.

Executives may play up the drama of negotiations to bide their time. Patience and diplomacy are critical so avoid showing anger at interruptions or delays.

Never put all of your cards on the table. Since time is on their side, **Latin Americans** do not mind waiting for a deal to be concluded in their favour. Never say "this is my best offer, take it or leave it." They will most likely leave it.

No decision will be made until trust is established between the two companies. Expect some bargaining.

If negotiations come to a standstill and you feel you are backed into a corner, stop, leave the room, and resume negotiating later from another perspective.

Deadlines are not usually met, be flexible. It is considered unbecoming to agree quickly on any business proposal.

Do not be too eager to please. Silence goes a long way and is a useful technique in getting what you want out of the negotiations.

Decisions are made solely by the top executive. Often they are made by gut instinct and rarely questioned.

**Mexican** negotiating teams will present a united front. All questions will be deferred to the most senior official present.

Unlike the rest of **Latin America**, where decisions come mostly from the top, in **Costa Rica** they are made by a group of people. This country has the most lawyers per capita in the world and they usually speak **English**.

All portions of a contract are subject to negotiation. Make sure all contracts are in due form backed up by letters of intent from the banks. This will help avoid delayed payments. All agreements should be put in writing.

Friendship and being simpatico must continue after a contract is signed.

## WOMEN

Overall, there is still a strong sense of "machismo ethics" in **Latin America**. The "boy's club" is still prevalent, and it can be difficult for women to do business in some parts of **Latin America**. However women are beginning to gain credibility in the workplace. One must earn the respect of one's peers first.

In **Argentina** more women than men have a college education. They are now playing a bigger role in politics and business. There are more professional women in **Chile** than anywhere in **South America**.

In **Bolivia** and **Ecuador** women are considered inferior to men and are responsible for managing the household.

**Costa Rican** women keep their own identity in all judicial, political, and business affairs.

In **Costa Rica** and **Uruguay**, a man who commits abduction, rape, or indecent assault on a woman is not charged with a crime if he declares his intent to marry his victim. The victim has to consent to the proposal.

In the **Bahamas**, women (maternal ancestors) can inherit property only if there are no paternal ancestors left.

In **Chile**, the husband runs all property in a marriage.

In **Venezuela**, a new constitution permits women to transfer their citizenship to foreign born husbands.

There are more women than ever in the working force in **Mexico**, but very few at the upper echelon.

Women in **Uruguay** are considered equal, but men still hold the major positions in business.

When doing business in **Latin America**, women should act strictly professional. Represent your company, not yourself.

## CORPORATE GIFTS

Do not give corporate gifts until after a deal has been closed. Present them in a social setting rather than a business environment. Gifts will be opened after you have left.

Acceptable gifts may include a bottle of fine Scotch, Cognac, or French champagne. Brand name items, designer pens, electronic gadgets, classical CDs, or something regional from your country are appropriate.

On subsequent trips bring gifts for the secretaries as well. A bottle of perfume or a scarf is a good choice; if you are a man tell them that your wife selected the gift. When you give a small item, put it in the receiver's hand instead of on the table.

Avoid gifts of knives or letter openers for they symbolize the rupture of a friendship. Handkerchiefs are associated with sorrow. Do not give personal items such as ties, shirts, or soaps, and wine is considered too common. Avoid silver, as it is a tourist item.

Do not openly admire objects, as they may feel it is necessary to give them to you.

When receiving a gift, open it immediately in front of the giver and say, "Thank you."

## BUSINESS ENTERTAINING

Business lunches are usually scheduled during siesta. Breakfast meetings are rare, except in **Mexico City**.

Business lunches are popular and take place between 13:00 and 17:00 and are often used to establish a working relationship of trust since very little business will be discussed. If you are invited to lunch, your host may be as much as half an hour late.

As lunch is the main meal of the day, business lunches can last up to four hours. In order to stop this practice in **Mexico**, the government declared business lunches no longer tax deductible and, since April 1999, government employees are limited to one-hour lunch breaks.

A power lunch will normally start with several cocktails and an assortment of appetizers. The main course is served with wine or more cocktails, desert, coffee, and brandy.

Dinners are for socializing and may start as late as 22:00. Never address business at dinner unless invited to do so.

When you extend a dinner invitation, always include the wives of your associates. To make a favourable impression, allow your guest choose the wine. Never get drunk, it is considered offensive.

The host pays for the entire meal. Do not offer to pay if you have been invited, instead reciprocate these invitations by suggesting a few elegant restaurants your associates can choose from.

When taking associates out for a meal always pay the bill privately or else they will not let you do it.

## HOME INVITATIONS & GIFTS

Although it is rare, if you are invited to dine in a home, arrive a little late but never early. Bring a small gift of imported candy, chocolates, or flowers for your hosts. Thank them at the door when you leave. Never show up at someone's home without a proper invitation.

Flowers for the hostess may be sent in advance or brought with you. Avoid giving white or purple flowers, calla lilies, or marigolds, as they are all associated with mourning. Yellow indicates contempt. Roses are the preferable choice, however red is believed to cast a spell.

## TABLE MANNERS

Dinner in **Latin America** generally begins later than in **Europe** or **North America**.

Drinks, such as vermouth, and snacks will be served before dinner. Allow your host to seat you and to commence the meal with a toast. Wait until everyone else has been served before beginning.

Formal dinners are served one course at a time, while casual meals are set out all at once. Wine is served throughout the meal. Never pour wine with the left hand or clutch the neck of the bottle — it is considered an insult. Scotch and liqueurs are offered after dinner.

**South Americans** use the continental method to eat. Keep your hands and wrists on the table but not your elbows. Do not rest your hands in your lap.

Never pick up food with your fingers, even fruit and chicken should be eaten with utensils.

Try a bit of each dish that you are offered or your hosts may feel that their food was not good enough. If you praise the food, a second helping will be served. It is customary to politely decline the first offer before agreeing to another portion.

Leave some food on your plate to indicate there was plenty of food to go around (except in **Bolivia**, **Paraguay, El Salvador**, **Belize**, **Guatemala**, and **Panama**). When you have finished, place your utensils parallel on your plate. Coffee is served after the meal. You should leave 30 minutes later.

**Argentines** cut meat with the fork upright in the meat and cut through the tines. When they are finished, they cross their knife and fork, tines down, in the middle of the plate.

## GOOD TOPICS OF CONVERSATION

Good topics of conversation include history, art, literature, museums, education, food, and sports (soccer, car racing). Compliment the hosts on their children, meal, and home. Discuss interesting destinations to visit in their country.

## TOPICS TO AVOID

Be aware of your words and actions. An off-colour remark or misunderstanding can put an end to a business or personal relationship. Always respect local customs and traditions.

Avoid inquiring about the family until your host brings up the subject.

Refrain from discussing earthquakes, religion, race, poverty, salaries or prices, politics, and illegal aliens.

Don't use the Lord's name in vain, especially in public.

Stay away from asking questions about terrorism, the illegal drug trade, and street children.

In **Brazil**, topics to avoid include **Argentina** and AIDS.

Do not ask a **Mexican** business person whether he is of Indian descent.

Abstain from making jokes about Montezuma's revenge (diarrhoea).

In **Bolivia**, it is an insult to call rural Bolivians Indios (Indians); instead, call them campesinos (farmers). Avoid discussing the border problem between **Chile** and **Bolivia**.

## CUSTOMS & TRADITIONS

An effort to respect their traditions will make you more respectable in the eyes of **Latin Americans**.

**South Americans** and **Mexican** are not impressed with self-made individuals or the nouveau riche as some **North Americans** are — they are traditionalists. Old money and family connections are more important. They believe that whether you are born rich or poor, that is your destiny.

Social status is very important in **Latin America**. The people are very class conscious. What you wear (starting with your shoes), your accessories (pens, watches and briefcases), how you hold yourself, and where you eat and stay will all be scrutinized. Make a good impression. The exception to this rule is **Costa Rica** where there is no class distinction and everyone is considered equal.

**Panamanians** no longer believe that the most powerful people should have endless privileges.

In **Uruguay** politics and business are influenced significantly by its large middle-class.

In **Argentina** the middle class governs politics while the upper echelons rule business.

Honour is of great importance to the **Latin American** people: never criticize, pull rank, or embarrass someone in public.

There is a big celebration when a girl turns fifteen, called a quinceanera, which is a sort of coming-out party.

**Brazil** is changing its civil code regarding marriage and divorce. The present code is nearly 100 years old — written at a time when machismo dominated **Latin American** culture. By 2003 the new code will ensure that women have rights in marriage and divorce and will also ensure that divorced fathers have a chance of gaining custody of their children.

**Colombians** generally do not respect lineups at taxi stands, bus stops, and in stores.

The criminal law in **Jamaica** prohibits consensual sex between same-sex couples, which is punishable by up to 10 years in prison with hard labor.

## GESTURES

**Latin Americans** stand closer to one another when they converse than **Europeans** and **North Americans**. People may even touch your shoulder or lapel. This is a show of friendship. Do not step back or you will be perceived as aloof and may put them off. However, men should avoid physical contact with women in public.



 

To beckon, extend your arm palm down, and make scratching motions with your fingers.

You may cross your legs, knee over knee, but avoid placing one ankle over your knee.

To indicate that something is so-so, hold your hand horizontally and wag your thumb up and down.

Hissing to get someone's attention is not considered rude.

In **Peru**, you point something out by pursing your lips in that direction. To warn someone, tug the corner of your eye down. To indicate that something is too much, loosely shake your hand up and down. If you do this with your elbow raised, it means "we went overboard."

## GESTURES TO AVOID

Hands on hips shows anger.

Yawning in public is impolite.

Do not point your fingers at people.

Brushing the chin outward with the back of the fingers expresses "I don't know or care."

The fig gesture, made by placing the thumb between the index and middle fingers is a phallic symbol.

It is bad manners to slap your fist into the palm of your other hand.

In **Argentina**, the **North American** sign for "he is crazy" (making a circular gesture with the forefinger next to the ear) could be misunderstood for "you have a telephone call."

When shopping in **Mexico**, place the money for your purchases directly in the clerk's hand, rather than on the counter. It is a sign of contempt to put your payment on the counter because it is perceived as meaning that you don't want direct contact with a lowly store clerk.

In **Brazil**, drivers insult other drivers by pretending to hold up an apple. Never do this yourself.

By holding your palm upward and spreading out your fingers you are saying that a person is stupid.

The **North American** OK gesture (thumb and index finger forming a circle) is regarded as obscene. It represents a bodily orifice.

Slapping the inside of the thigh near the groin is considered indecent.

To tap your elbow with your hand indicates the person you are discussing is stingy.

Do not put your feet on furniture or use your feet to point or move objects.

The "Hook 'em horns" (fist raised with index finger and little finger extended) implies marital infidelity, as does making a "V" sign and placing it below your nose.

## DRESS CODE

In **Latin America** city dwellers and business types dress much like people in **North America** and **Europe**. Attire tends to be a little more formal. Wear your best, paying attention to details.

A conservative suit, white shirt, tie, and black shoes are recommended for most business engagements. A jacket and tie are proper attire for social dining occasions.

A skirt and jacket or dress is more appropriate for women than a pantsuit. Avoid revealing garments and short skirts.

Shorts are resort wear for both genders.

Casual wear consists of pants and shirt or dress and sweater. When invited to an outdoor barbecue, nice casual clothes are in order.

For diplomatic functions a man is expected to wear a tuxedo, a woman an evening gown. For a formal occasion men may wear a dark suit and ladies a cocktail dress.

In **Mexico** the traditional *guayabera*, a shirt worn over trousers, is acceptable casual wear.

Never wear Indian clothes for casual outings, you may offend the native people and you will appear strange to your associates.

In **Brazil** do not wear yellow and green together because these are the colours of the flag.

## PHOTOGRAPHY

Ask permission before you take photos of people or religious ceremonies. Some will expect a fee, others may decline. Older people may still believe that the camera will capture their soul. During a parade or celebration, you may take pictures of a group.

Avoid taking pictures of official or government buildings. For security reasons, do not use your camera at the airport, train station, or port of call. Your camera may be confiscated and you may face a fine.

In **Brazil**, do not take pictures of voodoo ceremonies.

Latin **South America** is a photographer's paradise, take advantage of it. Always carry a camera with you when travelling, even when it is for business.

# Chapter 13

Terrorism

# Terrorism

## BE ALERT TO TERRORISM

The very real possibility of terrorist attack at home or abroad has most of us concerned with safety. Likewise, most of us have no idea how we should handle terrorist activity such as kidnapping, armed attack, bio-terror, and nuclear threat. Companies are so secretive about the subject, you probably don't even know whether your company has any plans in place for handling such emergencies. If you don't know, try to find out. If you are a company head, consider informing your employees of the company's plans, even if every detail cannot be disclosed for security reasons. Former victims have said they would have been better able to handle the situation if they had some knowledge and advice beforehand.

## TERRORISM ABROAD

The objective of terrorists is to get money or seek publicity for a cause and create fear. In the case of kidnappings, men are usually the targets. While almost anyone from a wealthy corporation will suit the purpose of kidnappers, high-profile individuals or companies are the most likely targets.

If you face an emergency in a foreign country, first call your company's head office, which has a strong commitment to protecting its employees. Then call the local police and your embassy.

Before you take a short- or long-term position abroad, here are some tips to prepare yourself.



## Do:

Get a security briefing of the area you will be working and travelling in.

Questions to ask are:

- Has there been terrorist activity in the region in the past?
- Were hostages taken?

Make sure your legal and immigration documents are in order.

Visit the Web site of your country's Department of Foreign Affairs and International Trade. Find out if the place you are going to is a hot spot for terrorist activity.

Check all the references and credentials of the people working with you.

Communicate your needs to the people hired to help you make your adjustment to the new location.

Provide a detailed account to your company of what you will need as far as security measures are concerned.

## IF YOU ARE A POSSIBLE TARGET

### Do:

Be aware of your surroundings and the people that frequent your place of business and come to your home.

Alert yourself to signs of being watched. Someone may be taking note of your routine.

### Don't:

Park in the same place every day. Always vary your route and consider using different vehicles.

Use a labelled parking stall, drive a car with vanity plates, or use identification tags on your belongings.

Dismiss the need to learn about the politics and culture of the new location.

## TIPS FOR SAFE BUSINESS TRAVEL

Here are some measures that you can take to protect yourself while travelling on business.

### Do:

Get the check-in clerks at airports and hotels to write down your flight number or hotel room rather than say it out loud. You don't want the wrong people to get this information.

Memorize your passport number and only take out your passport for immigration officials.

Keep your hotel room neat so that an intrusion will be noticeable.

Stay away from slums, poorly lit areas, and narrow alleyways.

Carry one credit card separately from the rest. That way, if your wallet gets stolen you will still have a source of money.

Use common sense when you go out to nightclubs, discotheques, and other late-night establishments. Arrange return transportation to your hotel.

Watch out for "honey traps." An extra-friendly companion may be trying to get you into a compromising and potentially dangerous situation.

Stay away from demonstrations and other large gatherings.

Keep a distance of at least two arms lengths from an inquiring stranger.

Choose taxis with care.

Drive in the centre lane of the road when possible. Keep a safe distance from the car in front.

Dress conservatively — no form fitting clothing — if you are a woman travelling in developing countries or male-dominated societies.

## Don't:

Resist armed attackers — give them your valuables. Do not carry large amounts of money or anything that you are not prepared to lose.

Use ATMs that are on low visible streets where criminals can observe your transactions.

Take unmarked taxicabs or get into any taxi carrying passengers you don't know.

Drive on narrow, quiet, and unlit streets, or after dark in the countryside.

Walk alone in remote areas, such as some beaches, trails, and among ruins.

### TERRORISM AT HOME

Terrorists around the world are working on more sophisticated approaches to mass destruction. To strengthen employee confidence, companies should provide guidelines on how to deal with terrorism. If you are the person who hires, look closely at whom is working for you.

For reassurance, bring in an expert to describe how to act and what to do in the case of an emergency (who do you call? where are the emergency exits? do you use the elevator? and if so, how many stairs? and how long does it take to get out?) Knowing is better then being left out in the dark.

## COMPANY GUIDELINES AFTER A CRISIS

After a crisis, hire a counsellor to deal with employees on an individual basis. An employee that is having problems will show signs of depression, a lack of self-worth, anxiety, lethargy, low self-confidence, anger, and/or cannot concentrate. This person will need extra help.

**What Managers Can Do:**

- Be alert.
- Stay visible.
- Let employees know that there are opportunities for them to contribute to and work with charity groups.
- Get the PR team to publicize the company's charity work both inside and outside of the office.
- Employees with a history of alcohol and drug problems are at risk during a critical time. Be aware that troubles at home might be worsened.
- Try to convince employees who work from home to come into the office for reinforcement, though allow them to continue working from home if they wish.
- Anger is a normal response to tragedy, but ensure that it's not directed at other people in the office.
- News reports — radio or television — should be limited in the office.
- Make yourself available to your staff. Go out to lunch with them.
- Show that you care.
- Thank staff members for a job well done.
- Control rumours by providing timely and accurate information on the condition of the company and the industry.

## DEALING WITH STRESS IN A CRISIS

Here are some ways you can deal with stress in difficult situations.

- Be physically active. It will help you to relax and improve your energy levels.

- Don't bottle up your feelings. Talk to a friend, a co-worker, or family member.
- Take time for yourself. Busy people need to be reminded to take time for a movie, a book, or a hobby.
- Maintain healthy eating habits. Alcohol, caffeine, sugar, fatty foods, and tobacco all work against the body's ability to deal with stress.
- Don't skip vacations. Our bodies need recharging.
- Organize your time better. Make priority lists and learn to say no when you have too much on your plate.
- Get a good night's sleep. Being overtired contributes to stress and anxiety.
- Volunteer. Helping others is a stress reducer.
- Laugh. Research shows that 100 laughs is as good for your heart as 15 minutes of bike riding.
- Relax. Do relaxation exercises such as yoga, meditation, or deep breathing.
- Ask for the help of a health professional if your depression or anxiety persists.

## WORLDWIDE TERRORISM GROUPS

### AFRICA

Some of the world's most tragic conflicts are in **Rwanda**, **Nigeria** (**Kano**), and **Algeria**.

The *Armed Islamic Group* (GIA) is located in **Algeria.** It is an Islamic extremist group whose objectives are to replace the secular Algerian regime with an Islamic state. Its activities involve attacks against civilians, journalists, and foreign residents.

The *Army for the Liberation of Rwanda* (ALIR) is located in the **Democratic Republic of the Congo** and **Rwanda** and seeks to control Rwanda's Tutsi-dominated government.

The *Revolutionary United Front* (RUF) is located in **Sierra Leone, Liberia**, and **Guinea**. It seeks to take over the current government of Sierra Leone and control the diamond-producing regions of the country.

The *People Against Gangsterism and Drugs* (PAGAD) is an anti-government and anti-Western group located in the **Cape Town** area of **South Africa**. It views the South African government as a threat to Islamic values.

## ASIA

The *Harakat ul-Mujahideen* (HUM) is based in **Pakistan**, primarily in **Kashmir**. It is an Islamic militant group whose operations are against Indian troops and civilian targets in Kashmir.

The *Islamic Movement of Uzbekistan* (IMU) is a coalition of Islamic militants located in **Afghanistan**, **Tajikistan**, **Uzbekistan**, and **Kyrgyzstan**. Its aim is to establish an Islamic state in **Uzbekistan**.

The *Alex Boncayao Brigade* (ABB) is located in **Manila** and central **Philippines**. It is a breakaway urban hit squad of the Communist Party of the Philippines New People's Army.

The *Abu Sayyaf Group* (ASG) is an Islamic separatist group located in the **southern Philippines**. It seeks to promote an independent Islamic state in **western Mindanao** and the **Sulu Archipelago**.

The *Al-Qaida* is believed to be headed by Osama bin Laden and is based in **Afghanistan**. It is dedicated to opposing "non-Islamic" governments and expelling Westerners and non-Muslims from Muslim countries.

The *Jaish-e-Mohammed* (JEM) is an Islamist group based in **Pakistan**. Its aim is to unite **Kashmir** with **Pakistan**.

The *Japanese Red Army* (JRA) is located somewhere in **Asia** or Syrian-controlled areas of **Lebanon**. Its goal is to overthrow the Japanese government and incite worldwide revolution.

The *Lashkar-e-Tayyiba* (LT) is a Sunni anti-US missionary organization based in **Pakistan**.

The *Liberation Tigers of Tamil Eelam* (LTTE) is located in **Sri Lanka**. Its aim is to establish an independent Tamil state.

Terrorism

The *New People's Army* (NPA) is a military wing of the Communist Party of the **Philippines**. Its goal is to overthrow the government and it opposes any U.S. military presence in the Philippines.

The *Aum Supreme Truth* (AUM) is a cult located in **Japan**. Its aim is to take over Japan, then the world.

The *Chukaku-Ha* (Nucleus or Middle Core Faction) is a domestic militant group located in **Japan**. It opposes Japan's imperial system and Western "imperialism."

## EUROPE (EASTERN & WESTERN)

In **Western Europe**, the most deadly and long-running terrorist campaigns have been waged in the name of Irish republicanism in **Northern Ireland** and **Basque** nationalism in **Spain**.

In the **former Soviet Union** and **Eastern Europe**, the fall of communist dictatorships has unleashed ethnic hatreds. Conflicts exist largely in **Bosnia**, **Nagorno-Karabakh**, **Georgia**, and **Chechnya** in the **Russian Federation**.

The *Armenian Secret Army for the Liberation of Armenia* (ASALA) is an **Armenian** terrorist group whose goal is to have the **Turkish** Government publicly acknowledge its responsibility for the deaths of 1.5 million Armenians in 1915 and make amends.

The *Kurdistan Workers' Party* (PKK) is located in **Turkey, Europe**, and **the Middle East**. Its goal is to establish an independent Kurdish state in **southeastern Turkey**.

The *Revolutionary People's Liberation Party/Front* (DHKP/C) is a Marxist, anti-U.S. and anti-NATO group located in **Turkey** and **Istanbul**.

The *Revolutionary People's Struggle* (ELA) is an extreme leftist group located in **Greece**. It is anti-U.S. and seeks the removal of U.S. military forces from **Greece**.

The *Revolutionary Organization 17 November* (17 November) is a radical leftist group located in **Athens, Greece**. It is anti-U.S., anti-Turkey, anti-NATO and seeks the removal of U.S. bases and the Turkish military presence from **Cyprus**.

The *Basque Fatherland and Liberty,* located in **northern Spain** and **southwestern France**, aims to create an independent homeland in Spain's **Basque** region.

The *First of October Antifascist Resistance Group* (GRAPO) is located in **Spain**. Its goal is to overthrow the Spanish Government and replace it with a Marxist-Leninist regime.

The *Irish Republican Army* (IRA) is a radical terrorist group located in **Northern Ireland** and the **Irish Republic**. It is dedicated to removing **British** forces from **Northern Ireland** and unifying **Ireland**.

The *Continuity Irish Republican Army* (CIRA) is also a radical terrorist group located in **Northern Ireland** and the **Irish Republic**. It is dedicated to the reunification of Ireland.

The *Real IRA* (RIRA) is a political pressure group located in **Northern Ireland** and the **Irish Republic** and is also dedicated to removing **British** forces from **Northern Ireland** and unifying **Ireland**.

The *Loyalist Volunteer Force* is located in **Northern Ireland** and **Ireland**. It is opposed to a political settlement with Irish nationalists in **Northern Ireland**.

The *Orange Volunteers* (OV) is an extremist Protestant terrorist group located in **Northern Ireland**. It also seeks to prevent political settlement with Irish nationalists in **Northern Ireland**.

The *Red Hand Defenders* (RHD) is an extremist terrorist group located in **Northern Ireland** that also seeks to prevent political settlement with Irish nationalists in **Northern Ireland**.

## MIDDLE EAST & GULF STATES

Some of the most significant terrorist activity takes place in the **Middle East**. This activity generally falls into the following groups:

- Palestinian Islamic groups that bitterly oppose the Declaration of Principles agreement between PLO leader Yasser Arafat and the Israeli government. Terrorist activity is largely used against Israeli targets in the Occupied Territories, but also against Israeli and Jewish targets elsewhere.



Terrorism

- Extreme Islamic fundamentalists in most **Muslim** countries who want to replace pro-Western **Arab** régimes with their own Islamic republics. The Islamic revolutionary régime in **Iran** actively supports these groups to wage *Jihad* (Holy War).
- Islamic fundamentalists who frequently target Westerners living or working within their country.
- Outside the **Middle East**, the threat of terrorism may come from those not directly sponsored by a state or major terrorist player. Islamic fundamentalists may try to recruit members from the expatriate community. Such groups could emerge in Western countries with large Muslim minority populations such as the **USA, Canada, France, Britain, Germany, and Australia.**

The *Mujahedin-e Khalq Organization* (MEK or MKO) is an armed Iranian dissident group based in **Iraq**. It opposes the Iranian Government.

The *Palestine Liberation Front* (PLF) is a militant Palestinian group based in **Iraq**.

The *Abu Nidal Organization* (ANO) is an international terrorist organization based in **Iraq, Lebanon, Sudan**, and **Syria**. Its targets include the **United States**, the **United Kingdom, France, Israel**, moderate Palestinians, the PLO, and various **Arab** countries.

The *al-Jihad* is an **Egyptian** Islamic extremist group operating in the **Cairo** area. It aims to overthrow the **Egyptian** Government and replace it with an Islamic state.

The *Democratic Front for the Liberation of Palestine* (DFLP) is a Marxist-Leninist organization in **Syria, Lebanon**, and **Israel**.

The *Al-Gama'a al-Islamiyya* is a large militant group based in **Egypt**. Its goal is to overthrow the **Egyptian** Government and replace it with an Islamic state.

The *HAMAS* is an Islamic Resistance Movement in **Israel**. It aims to establish an Islamic Palestinian state in place of **Israel**.

The *Hizballah* (Party of God) is a radical Shia group in **Beirut** and **Lebanon**. Its goal is the removal of all non-Islamic influences from **Lebanon** and the creation of an Islamic republic in **Lebanon**.

Terrorism

The *Kach and Kahane Chai* is an organization based in **Israel** and **West Bank** settlements dedicated to restoring the biblical state of **Israel**.

The *15 May Organization* was formed from remnants of the Special Operations Group of the *Popular Front for the Liberation of Palestine* and is located in **Iraq**.

The *Palestine Islamic Jihad* (PIJ) is based in **Syria** and is dedicated to the creation of an Islamic Palestinian state and the destruction of **Israel** through holy war.

The *Popular Front for the Liberation of Palestine* (PFLP) is a Marxist-Leninist group in **Syria, Lebanon**, and **Israel**.

The *Popular Front for the Liberation of Palestine-General Command* (PFLP-GC) split from the PFLP in 1968 and is opposed to Arafat's PLO. It is based in **Damascus** and **Lebanon**.

## NORTH AMERICA (CANADA & UNITED STATES)

Many terrorist groups use **Canada** and the **United States** as a place to hide, raise money, and recruit people from ethnic communities for their cause.

In **Canada** and the **United States**, some extreme right groups are quite active. These include white supremacists, skinheads, neo-nazis, anti-government, anti-abortion, anti-religion, and other insurgency groups.

Violent attacks by hate groups motivated by extreme right ideology are likely to increase. However they remain in localized regions and show no signs of developing on an international scale.

## LATIN AMERICAN (INCLUDING MEXICO)

The *National Liberation Army* (ELN) is located in **Colombia** and is a pro-Cuban, anti-American guerilla group.

The *Revolutionary Armed Forces of Colombia* (FARC) is the military wing of the Colombian Communist Party. It takes action against **Colombian** political, military, and economic targets.

The *Shining Path* is located in **Peru**. Its goal is to destroy existing Peruvian institutions and replace them with a communist peasant revolutionary regime.

The *Tupa Amaru Revolutionary Movement* (MRTA) is a Marxist-Leninist revolutionary movement located in **Peru**. It aims to establish a Marxist regime and replace Peru's imperialist elements.

The *United Self-Defense Forces/Group of Colombia* (AUC) is located in **Colombia**. Its goal is to protect its sponsors from insurgents.

## BIOLOGICAL AND CHEMICAL WARFARE

The main objective of terrorists is to cause extreme fear and even panic among civilians. Terrorists may use biological or chemical weapons, which they may obtain from sympathetic régimes or from renegade scientists who defected during the Cold War. Countries who sponsor international terrorists are **Iran, Iraq, Syria, Libya, Cuba, North Korea**, and **Sudan**.

### Facts about Anthrax

Anthrax is a lethal disease caused by the bacterium Bacillus anthracis. Symptoms usually occur within seven days after exposure. The inhalation of anthrax may resemble a common cold and progress to severe breathing problems and shock. The inhalation of anthrax is often fatal. Anthrax can also be contracted by contact with the skin as well as intestinally. Anthrax does not spread from one person to another.

Anthrax is stocked in culture collections or germ banks around the world, including **Iraq, Egypt, Syria, North Korea, Russia**, and the **U.S.** It can be sent in the mail as a powder or aerosolized.

### Treatment

In persons exposed to anthrax, infection can be treated or be prevented with antibiotics such as penicillin, ciprofloxacin, or doxycycline. A vaccine is also available, but in limited quantities.

People may be decontaminated in a shower of detergent and bleach. Clothes should be tested or destroyed.

### Facts about Botulism

Botulism is a muscle-paralyzing disease. Symptoms occur 18 to 36 hours after exposure and include blurred vision, drooping eyelids, slurred speech, difficulty swallowing, and dry mouth, followed by paralysis and respiratory failure.

The toxin is typically found in contaminated canned foods and ingested. Botulism is not spread from one person to another. Wounds can also be infected with the bacteria C. botulinum toxin, with symptoms beginning within six hours to two weeks. Infant botulism is caused when a baby ingests the bacteria. It then grows in the intestine and releases the toxin.

Samples of this naturally occurring bacteria are held in many micro-organism culture collections and at least six countries may have tested it in the form of a weapon. It can be dispersed as an aerosol or released into food or water supplies.

### Treatment

If diagnosed early, it can be treated with antitoxin (expect for infant botulism) and assisted ventilation. Wash clothing and skin with soap and water.

While potent, botulinum toxin is easy to destroy. Heating it to an internal temperature of 85°C for at least five minutes will detoxify contaminated food or drink. Extreme temperatures and humidity will degrade the toxin, and fine aerosols will eventually dissipate into the atmosphere. You get some protection by covering your mouth and nose with clothing. Intact skin is impermeable to botulinum toxin.

The toxin will naturally degrade within hours to days, however contaminated objects or surfaces can be cleaned with 0.1 percent hypochlorite bleach solution.

### Facts about Bubonic and Pneumonic Plague

Plague is an infectious disease of both animals and humans. It is found in rodents and their fleas in many areas around the world. The two types, bubonic and pneumonic plague, are caused by the bacterium Yersinia pestis, which is transmitted from person to person or by the bite of a flea that fed on an infected rodent.

Pneumonic plague infects the lungs and symptoms are fever, headache, weakness, and a cough producing bloody or watery sputum. Without treatment, septic shock and death usually occurs in three days. Bubonic plague is characterized by chills, fever, vomiting, diarrhea, and the formation of buboes (swollen inflamed lymph nodes).

Plague can be disseminated by aerosol. The U.S., Russia, North Korea, and Egypt may have cultivated plague as a weapon.

### Treatment

Early treatment with antibiotics is an effective treatment for plague. There is no vaccine.

Wear a surgical mask, gown, gloves, and eye protection around an infected person.

Heat, disinfectants (2 to 5 percent hypochlorite), and exposure to sunlight renders the bacteria harmless.

### Facts about Smallpox

The variola virus causes this highly contagious killer. Symptoms include high fever, fatigue, headaches, backaches, and a characteristic rash with flat red lesions. Smallpox is spread by face-to-face contact with an infected person.

The spread of smallpox via aerosol would have devastating results. If it initially infected 50 to 100 persons, it would rapidly spread by a factor of 10 to 20 times.

The only two official stocks of smallpox are in Russia (whose supply may have been stolen) and the United States. Egypt, North Korea, and Iraq possibly have stores of smallpox.

### Treatment

If the smallpox vaccine is taken within four days of exposure, the disease is less severe. There is no proven anti-viral treatment. Death occurs in 30 to 50 percent of cases.

Individuals in whom smallpox is suspected should be isolated immediately. Anyone in a household of an infected person or who had face-to-face contact with an infected individual should be vaccinated and monitored.

Terrorism

### Facts about Sarin

Sarin is a colourless, odorless nerve gas. Initial symptoms may be a reaction at the point of contact, localized sweating, muscular twitching, runny nose, tightness of the chest with shortness of breath, and dim vision. In more severe exposure, symptoms include headache, cramps, nausea, vomiting, involuntary defecation and urination, twitching, jerking, staggering, convulsions, drowsiness, coma, and respiratory arrest. Death may occur. Appropriate chemicals can destroy most nerve agents.

### Treatment

People should be immediately decontaminated, usually with a mixture of chlorinated lime and magnesium oxide.

Acute exposure to sarin may require life support for the victims. Do not perform mouth-to-mouth resuscitation when someone's face is contaminated.

## COMBATING TERRORISM

The international community should face terrorism head on. Among the general principles for reducing terrorism, Professor Paul Wilkinson from the University of St. Andrew's, Scotland, suggests the following:

- Don't surrender to terrorists. Make no deals or concessions, even when facing extreme intimidation and blackmail.
- Increase efforts to bring terrorists to justice by prosecution and conviction before courts of law. Work within the framework of the rule of law and the democratic process.
- Penalize state sponsors who give terrorists safe haven or other support.
- Never allow terrorist intimidation to stop international diplomatic efforts to resolve major political conflicts.

Terrorism

# BIBLIOGRAPHY

BIBLIOGRAPHY

BIBLIOGRAPHY


Aizenman, Nurith. "Women of the World Update". Marie Claire Report, July, 2000.

Alexander, Anne. "Understanding Voice Male Gender in the Workplace." Look West Magazine.

*Amex Pocket Guide to Hong Kong, Singapore and Bangkok.* Amex Publishing, 1988.

Amir, Datin Noor Aini Syed. *Malaysian Customs & Etiquette.* Times Books International, 1991.

Amparano Lopez, Julie. "Hiring Hopes." Wall St. Journal, 1993.

Anzelowitz, Lois. "Luggage: On a roll." Working Woman, 1994.

Appelbaum, Judith. *How to Get Happily Published: A Complete & Candid Guide.* Harper Collins Canada, Limited, 1992.

Appleton, Dr. William S. *It takes More than Excellence.* New York: Prentice Hall Press, 1986.

Ash, Mary Kay. *Mary Kay on People Management.* New York: Warner Books, 1984.

Asia Pacific Foundation of Canada. "Asia Pacific Backgrounder", All of Asia's Backgrounder. Vancouver, B.C., September 1993.

Asia Pacific Foundation. "Canadian Women Doing Business in Asia." Industry, Science and Technology Canada Booklet, March 1995.

Asia Speak: Status - Formality - Trust.

Axtell, Roger E. *Gestures: The Do's and Taboos of Body Language Around the World.* New York: Wiley, 1991.

Axtell, Roger E. *The Do's and Taboos of Hosting International Visitors.* New York: Wiley, 1990.

Baldrige, Letitia. *Complete Guide to Executive Manners.* New York: Rawson Associates, 1985.

Barnett, Vicki. "Crossing the Cultural Divide." Edmonton Journal, The.; Calgary Herald.

Bartholomew, Edinburgh. *Kenya: A world travel guide.* Edinburgh: Bartholomew, 1991.

Beijing Platform for Action. From June 5 - June 9, 2000, government delegates and NGO representatives from more than 180 countries gathered in New York for a Special Session of the United Nations General Assembly to review implementation of the Beijing Platform for Action. For more information go to *www.equalitynow.org.*

Bell, Robert. *You Can Win at Office Politics.* New York Times Books, 1984.

Berman, Steve. *How to Create your own Publicity for Names, Products or Services and get it for Free.* New York: Frederick Fell, 1977.

Bixler, Susan. *The professional image: The total program for marketing yourself visual*ly. New York: Putnam, 1984.

Book of "Li": Etiquette - Ceremony - Protocol, The

Boyle, Mathew. "Nothing really matters." Fortune Magazine, October 15, 2001.

Brennan, Lynne and David Block. *The Complete Book of Business Etiquette.* Judy Piatkus Ltd., 1991.

Byram, Marie-Therese. *Simple Etiquette in France* (Simple Etiquette Series). P. Norbury Pubns Ltd. UK: 1992.

*Caribbean Islands Handbook.* Prentice Hall, 1993.

Carnegie, Dale. *Speak more Effectively.* New York: Association Press, 1962.

Carnegie, Dale. *The Quick and Easy way to Effective Speaking*, revised by Dorothy Carnegie. New York: Pocket Books, 1962.

Carson, Gayle. *Winning Ways: Techniques That Take You to the Top.* Berkley Pub, 1991.

Castle, Dennis & John Wade. *Teach Yourself Public Speaking.* The Chaucer Press Ltd., 1985.

Chesanow, Neil. *The World-Class Executive.* Rawson Associates, 1985.

Christmas, Rachel Jackson & Walter. *Bermuda and Bahamas.* Fielding, 1994.

BIBLIOGRAPHY

Chambers, Kevin. *The travelers' guide to Asian Customs & Manners*. Distributed by Simon & Schuster. New York: Meadowbrook, 1988.

Coffin, Royce A. *The Negotiator: A manual for winners*. Amacom, 1973.

Collins, Eliza G.C. "Power Protocol in Getting to the Top." Harvard Business Review.

Collins, Eliza G.C. "Upward Mobility: The Etiquette of Ambition." Harpers Bazaar Magazine.

Condé Nast Traveller. "Jet Lag."

Coolidge, Shelley Donald with The Christian Science Monitor. "Times and Offices are Changing." Edmonton Journal, The, March 20, 1999.

Copeland, Lennie & Lewis Griggs (Contributor). *Going International: How to Make Friends and Deal Effectively in the Global Marketplace*. New American Library Trade, April 1990.

Crowther, Geoff and Hugh Finlay. *Lonely Planet - East Africa*. Oakland, CA: Lonely Planet Publications, 1997.

Crowther, Geoff. *Lonely Planet - Korea and Taiwan*. Oakland, CA: Lonely Planet Publications, 1985.

Davidson, Jeffrey P. *Power and Protocol for Getting to the Top*. New York: Shapolsky, 1991.

De Mente, Boyle L. *Korean Etiquette & Ethics in Business*. NTC/Contemporary Publishing Company, 1994.

Department of Foreign Affairs and International Trade, *www.dfait-maeci.gc.ca/travelreport/ menu_e.htm*.

Devine, Elizabeth & Nancy L. Braganti. *The Traveler's Guide to Asian Customs and Manners*. New York: St. Martin's Press, 1986.

Devine, Elizabeth & Nancy L. Braganti. *The Traveler's Guide to European Customs and Manners*. Deephaven, MN: Meadowbrook Books, 1984.

Devine, Elizabeth & Nancy L. Braganti. *The Traveler's Guide to Latin American Customs & Traditions*. St. Martin's Press, Inc., 1988.

Dienhart, L, and M. Pinsel. *Power Lunching.* Turnbull & Willoughby Publishers, Inc., 1984.

Doyle, Thomas F. Jr. *How to Write a Book about your Specialty.*

DuBrin, Andrew J. *Winning at Office Politics.* New York Van Nostrand Reinhold, 1978.

Dunekel, Jaqueline. *Business Etiquette.* Self-Counsel Press, 1992.

Economist, The. "Arabian Peninsula" business travellers' guides.

Economist, The. "A Survey of Britain." September 21, 1996.

Economist, The. "A Survey of Canada." July 24, 1999.

Economist, The. "A Survey of East Asian Economies." March 7, 1998.

Economist, The. "A Survey of France." June 5, 1999.

Economist, The. "A Survey of Germany." February 6, 1999.

Economist, The. "A Survey of India." February 22, 1997.

Economist, The. "A Survey of Iran." January 18, 1997.

Economist, The. "A Survey of Latin American Finance." December 9, 1995.

Economist, The. "A Survey of Mexico." October 28, 1995.

Economist, The. "A Survey of Philippines." May 11, 1996.

Economist, The. "A Survey of Russia." July 21, 2001.

Economist, The. "A Survey of Sub-Saharan Africa." September 7, 1996.

Economist, The. "A Survey of Tomorrow's Japan." July 13, 1996.

Economist, The. "Business in Europe." November 23, 1996.

Economist, The. "Spain in Transit." December 14, 1996.

Else, David, with Alex Newton, Jeff Williams, Mary Fitzpatrick, and Miles Roddis. *Lonely Planet - West Africa.* Oakland, CA: Lonely Planet Publications, 1992.

Ehrlich, Eugene & Gene R. Hawes. *Speak for Success.*

BIBLIOGRAPHY

Elphick, Art. *Winning: How to make yourself more likeable.*

Exner, Raquel. "Remember Your E-mail Manners." Edmonton Journal, The, Fall, 1999.

Finnerty, Amy. "The Waiting Game." Oprah Magazine, June, 2001.

Finnish Foreign Trade Association and Chamber of Commerce of Finland. "Finland in the 1990s".

Fisher, Roger & William Uey. Getting to Yes: Harvard negotiating project. New York: Penguin Books, 1983.

Flemming, Charles. "Europe is All Over the Map When It Comes to Offices." Wall Street Journal, Paris, July 1999.

Florence, Mason. *Lonely Planet - Vietnam: A travel survival kit*. Oakland, CA: Lonely Planet Publications, 1999.

Fodor's. *Australia & New Zealand: A complete Guide including the Great Barrier Reef.* Fodor's Travel Publications, Fodor's Travel, 1994.

Fodor's. *Jordan and the Holy Land.* Fodor's Travel Publications, Fodor's Travel, 1994.

Fodor's. *Morocco.* Fodor's Travel Publications, Fodor's Travel, 1991.

Fodor's. *Singapore: The Complete Guide with Excursions to Malaysia and Indonesia.* Fodor's Travel Publications, Fodor's Travel. 7th ed. 1993.

Fodor's. *South East Asia, Philippines.* Fodor's Travel Publications, Fodor's Travel, 1993.

Fodor's. *Turkey.* Fodor's Travel Publications, Fodor's Travel, 1993.

Foreign Trade magazine. Sept./Oct. 1991, Nov./Dec. 1991, May/June 1992, July/Aug. 1992.

Foxworth, Jo. *Boss Lady's Arrival and Survival Plan.* New York: Warner Books, 1986.

Fraser, Sarah. "What's in a bag?" Business Traveler Magazine, July 1994.

French, Carey. "Report on Business Travel." The Globe & Mail, September 29, 1998.

Gawain, Shakti. *Creative Visualization.* San Rafael, Calif.: New World Library, 1978.

Globe & Mail, The. "Report on Business." Feb. 1992, Sept. 1992.

Globe & Mail, The. "Report on Business Travel." February 28, 1995.

Globe & Mail, The. "The eight deadly e-business assumptions" and "Mastering the Web." June 15, 2000.

Grothe, Mardy, and Peter Wylie. *Problem bosses: Who They Are and How to Deal With Them.* New York: Facts on File, 1987.

Hall, Edward T., U.S. anthropologist. Quoted in article written by Jon Bowen in the Globe and Mail, September 16, 1999. Page C3.

Harper, Damian. *Lonely Planet - Hong Kong.* Oakland, CA: Lonely Planet Publications, 1998.

Harper, Peter and Peplow, Evelyn. *Philippines Handbook.* Moon Publications, 1991.

Harris, Morgan, and Patti Karp. *How to make News and Influence People.* Blue Ridge Summit, PA: Tab Books, Inc., 1976.

Hegarty, Christopher, with Phillip Goldberg. *How to manage your Boss.* Random House, Incorporated, 1985.

Hill, Napoleon. *Think and Grow Rich.* New York: Fawcett, 1960.

Hobica, George. "100 All Time Best Travel Tips." Travel Holiday Magazine.

Humphreys, Andrew, Siona Jenkins, Leanne Logan, Geert Cole, and Damien Simonis. *Lonely Planet - Egypt and the Sudan.* Oakland, CA: Lonely Planet Publications, 1999.

Hunter, J.B. "Your personal column will help you win recognition, enhance your stature and influence in the community and your profession."

Insight Guides. "Australia," 1989.

Journal of the AMA (JAMA).

Jeffrey, Barbara. *Wedding Speeches and Toasts.* W. Foulsham & Co. Ltd., 1971.

BIBLIOGRAPHY

Johnson, Dorothea & Hester Beall Provensen. "Savvy Presentation Skills" article. The "How" for the Executive, Effective Broadcast Interviews.

Johnston, Tony, Senior Vice-president of Corporate Affairs at Calgary-based Westaim Corp. Quoted in article written by Catherine Mulroney, Globe and Mail, March 31, 2000. Page E10.

Kennedy, Angus J. *The Internet & World Wide Web - The Rough Guide*. The Penguin Group, 1998.

Kennedy, Marilyn Moats. *Glamour Guide to Office Smarts*. Fawcett Publications, 1986.

King, Jane. *New Zealand Handbook*. Moon Publications, 1987.

Korda, Michael. *Power!: How to get it, how to use it*. New York: Random House, 1975.

Korda, Michael. *Success: How every man & woman can achieve it*. New York: Random House, 1977.

Lamb, Christina. "Pakistan women fight murder by fire." Daily Telegraph, London.

Leboeuf, Michael. *Take Control of Your Time and Your Boss*. (audio cassettes).

Leppert, Paul. *Doing business with the Thais: A handbook for executives*. Sebastopol, Calif.: Patton Pacific Press, 1992.

Lewis, H. Gordon. *How to handle your own Public Relations*. Chicago: Nelson-Hall Inc., 1976.

Longman. *Business guide to the United Arab Emirates*. World of Information, 1985.

Lublin, Joan. "Lost promotions have silver linings." Wall Street Journal, September 08, 1993.

MacKillop, Malcolm. "How to deal with a boss who's a bully." Globe and Mail, September 25, 2000.

Marjabelle, Stewart Young. *The New Etiquette*. St. Martin's Press, 1987.

Marlin Traveller. "Beating Jet lag." 1996.

Martin, Judith. *Miss Manners*. Warner Books, 1983.

Marshall, Sol, H. "Establish yourself as an Authority."

McArthur, Douglas. "It's a scary world for corporate travellers." Globe and Mail, August 30, 2000.

McGuinness, Victoria Miranda. *Simple Etiquette in Spain (Simple Guides. Customs and Etiquette).* Midpoint Trade Books, Incorporated, 1993.

Molloy, John T. *New Dress for Success*. Warner Books, Incorporated, 1987.

Morrison, Terri, with Wayne A. Conaway & George A. Borden;[with a foreword by Hans Koehler]. *Kiss, bow, or shake hands: How to do business in sixty countries.* Holbrook, Mass.: B. Adams, 1994.

Morrow, David J. "Dealing with Absent Bellhops and Unexpected Roommates." New York Times, Sunday, April 28, 1996.

Murphy, Joseph. *The Power of Your Subconscious Mind.* Prentice Hall, 1988.

Nabou.com. "Terrorist Organisations", *www.terrorismfiles.org.*

Nash, Nathaniel C. "A new look into Latin America." New York Times, April 11, 1993.

Newton, Alex. *Lonely Planet - Central Africa*. Oakland, CA: Lonely Planet Publications, 1994.

Nierenberg, Gerard I., and Henry H. Calero. *Fundamentals of Negotiating*. Simon & Schuster Trade, 1973.

Nierenberg, Gerald I., and Henry H. Calero. *How to Read a Person like a Book.* Random House, 1985.

Nundy, Julian. "French Women to Get Greater Role in Government." Globe and Mail, The, September, 1999.

O'Brien, Richard. *Publicity: How to get it.* Harper & Row, 1977.

Pascoe, Robin. *The Wife's Guide (Surviving Overseas).* Times Books International, 1992.

Pang, Guek Cheng & Robert Barlas. *Culture Shock Canada.* Graphic Arts Center Publishing Company, 1992.

BIBLIOGRAPHY

Panté, Robert. *Dressing to win: How to have more money, romance, and power in your life!* Garden City, N.Y.: Doubleday, 1984.

Perrin, Wendy. "How to Get the Perfect Hotel Room." Condé Nast Traveler, August 1996.

Perrin, Wendy. *Perrin Report.* June 1999.

Perrin, Wendy. "Perrin, the Report." Condé Nast Traveler, January 1997.

Peters, Jens. *Lonely Planet - Philippines.* Oakland, CA: Lonely Planet Publications, 1997.

Pizzuto, Joseph J. *Fabric Science.* Revised by Arthur Price & Allan C. Ghen. Fairchild Publications, 1994.

Ponder, Catherine. *Open your Mind to Prosperity.* DeVorss & Company, 1984.

Porat, Karin. "Get Your Net Working." Look West Magazine.

Post, Elizabeth L. *Emily Post on Business Etiquette.* Harper Collins Canada, Limited, 1992.

Post, Elizabeth L. *Emily Post's Etiquette.* Harper Row, 14th Edition, 1984.

Post, Emily. *Etiquette, a Guide to Modern Manners.*

Department of Health and Human Services U.S.A. "Public Health Emergency Preparedness."

Ramsey, Laura. "Banishing the Cube." Financial Post, September 1999.

Ramsey, Laura. "Big Bucks Not the Only Bait." Financial Post, September 6, 1999.

Ramsey, Laura, [columnist]. "Office Politics." National Post, p10-11, May 10, 1999.

Roberts, Wess. *Leadership Secrets of Attila the Hun.* Warner Books, 1987.

Robison, Gordon. *Lonely Planet - Arab Gulf States.* Oakland, CA: Lonely Planet Publications, 1996.

Rowland, Diana. *Japanese Business Etiquette.* Warner Books, 1985.

Rubenstein, Hal & Jim Mullen. "I'm a Travelin' Man." New York Times, 1996.

Reuter, Michael Conlon. "To Avoid Cultural Gaffes, Watch Your Feet and Hands." Vancouver Sun, The, October 4, 1997.

Russell, Malcom B. *The Middle East and South Asia.* (The World Today series), 1992.

Sackheim, Maxwell. *How to Advertise Yourself: Five Basic Steps to Selling Your Appearance, Your Thoughts, Your Words, and Your Experience to Any Individual or Group.*

Schlosberg, Jeremy. "Complaints That Get Results." Condé Nast Traveler.

Shea, Michael. *Influence: How to make the system work for you.* London: Century, 1988.

Schiffman, Stephan. *LDD Calling Techniques.* Bob Adams Inc., 1987.

"Special Report on Workspace." National Post Business, July, 2001.

Stafford, Diane. "Companies Expect Some Salary Negotiations." Edmonton Journal, The, August 7, 1999. Knight-Ridder Newspaper.

Stafford, Diane. "Keeping Sane in Your Shrinking Cubicle." Kansas City Star, The, Fall 1999.

Staten, Clark L. "Emergency Response to Chemical/Biological Terrorist Incidents." Emergency Response & Research Institute, 1997.

Stone, A.C. *Golf Etiquette.* October 2, 1995.

Tausz, Andrew. "The Worst Seats in the House." Globe & Mail, March 11, 1999.

Thompson, Jacqueline (ed.). *Image Impact for Men.* NY: A & W Publishers Inc., 1983.

Tilbury, Neil, Paul Hellander, and Andrew Humphreys. *Lonely Planet - Israel: A travel survival kit.* Oakland, CA: Lonely Planet Publications, 1999.

Travel advisories in Canada: 1-800-267-6788 or visit *www.dfait-maeci.gc.ca/travelreport/menu_e.htm.* In the U.S. contact the U.S. state Department at *www.travel.state.gov/travel_warnings.html.*

United States Department of State. "Patterns of Global Terrorism, 2000." April, 2001.

Veltman, Laura. *How to Live and Work in Australia: A Handbook for Emigrants.* Unsourced Publishers Pub., 1990.

Wall Street Journal. "Report on China." Dec 10, 1993.

Wall Street Journal Guide to Business Travel. "International Cities."

Waltraud, Coles, and Uwe Koreik. *The Simple Guide to Customs and Etiquette in Germany (Simple Guides. Customs and Etiquette).* Talman Company, 1995.

Warschaw, Tessa Albert. *Winning by Negotiation.* McGraw-Hill, 1992.

Waitley, Denis. *Winner's Edge: The Critical Attitude of Success.* Berkley Pub Group, 1994.

Web sites: *www.hrw.org*, Human Rights Watch, Women's Rights Division; *www.equalitynow.org*, Equality Now; *www.now.org*, National Organization for Women; *www.iwdc.org*, International Women's Democracy Center; *www.rawa.org*, Revolutionary Association of the Women of Afghanistan (RAWA).

Weisel, Al. "How Secure is that Metal Safe." Travel Leisure, March 1999.

Weisel, Al. "Prescription for Trouble." Travel Leisure, April 1999.

Wheeler, Tony, and Geoff Crowther. *Lonely Planet - Malaysia, Singapore & Brunei: A travel survival kit.* Oakland, CA: Lonely Planet Publications, 1991.

Wheelwright, Gay. "PC Cards." Financial Post, May 17, 1999.

Wilder, Lilyan. *Talk your way to Success.* New York: Simon & Shuster Inc., 1986.

Wilkinson, Paul. "Terrorism: Motivations and Causes." Canadian Security Intelligence Service Publication, Commentary No. 53.

*World Business Travel Guide.* Uniglobe. Summerhill Press Ltd., 1990.

Wyse, Lois. *Company Manners: An Insider Tells How to Succeed in the Real World of Corporate Protocol & Power Politics.* Crown Publishing Group, Incorporated, 1993.

Yager. Jan. *Business Protocol: How to Survive & Succeed in Business.* Hannacroix Creek Books, Incorporated, 1999.

Yeomans, Mathew. "Carry on War." Travel Leisure, February 1999.

Yeomans, Mathew. "Functional Chic." Travel Leisure, January 1999.

Yeomans, Mathew. "Telephone Zone." Travel Leisure, June 1999.

Young, Pamela. "Bad Times - Better Meetings." Business Traveller, 1996.

Zartman, William. *The Negotiation Process.*

Every effort was made to accurately reflect the research information used in the development and compilation of this book.

Excellent information was obtained from Condé Nast Traveller, National Post, The Globe & Mail and other sources too numerous to list.

# Index

Index

## A

## B







Index

## C

Index

## D

## E

Index

## F



## G

## H

## I

## J



## K



## L

## M

## N

## O



## P



Index

## Q







Index

## R



## S

## T

## U



## V



## W

## Y



Index

Index

ISBN 155212380-4

9 781552 123805